Exposé of Polygamy
A Lady's Life among the Mormons

Volume 10
Life Writings of Frontier Women

Fanny Stenhouse.

Exposé of Polygamy:
A Lady's Life among the Mormons

Fanny Stenhouse

Edited by
Linda Wilcox DeSimone

UTAH STATE UNIVERSITY PRESS
LOGAN, UTAH
2008

Utah State University Press
Logan, Utah 84322–7800
www.usu.edu/usupress

Manufactured in the United States of America
Printed on acid-free paper

ISBN: 978–0–87421–713–1 (cloth)
ISBN: 978–0–87421–714–8 (e-book)

Library of Congress Cataloging-in-Publication Data

Stenhouse, T. B. H., Mrs., b. 1829.
  Exposé of polygamy : a lady's life among the Mormons / Fanny Stenhouse ;
edited by Linda Wilcox DeSimone.
     p. cm. – (Life writings of frontier women ; v. 10)
  Originally published: New York : American News Co., 1872.
  Includes bibliographical references and index.
  ISBN 978-0-87421-713-1 (cloth : alk. paper) – ISBN 978-0-87421-714-8 (e-book :
alk. paper)
  1. Mormon Church–Controversial literature. 2. Church of Jesus Christ of
Latter-day Saints–Doctrines. 3. Mormon Church–Doctrines. 4. Polygamy–
Religious aspects–Mormon Church. 5. Stenhouse, T. B. H., Mrs., b. 1829. I.
DeSimone, Linda Wilcox. II. Title.
  BX8645.S67 2008
  289.3'79225–dc22
  [B]
                              2008008575

Contents

Preface

I first want to thank Maureen Ursenbach Beecher, formerly the general editor of the *Life Writings of Frontier Women* series from Utah State University Press, who is responsible for the birth of this book. One day when she and I met for a catch-up lunch, she suggested the possibility of a project in the series that would bring Fanny Stenhouse's first book about her experiences in Mormonism and polygamy back into print. Although I was interested in the project (especially since my daughter had recently married into the Stenhouse family), it took another several months for me to contact her again about the project and begin to flesh out with her the framework for moving forward. Maureen generously shared with me her own copies of several versions of Stenhouse's book and provided ongoing encouragement as well as the benefit of her felicitous phrasing. John R. Alley, executive editor at the Utah State University Press, has also been a constant source of support. His quick response to questions, his patience in providing technical information, and his helpful editorial suggestions and guidance all have alleviated anxieties and smoothed the way.

Many special thanks go to Stenhouse descendants Douglas Simms Stenhouse and Carolyn Young Hunsaker. Douglas, a grandson of Fanny Stenhouse's seventh child, T. B. H. Jr., shared with me at our first meeting the work he had collected on his family's history, including an account he had written of the lives of his ancestors T. B. H. and Fanny Stenhouse. He also put me in touch with Carolyn Young Hunsaker, a descendant through Fanny Stenhouse's eldest daughter, Clara. Carolyn has been extraordinarily generous and helpful in sharing her own research and family stories—as well as those of her aunt LeJeune Young Decker—answering innumerable questions, showing me artifacts from the family's pioneer heritage, and in general providing an accommodating sounding board that helped me work through the many pieces of the Stenhouse family history.

I have also benefited from the assistance of the staff at L. Tom Perry Special Collections in the Harold B. Lee Library at Brigham Young

University—especially David Whittaker and Russell Taylor, who made it possible for me to locate and compare the various versions of Stenhouse's work more easily. The staffs at the Utah State Historical Society/Library Research Center and the Church History Library of the Church of Jesus Christ of Latter-day Saints were similarly accommodating.

෯෯

In reproducing the text of Fanny Stenhouse's *Exposé of Polygamy: A Lady's Life among the Mormons,* I have retained the spelling, punctuation, capitalization, and wording of the 1872 first edition so as to provide here an exact transcription of her first book.

Reckoning with Fanny Stenhouse

The name Fanny Stenhouse may bring to the mind of someone vaguely familiar with it associations such as Fanny Stenhouse = anti-Mormon, anti-polygamy crusader, lurid exposé author. Her reputation or, in some minds, notoriety is largely based on her massive exposé, "*Tell It All*," in which she describes in fascinating detail her experience as a Mormon, the unusual doctrines and practices of Mormonism, and especially the damaging effects of polygamy as she observed and experienced them. Stenhouse and her book became national and even international phenomena. The book went through many editions, and she went on the lecture circuit and testified before Congress as part of the national debate on Mormons and polygamy.

Yet this was not Stenhouse's original telling of her story. Two years before the 1874 publication of the wildly popular "*Tell It All*" and soon after her break with Mormonism, she wrote a shorter memoir. This version, titled *Exposé of Polygamy in Utah: A Lady's Life among the Mormons. A Record of Personal Experience as one of the Wives of a Mormon Elder during a Period of more than Twenty Years*, reveals a different woman and a different voice from the more highly colored ones of the later, longer book. The first account of Stenhouse's experience has been sidelined, largely forgotten and subsumed in the image of the later Fanny Stenhouse. But that early version lets us see a sensibility more immediate and honest, experience a forthright and restrained writing style, and make acquaintance with a more human and sympathetic woman.

A detailed description of the book's contents is unnecessary, since Stenhouse is a compelling storyteller and makes it easy for readers to discover and understand her experiences on their own. Along with Stenhouse's own personal history we find illuminating pictures of general Mormon life and society; extensive descriptions, comments, and analyses of polygamy in its many forms and ramifications; and a fair amount of Stenhouse's philosophy regarding life, God, human nature, and love.

1

Stenhouse's personal history is simply told. She briefly recounts her early life, conversion to Mormonism, missionary work with her husband in Switzerland, church experiences in England, and life in New York and eventually Salt Lake City. Her description of herself when young as religiously oriented, a seeker and Bible reader, makes it easy to understand why she would find Mormonism—with its stories of angels, apostles, and continuing revelation—attractive and compelling. She goes on to describe her gradual disillusionment with the Latter-day Saints after a long struggle with the doctrine and practice of polygamy and how she and her husband finally left the church.

In giving an account of her own life, Stenhouse provides glimpses into the hierarchal structure and community life of Mormon society. She shows us the workings of the church both in England and Switzerland—the activities of the proselytizing elders and visiting church authorities, including their behaviors and foibles, and how missionary work and emigration was funded and organized. She recalls her favorable impressions, upon reaching Salt Lake City, of Brigham Young and his wives, whom she generally treats fairly. She provides a restrained account of going to the Endowment House—where church leaders administered sacred ordinances, including those concerned with plural marriage—minus the confidential details she later provided in "*Tell It All.*" In her descriptions of balls, social events, and encounters with church authorities in daily life, Stenhouse shows herself to be a sharp-eyed social observer with keen psychological insight into human behavior. Her portrayal of Mormon society helps to set Stenhouse's experiences in the wider context in which she lived them.

What by far looms largest throughout her memoir is Fanny's nemesis—polygamy. The title of her book, *Exposé of Polygamy in Utah,* says it all. Without the practice of polygynous plural marriage in the Mormon church, we would not have this book. Fanny Stenhouse probably would have settled into her life within Utah Mormondom and remained there. Even if, in that alternative, imaginary, monogamous culture, she had become sufficiently disillusioned with Brigham Young's leadership of the church, it is more likely that she would have exited Mormonism quietly than that she would have felt impelled to write the story of her experiences as a Mormon, and it is even less likely that her story would have found a publisher. It was the institution of religious polygamy that fueled her distress, produced her writings, and made them popular.

The origins of polygamy in the Mormon church are shadowy.[1] Joseph Smith, the founder, spoke of the ancient Israelite practice of polygamy soon after the 1830 organization of his new church, and there were rumors in the first few years of his unseemly conduct toward other women. Fanny Alger, a young servant girl in Smith's household in Kirtland, Ohio, may have been his first plural wife in the mid-1830s, although the first official record of such a marriage dates to April 1841, when Smith was sealed to Louisa Beaman. During the three years before his death in 1844, Smith secretly introduced the doctrine to his inner circle and commanded them to take additional wives. He was himself taking them at a furious rate (more than thirty total), among them women already married to other men. It was not until July 12, 1843, that Smith dictated and thus committed to writing the "Revelation on Marriage" (now section 132 of the Doctrine and Covenants, accepted as scripture by the Utah Mormon church, officially the Church of Jesus Christ of Latter-day Saints), which provided the rationale and justification for plural wives. The revelation lays out the path to reach the highest level of heaven through sealing in a celestial marriage for time and eternity. It explains that all earthly contracts, including marriage covenants, end at death, but those who marry in the "new and everlasting covenant" and are sealed by the priesthood power given to Joseph Smith will be exalted in heaven, have thrones and kingdoms and eternal increase of children, and be gods themselves. Moreover, a man can, with the consent of his wife, take additional wives in order to "multiply and replenish the earth." The justification rests on God's apparent approval of Abraham and other Old Testament patriarchs having multiple wives and concubines; the recipients of the revelation are exhorted to go and do likewise. God reassures Smith that his sins are forgiven, his throne is prepared, and he will be exalted, while also strongly warning his wife Emma that she must accept "all those given to Joseph" and cleave to him or be destroyed.

From the early years of the church until the time of Joseph Smith's death, there were rumors, charges and countercharges within the church membership, about licentiousness, polygamy, adultery, and "spiritual wives." Official denials alongside the truth known to a few but suspected by many created unstable social tension and resulted in several church members, many of them close associates of Smith, either leaving the church or being excommunicated as apostates. The tension over polygamy was one of the factors that led to Smith's death and the abandonment of the city of Nauvoo, Illinois, where Mormons had settled, on the banks of the Mississippi River.

Amid the chaos and uncertainty after the death of Joseph Smith, Brigham Young, as head of the powerful Council of the Twelve Apostles, successfully fought off other claims to legitimacy and assumed leadership of what eventually became the Utah branch of Mormonism. Young and several other apostles were already secretly engaged in polygamy, allowing the practice to continue surreptitiously during the next year or two while the faithful were busy completing a temple in Nauvoo and looking forward to the new blessings promised once sacred ceremonies could be performed there. However, the Mormons were forced to leave Nauvoo soon after the temple's completion, beginning their long trek westward in early 1846 and settling in the area that became Utah in 1847.

By the time of the westward migration, those who had stayed with Brigham Young and the Twelve instead of following any of several splinter groups had generally come to accept the open secret of polygamy, and isolation in the West initially allowed the Utah Mormons to practice plural marriage with a minimum of outside interference. Efforts to achieve statehood quickly were not successful, though, and rumors continued to circulate, both in the United States and abroad, about Mormon marriages. Soon after Fanny Stenhouse converted to Mormonism in England in 1849, she became aware of whispered conversations, rumors of multiple wives, and denials by church elders. Finally Apostle Orson Pratt announced polygamy as the official policy and practice of the church in an August 1852 address.

That announcement offered religious justification for the practice by harkening back to the prophets of the Old Testament and also explicating a theology of polygamy as a means of providing more bodies for pre-existent souls and quickly building up the Kingdom of God on earth. Pratt stressed that polygamy was incumbent on the Saints because it was a revelation to Joseph Smith and claimed it would help prevent social problems such as adultery and prostitution.

Even after the public acknowledgment of polygamy, however, there was less than unanimous support and enthusiasm for the practice among Mormons. What became known as the Mormon Reformation of 1856 and 1857 was the most strident of periodic attempts on the part of church authorities to motivate members to live the law of polygamy more fully. This was done through exhortations, sermons, rebaptisms, and other forms of ecclesiastical and group pressure. Still, though scholars' estimates vary and have generally increased in recent years, polygamy remained a minority's practice among Mormons. It was more common among church leaders and the elite in the community than among rank and file members, partly because of greater pressure on prominent members to conform and partly because such men had greater economic ability to support additional wives.

Such a great change in family structure and relationships, without a clear road map for implementing it, left each new polygamous household to work out functional details, at least in the beginning. There was no one-size-fits-all solution, so a variety of patterns were established by families. Fortunately, the inevitable tensions inherent in polygamous families had a safety valve in the surprisingly liberal divorce laws enacted in the territory in 1852. In general, women could more easily procure divorces than men, so the initiative mostly lay with women in cancelling a marriage if it became unworkable.

The world outside of Utah continued to be appalled by polygamy, and within a few years of the 1852 announcement the Republican presidential platform of 1856 labeled polygamy and slavery as the "twin relics of barbarism." In 1857 President James Buchanan sent federal troops to Utah to curb Mormon resistance to territorial government. Although in that case polygamy was not a direct cause, it no doubt contributed to an atmosphere of mutual distrust. After a period of relative tranquility in the 1860s and early 1870s, virulent hostility toward polygamy increased later in the 1870s (partly due to books like Stenhouse's), culminating in congressional legislation against it, legal prosecution and disenfranchisement of practitioners and believers, dismantling of the Mormon church's corporate structure, and the eventual surrender of the church via an 1890 Manifesto of its leader counseling members to henceforth refrain from polygamous marriages.

Stenhouse presents her awareness of polygamy as growing gradually. After overheard whisperings, rumors, and denials, she soon confronts the reality of the doctrine and is instructed to teach it to other women in Switzerland. Later she describes how polygamy is practiced in England, New York, and Salt Lake, and finally, as her husband courts and marries another woman, she adjusts to having to share him. She is adamant, however, that whatever the adjustments, women never do "get used to it."

As she recounts her struggles to understand and accept polygamy, Stenhouse also takes on the documented source of the doctrine, "The Revelation on Marriage." She reveals her horror at her first exposure to a written copy, which she throws down without reading it fully. Years later, when her husband's courtship of an intended third wife has not gone well, she decides to examine Mormon origins more closely, reads the Revelation thoroughly, and experiences her own "revelation" as to its human rather than divine origin. This is the catalyst that sends her belief in the rest of Mormon doctrine crumbling and results in her leaving Mormonism.

She provides her assessment of "The Revelation on Marriage" as well as a complete copy of it in an appendix to her book, "so the reader will be able to form his own judgment from the document itself." She acknowledges that readers will approach it differently depending on their background. Faithful Mormons will see it as sacred writ, while others will see it as either an outright fake or a "strained effort" by Smith to "justify, under the sanction of a commandment, the leadings of his own passions." For Stenhouse, "There is no evidence of God in it. From beginning to end, it is man, and weak man only."

Stenhouse bolsters her belief in the revelation's earthly origin with several arguments. For one, she slyly notes that "it entirely escaped the notice of 'the Lord,' that the Patriarch Isaac was not a Polygamist."

Second, she quotes Joseph Smith's son, Alexander H. Smith, who discussed at some length the reasons for his belief that the revelation did not come to his father from God. Rather than accepting his points uncritically, Stenhouse disagrees with some of his analysis but also makes use of his arguments from the text itself that question the claim of divine origin.

Stenhouse herself analyzes the wording of the revelation, noting that claims of heavenly origin are undercut because, as one example, "The subtle way in which the priesthood therein entwines its authority around the woman, threatening her at one moment with damnation and the next attracting her with promises of glory, evinces too much system and calculation for such an origin." She concludes that the revelation was the result of a battle between Smith and his wife Emma: "The true story is the best—Joseph had himself entered into practical Polygamy, and a revelation was necessary to appease his wife, Emma, and to satisfy his brother, Hyrum, who had some 'conscientious scruples.'"

With her critique's techniques, Stenhouse shows that her opposition to the revelation is not based only on emotional repugnance but that she has rational arguments based on textual analysis, logic, a knowledgeable authority, and her own ability to recognize attempts at manipulating women.

In addition to her personal reactions and experiences, Stenhouse contrasts the theory of how polygamy is supposed to be entered into with the broader reality of how additional wives are taken. Having given illustrative accounts in the *Exposé* of what she had observed living in polygamy to be like, Stenhouse provides in her appendix extensive quotations from church authorities showing both the ideal in polygamous households—all peace, harmony, and joy—and the reality of deep dissatisfaction and unhappiness. She thereby buttresses her personal experiences and observations with statements from high-ranking church leaders, increasing the credibility and authenticity of her writing. But then she also includes in her "choice extracts from modern apostles" passages that seem designed mainly to highlight the most exotic elements of Mormon speculative theology—such as God being "first Husband" to Mary in the flesh in order to produce Jesus's earthly body, and Jesus being married with children, even possibly a polygamist, excerpts which were likely chosen at least partly for their shock value. Here, at the end of *Exposé*, we begin to see the seed of the more flamboyant style and approach that characterized her later revision of the book.

Stenhouse also describes how polygamy functions in practice: where the wives are housed, how households are managed and duties assigned or shared, how the husband distributes his time and attention. Offering insights into how a "woman's choice" functions in polygamy and how divorce is handled, she also explains marriage for the dead and marriages for time compared with eternal sealings. More important, Stenhouse recounts in great detail the deleterious effects she perceives polygamy as having on all those involved. Understandably, her primary sympathies are with first wives, who deal with being displaced in their husbands' affections or at least having to share them with other women. But she also notes the difficulties faced by later wives, who do not have the strong original bond or history with the husband that the first wife usually has, who necessarily feel like intruders into another woman's home, and who may fall under the thumb of a dominant or even cruel first wife who still is in charge of the household.

And, although she frequently expresses an antipathy toward men bordering on hatred for the entire gender because of polygamy, Stenhouse also shows understanding and sympathy toward the men involved. As much as she is angry at church elders for their deception in hiding and denying the truth about polygamy, she feels their hearts were likely in the right place in trying to make the doctrine, little by little, more easily acceptable to women. It is worth noting that even when pointing out the follies of some of the elders in England she takes pains not to overdo the criticism, attributing much of the silliness she observes to the temper of the times and general fanaticism about end times during that period. She also expresses respect for those men who are sincerely trying to perform what they see as a religious duty as best they can. Stenhouse recognizes the difficult position of a polygamist husband attempting to treat his wives equally and yet always aware they are watching him closely for signs of favoritism.

Such a system leads inevitably to estrangement between husband and wife, Stenhouse contends. The wife hides her true feelings rather than let her jealousy or hurt show and no longer feels she can confide in her husband. Because it is too painful to love him deeply when his affections are divided, she also stifles her own affection for her husband. For his part, the husband increasingly goes through the motions without true feelings, to maintain even treatment among his wives. The result is, in the best cases, calm in the household but, as Stenhouse says, not the calm of sleep but of death, the death of real love.

As Stenhouse tries to understand and cope with the polygamy doctrine, she shares her thoughts about God and religion, human nature, and love. Finding it hard to reconcile her idea of a loving God with a deity who would require such sacrifice of his children, she writes, "I can never believe that the great God created our natures, such as they are, and then gave us laws that would outrage them." The strength of her own love for her husband turns out to be a thorn in her path to accepting sharing him with another. "Why did the Lord implant this love in my nature?" she cries. "If it is wrong, He could have created me without it. Or was it for the pleasure of torturing His daughters that this was done?" By the time her husband was courting a potential third wife, Stenhouse felt she had tried and tried to mold her feelings and behavior to the expected standard but nevertheless began to wonder whether this was really God's intention, as her concern broadened beyond her own pain to encompass the plight of all women living in polygamy: "I had striven hard to do His will; but I had failed in every single instance to see, in what I was called upon to suffer, any indication of a God of justice. 'How,' said I, 'could the humiliation, abasement, and misery of thousands of women contribute to the glory of God?'" In Stenhouse's view, love cannot thrive in polygamy, and human nature becomes twisted from the deception and emotional withdrawal required to live the principle.

Was Stenhouse's depiction here of nineteenth-century Mormon polygamy accurate? I think she got it right, for the most part. The various permutations she describes did in fact exist, although it is difficult to assess the extent of any particular form or consequence of polygamy in practice. While her feelings were likely stronger and certainly more openly expressed than those of many Mormon women, her struggle to live her religion and somehow deal with the emotional pain the doctrine of polygamy created was typical. Although Leonard Arrington and Davis Bitton say that "for the most part Mormon women saw the anxieties and frustrations of polygamy as no greater than the tensions of the monogamous marriages some of them had known in their younger days," the wealth of information now available makes it clear that plural marriage brought a very different level and type of heartache and pain to the women involved. Later studies of Mormon women in polygamy indicate that the main justification for polygamy was religious obligation and that "the reality for most women was probably a mixture of faith and frustration," much as Stenhouse describes.[2]

What Stenhouse has provided is a thorough summation of the ways in which the challenge of sharing a husband changed the dynamic of husband-wife relationships and a troubling accounting of the emotional distress suffered by all parties involved. Probably most women experienced polygamy much as Stenhouse describes it; they just didn't publicize it as she did. Mormon women supported plural marriage vigorously in comments to visitors (as Stenhouse did), with apparent conviction in marches and meetings, and to varying degrees in their hearts, but it is doubtful that most of them warmly embraced the principle and truly enjoyed living in plurality.

Besides assessing the accuracy of Stenhouse's depiction, what can we conclude about her motivation? She presents herself as "impartial" and "truthful" and as telling her story as simply and directly as possible, and what emerges is a picture of a woman honestly attempting to convey the personal truth of her experiences. One must wonder, however, if there was not some calculation in her presentation. If so, what else might she have wanted to accomplish? Clearly, she wanted to tell her story— "What I *know* about Polygamy" is how she puts it—and rather than writing a book simply to vent her feelings, she anticipated an audience of both the women of Utah and general readers in the outside world who might not be very knowledgeable about Mormonism. She even expresses hope that members of Congress will consider her experience as they deliberate the "Mormon question."

But Stenhouse had other reasons too for writing at this particular time. She alludes to "Very recent and unforseen circumstances" that impelled her, without explaining further. These circumstances may have involved encouragement from friends or being snowbound for several weeks, but it is also possible that money was a factor since her family's economic fortunes had fallen in the wake of their break with the Mormon church. Beyond this, however, the *Exposé* shows no evidence that Stenhouse had ulterior motives, such as vindictiveness or meanness of spirit, to share her story. Aside from her early personal history and the appendix, the book is for the most part simply episode after episode of what she observed or experienced, usually described in a direct and sympathetic manner.

The *Exposé* has the feel of having been written in a rush of emotion, and if it was indeed composed in just two or three weeks, as Stenhouse claims, it is a remarkable evidence of her literary skill. The narrative is full of energy, verve, passion, and emotion. She does not shrink from detailing the depth and extent of her emotional experiences, and she gives vivid accounts of the distress of others. While "emotional writing" has at times been criticized from a rationalist, masculinist point of view, I believe such criticism must be rejected here. The emotional tone of Stenhouse's *Exposé* is credible, given the circumstances she lived under and recounts. The powerful, genuine emotion she expresses in no way invalidates her story and conclusions but rather contributes to their believability.

While Stenhouse, like any author, would want to be seen in a favorable light, she also lets us see her failings and shortcomings. Admitting to a rebellious nature and to what she calls wicked and disobedient tendencies, she is no stranger to jealousy and doubt. Owning up to stealing letters on more than one occasion, she also shares instances of marital disharmony—for example, that her husband "told me that I was a great clog to him, and more than once he said he could not enjoy the Spirit of God and live with me." In short, she was no paragon of wifely or womanly virtue and does not pretend to be.

Fanny Stenhouse.

She was, however, a woman of strong spirit—perhaps a positive way of viewing what she describes as "rebelliousness" and most likely how she would really want to be perceived. She stands up to church authorities who try to push her into emigrating while she and her child are experiencing serious health problems. She has a strong sense of self and self-worth, clearly believing that women deserve equal respect with men, which is why her first impression of the polygamy doctrine is that it is "a degradation to womankind."

At the time Stenhouse broke with her Mormon past, she and her family had been in Utah eleven years. When they arrived in 1859 they were well known to the leadership of the Mormon church. Her husband, Thomas Brown Holmes (known generally as T. B. H.) Stenhouse, had been a dynamic missionary in England and Italy, and she had accompanied him in his missionary work in Switzerland for more than three years. They had also served for three and a half years in New York, where T. B. H. had worked on the church newspaper *The Mormon* and been in charge of the Eastern States Mission. With such prominence and record of service, they were readily welcomed into Mormon society in Salt Lake City.

Fanny Stenhouse, however, arrived too late in Utah to hold a position in the higher echelons of the Mormon women's organizations,[3] nor did her husband hold any notable ecclesiastical offices. He was, however, publisher of the *Salt Lake Telegraph*, the city's first daily newspaper,[4] and as the Stenhouses were among the most educated, intellectual, and socially adept of the Mormon flock, they were quickly involved in the social circle of Brigham Young and other leaders. T. B. H. was often called upon to escort visitors around the town, so many of them met his wife Fanny as well and commented about her in their writings.

The descriptions of visitors validate the impression of Fanny Stenhouse as among the more highly educated and cultured of Utah's residents. Sir Richard Francis Burton, the well-traveled English gentleman and explorer, visited Salt Lake City in September of 1860, about a year after the Stenhouses' arrival. Upon meeting Fanny, he noted that she "spoke excellent French, talked English without nasalisation or cantalenation, and showed a highly cultivated mind." She was also, he said, the first woman he heard provide a strong defense of polygamy on religious grounds.[5] William Hepworth Dixon, visiting in 1868, described her as "a clever, handsome woman,"[6] and a famous French feminist, Olympe de Joaral Audouard, said Stenhouse was "a sociable, kindly, charming woman, very well-educated, a good musician . . ." (which we assume is more accurate than her report that she was a Catholic and had thirteen children).[7] Among her many talents, Stenhouse occasionally performed in dramatic productions at the Salt Lake Theatre, such as her role as the Duchess of York in *Richard III*. She also is said to have acted as a midwife, delivering at least a few babies in her time.[8]

Along with the picture of daily life that Stenhouse paints and the images captured by visitors who met her, it is helpful to keep in mind that much of her time and attention would have been taken up with her ten children, born over a period of eighteen years from 1850 through 1868. In other words, throughout almost the whole of her married life until just a few years before she published her *Exposé*, Stenhouse was bearing children at a slightly faster rate than one every two years. The children are rarely mentioned in her book, and although she had the help of a young girl the family brought with them from Switzerland, the care and well-being of the children must have been a daily concern and responsibility for her. By the time her book was published, the eldest two were married, which still left eight children at home, the youngest not yet four years old.

(Clara had married Joseph A. Young, a son of Brigham Young in 1867, and Lorenzo had married Flora J. Young in 1869.)[9]

Stenhouse's account of her life essentially ends in 1870, after she and her husband had asked that their names be removed from church membership rolls. But her life between then and publication of her book in 1872 was far from quiet. Fanny and T. B. H. had become part of the New Movement, which is commonly called the Godbeites after one of its leaders, as they began to question Brigham Young's infallibility, especially his counsel and control regarding economic and commercial matters.[10] Stenhouse served as president of the Women's Mutual Improvement Society of the New Movement and worked for women's suffrage. In July 1871 national suffrage leaders Susan B. Anthony and Elizabeth Cady Stanton visited Utah and spoke at one of the Society's meetings, over which Stenhouse presided. Susan B. Anthony commented as follows: "On Wednesday p.m., after the fourth, we met with the Women's Mutual Improvement Society, in the new Hall. Some three hundred were present. Over one hundred joined the Society and paid their admission fee. Mrs. Stenhouse is President. She is a noble woman, and has been through the fires of persecution for leaving the Mormon church."[11] Stenhouse addressed the Society on occasion and volunteered to teach classes in English to French women as part of the Society's educational efforts in providing evening classes, a library, and other means of personal improvement for women.[12]

In early 1872, when it appeared that church leaders seemed willing to disavow polygamy to obtain statehood, Stenhouse wrote a fierce letter to the *Salt Lake Daily Tribune* pointing out the hypocrisy of giving up for political gain what had been presented as a divine law:

> How dare they vote away polygamy if it is, as they have always told us women, a divine law of heaven without which no man or woman can enter the celestial kingdom? . . . Women of Utah, rise up in the dignity of your womanhood and tell Brigham Young that he has been deceiving you all these years, or that he meditates to deceive the nation now, either of which is an abomination. I would have respected Brigham Young, had he said it is a divine law and, State or no State, we dare not lay it aside. Then I should have said he is honest; . . .[13]

This letter was written just as *Exposé of Polygamy* was being published. On the same date her letter was published in the Tribune, March 20, an advertisement appeared noting that her book would be available "about the first of March." The publisher, American News, enthused:

> In presenting this volume to the trade, it is perhaps almost unnecessary to observe that, at the present moment, a book of this description is urgently called for, and is particularly calculated to "take" with the public. "The Mormon Question" is laid before the world by countless daily papers, magazines, &c.; but after all, the subject is very little understood outside of the Mormon homes, while at the same time reliable information is eagerly sought for. *This work is a record of facts.*[14]

The price was $1.50. By the end of March the book was available in Salt Lake City, and notices throughout the first half of April indicated a second supply was available. By mid-April Stenhouse's book was heading into its third edition. The first had sold out in ten days, and the third was expected to be gone within thirty.[15]

Interestingly, at the same time Stenhouse's book came on the market, an announcement appeared of a forthcoming new publication for women—the *Woman's Exponent,* due out the beginning of May (although its appearance was delayed until early in June). The *Exponent*—"the first magazine published by and for women west of the Mississippi" (with one short-lived exception)—became, for over forty years, the premier voice for Mormon women and, for a time, essentially the voice of the church's Relief Society organization, although it was not an official church publication.[16]

Even as her first book was being introduced, Stenhouse's husband announced that her second book was already planned, its title being *"Tell It All."*[17] This news may have occasioned a small note in the *Deseret News:* "'*Tell It All*': The old adage says, 'A fool tells all he knows.'"[18] Within three months, Harriet Beecher Stowe had not only agreed to provide a preface for the upcoming book but had already written it.[19] A great-granddaughter of both Fanny Stenhouse and Brigham Young has suggested that Harriet Beecher Stowe actually pushed Stenhouse in the beginning to write her first book as well as insisting that she expand it into a more complete story.[20]

Predictably, the reception of the *Exposé* differed between the Mormon community and the "outer world." The Mormon-oriented newspapers largely ignored the book, apparently deciding not to give it further publicity. On the national scene, a penny pamphlet's description is perhaps typical:

> This book is replete with Incidents of the Inner Workings of domestic life in Utah, showing the unhappiness engendered by the practice of Polygamy. The heartburnings, the jealousies,

and the grievances of the wives, when another is added to
the household, are depicted in terse and very forcible language. . . . On the whole, this book, coming authoritatively
as it does, from one who has been a Mormon wife for twenty
years, gives a better insight into the inner life of that sinful
sect than anything ever before published. It can but enlist the
sympathy of every honest man and woman for the suffering,
down-trodden Polygamic wives of Utah."[21]

A book review in *Harper's* of "*Tell It All*" when it was published two years
later provides some analysis that just as easily applies to the earlier *Exposé*
and that Stenhouse would have likely agreed with:

To the psychological student, to whom Mormonism is a men-
tal problem insoluble, and the seemingly stolid acquiescence
of woman in her own shame an inexplicable mystery, not the
least interesting feature of this volume will be the fact that it
traces so clearly the process by which superstition gained, first
an influence, then an absolute control, over a mind originally
intelligent and over a will originally independent.[22]

The popularity of Fanny's first book, the *Exposé*, launched her on
a lecture tour that began in the fall of 1872 in Corinne, Utah, and proceeded to other cities in the West.[23] She spent the winter in the East, from
which she returned to Utah a year after the *Exposé's* first publication.[24] She
lectured in several large cities, including Washington, D.C., and Boston.
Her lecture in Boston at the Tremont Temple was praised by no less a
luminary than Lucy Stone, founder and editor of the *Woman's Journal* and
a prominent suffragist and reformer.[25]

In the summer of 1873 a laudatory article appeared in *Harper's Bazar*
reviewing the *Exposé* and mentioning the "more than ordinary interest"
that had been "excited" by her lecture in the eastern states. The article
gave a physical description of Stenhouse as being "of medium height,
inclining to *embonpoint*, ladylike, modest, and unpretending, attractive
rather from her quietness of manner than from any special characteris-
tics. She evidently possesses in a remarkable degree a reserve of latent
power which qualifies her to do any thing which she believes it is her duty
to undertake." The review pointed out, referring to Stenhouse, that, "The
usual troubles of the first wife under the 'plurality' system were intensi-
fied and rendered more acute, as might be expected, to a lady of refine-
ment and cultivation than perhaps they might have been to one of a cold
or unthinking disposition."[26]

Stenhouse spent the latter part of 1873 and early 1874 in Hartford, Connecticut, working on her second book, returning to Utah in April. *"Tell It All"* was published later in 1874 and sold briskly in Salt Lake City. A November newspaper notice mentioned that it had sold five hundred copies in the past three weeks and a third edition was being issued.[27]

Over the next two or three years Stenhouse lectured in Utah on multiple occasions, her subjects being "Polygamy" and "Brigham Young."[28] She also lectured in Nevada, the Pacific states, and even Australia. Her lecture tours were so financially successful that she focused on them and eventually moved away from Utah.[29]

One particularly powerful effect of Stenhouse's original book, the *Exposé*, was the impact it had on Ann Eliza Webb Young, who married Brigham Young in 1868 but by 1873 chafed under the privations she was experiencing. She read Stenhouse's *Exposé* and was deeply moved. As she told audiences later, the book "showed me things in a clearer light than I had seen them before. I knew every word was true from my own sad experience, and it encouraged me to leave the hateful polygamic life." Later that same year, Ann Eliza left her marriage (she eventually won a divorce in 1876) and gave her first lecture against polygamy and Brigham Young. She soon became a sensation on the lecture circuit as well. The books and lectures of Fanny Stenhouse and Ann Eliza Webb Young contributed greatly to the growth of anti-Mormon sentiment in the country in the 1870s.[30]

Ann Eliza Webb Young may also have provided a glimpse into Brigham Young's response to Stenhouse's *Exposé*:

> I remember once going into his office, and finding him examining the advertising circular of a book on Mormonism, written by a lady who had for a time been a resident of Utah. He commenced reading it aloud to me in a whining voice, imitating the tone of a crying woman. Yet, notwithstanding this attempt to make a jest of it, I knew that the publication of this book annoyed him excessively, and that he was both curious and anxious concerning the contents, and the effect they would produce.[31]

The sculptor Mahonri Young is said to have also recalled his grandfather Brigham Young's concern about Stenhouse's writings, telling his niece: "Winifred, do you know that your great-grandmother Stenhouse was the only person of whom Brigham Young was ever afraid? You have probably heard that when he saw this book [*"Tell It All,"* a copy of which Winifred was showing Mahonri during his 1946 visit] Brigham ordered the plates destroyed in Connecticut and every copy that could be found, burned."[32] If true, it appears that Young's orders fell short of their objective.

Since Stenhouse's revised book continued to be published in additional editions until 1890, there was clearly an audience for her story for many years after its original appearance. Although she continued to tour and lecture, she had moved out of Utah by 1875. She lectured in Nevada in February of that year, joining her husband T. B. H., who was writing a series of letters about the mine fields, and by June they were residing in San Francisco. By then she also had completed a new project—a play called *Saints and Sinners*, co-written by G. B. Densmore, who had dramatized Mark Twain's *The Gilded Age* with great success. The hero was to be General P. E. Connor, formerly in charge of Salt Lake's Fort Douglas. Brigham Young would be the villain, and Apostle George Q. Cannon the "low comedy man." Although plans were announced to produce the new play not only in San Francisco and New York but London and Australia, it apparently never reached the stage.[33]

Stenhouse undertook an extensive lecture tour in Australia, beginning her first lectures there in September 1875 and returning to San Francisco in July of the following year. Upon her arrival in Australia, one of the Sydney newspapers reported that Stenhouse's motive was to "forewarn, and thus forearm, the public of Australia against the preachings and machinations of the six Mormon elders who were sent as missionaries from Utah some months ago, by Brigham Young, to make converts in these colonies, and who we believe have actually arrived in our midst." It went on to point out that she had a slight head start on the missionaries and wished her much success.[34]

By this time Stenhouse's books were estimated to have sold over fifty thousand copies, and she was likely at the height of her lecturing abilities. It was noted that she was "the first lady lecturer who has appeared in Sydney," and her platform appearance and demeanor were described in complimentary terms: "She has bright, expressive eyes, a well moulded figure and a ringing voice, exquisitely modulated to the exigencies of the lecture whether it be for imitation, drollery, denunciation or declamation, in all of which she excells." Another report also had nothing but praise for her performance and her person:

> Every statement made by Mrs. Stenhouse has the genuine ring of truthfulness; the only thing which we perceive at all calculated to throw doubt upon her story of woman's degradation at Salt Lake is the lecturer herself. Can polygamy, after all, be so bad a thing, when it can turn out such a graceful, self-possessed, intelligent, accomplished, sympathetic, and able a lady lecturer as Mrs. Stenhouse?[35]

The year following her return from Australia, we get a glimpse of Stenhouse's situation in San Francisco through the eyes of the well-known Salt Lake photographer, Charles R. Savage. Savage had been converted to Mormonism in England by T. B. H. at the age of fifteen and had known the Stenhouses well. On a trip to California in 1877 he visited Fanny, finding her in a "lowly abode" in San Francisco. She appeared to him "very matronly, hair turned grey." They spoke about family matters, Stenhouse noting that her daughter Ida was doing well in school and developing a good operatic voice. She explained that although she was no longer a believer in religion, she was allowing her daughters to attend an Episcopal church as a way of introducing them into good society, but that she took pains to let them know that religion was "all humbug."

She hinted that her husband, Thomas, was "given up to drinking" since leaving the Mormon church and that she was supporting the family. Although she had made $7,000 from the sale of her book, she complained that her publisher "had robbed her of $1,000," and noted that she was currently considering "brilliant offers" to go on the lecture circuit once again.

Upon learning that Savage had another wife, she "gave me a short venomous harangue against Everything Mormon, and Polygamy in particular," yet she said she thought highly of the people of Utah and would even like to live there. Savage was impressed that she "spoke of my wife in the most endearing manner how much she loved her &c &c—I discovered for the first time her intense love for my wife." He reflected afterward that "whatever success she had had in pulling down the Mormon faith it had not been a source of comfort to her," and that it was best he not continue the friendship.[36]

However, the following year found him visiting her again, this time finding her "more agreable [*sic*] and less vinager [*sic*] in her talk" and noting that he "should rejoice to see her back among her old friends, she told me that, she cared more for her old friends than for any new ones she had made."[37] Savage seems to have maintained his attachment to Stenhouse in some form, since even as late as 1895 he made a note in his diary of her address in Los Angeles.[38]

By 1895 Stenhouse had suffered many difficult losses. T. B. H. had died in 1882, only four years after Savage had last visited. Fanny Stenhouse was still lecturing in the early 1880s, having "delivered to a large audience an intensely 'anti-Mormon' lecture which was reported in the papers" in San Francisco shortly before her husband's death. We know this because the Mormon church's historian still kept track of her, including the notice of her appearance in the clipping file the church maintained as a historical record.[39]

HOUSEWORTH · PARLORS,
No. 12 Montgomery Street, opposite the Lick House, San Francisco.

*Fanny Stenhouse in a photograph taken
in San Francisco.*

Her oldest daughter Clara had died in 1893 from typhoid fever at the young age of forty-two and had left seven children from ages eight to twenty-five.[40] Then in 1894 while living in San Francisco, Fanny Stenhouse was "bumped" by a street car at a turnaround, which caused her to lose part (or all, it is not known for sure) of her sight. Family memories indicate that she also had glaucoma and had undergone a "keyhole" operation whereby a piece of the iris had been removed to alleviate pressure on the optic nerve.[41]

Soon after this incident Stenhouse moved to Los Angeles, where she lived with her daughter Fanny Maud; she also spent time in Ensenada, Mexico, with another daughter, Minnie (Emelia Eliza) Godbe. Minnie had married in 1873 Anthony Godbe, the younger brother of William Godbe, leader of the Godbeite reform movement in which the Stenhouses had been involved.[42] Stenhouse apparently still traveled, as her great-grand-daughter Winifred Young recounts how much she enjoyed Stenhouse's stories when Stenhouse visited Young's family in Montclair, New Jersey, saying that Stenhouse and Aunt Susa Young Gates were "real storytellers and out to please."

In 1901 Stenhouse stayed with Winifred Young's family just before embarking on a trip around the world. She was heading first to England and then to revisit the place of her childhood on the Isle of Jersey. She also planned to go to France and Switzerland before sailing back to California by way of the South Seas. Six-year-old Winifred had not been told that her great-grandmother could not see, only that she should be very nice to her, so she "submitted quite generously if a bit impatiently to great-grandmother's various pats, smoothings, and caresses," and soon realized that "she *sees* with her fingers!" She was impressed with Stenhouse's deter-mination to travel: "But if her sight was gone, her spirit was not, and the incongruity of traveling to see the world without eyes to see with seems now, as then, only a natural demonstration of tremendous eagerness to know at first hand what was going on." Winifred also shares this picture of Stenhouse, now in her seventies:

> I did not know her until 1901 after she had been blinded in an accident, but young as I was [six years old], a serenity of face and manner impressed me almost as much as her sto-ries. Could she have had a change of heart since writing the book "Tell It All" even though tragedy struck time and again through the intervening years? This we shall never know.[43]

Winifred's family received a letter postmarked France from Stenhouse. Her handwriting was "large but quite clear, as usual." She reported having a wonderful time in England, where she had been met by Flora Bella Stenhouse Arnold (daughter of Fanny's "sister-wife," Belinda Pratt) and her husband, Gus Arnold. She also spent time with other family members, most likely her daughter Ida and her family, who lived in London. (Walter Stenhouse Young also spent "a few weekends at his Aunt Flora's charming estate just outside of London" during a trip to England the following year.) In France Stenhouse was staying with the family of "Madame Odouard" (Olympe de Joaral Audouard), who had

This photograph of Fanny Stenhouse was probably taken after she had lost her eyesight.

met and written about Stenhouse more than thirty years before, and she mentioned that they had been urging her to look up members of the De Bosque family (her former fiancé) as well. Stenhouse went on to describe her special experience of what it was like to revisit the sites of her early life without the faculty of sight:

> You know it is a very strange thing, Walter, but perhaps because I can't see at all, every detail of my life has passed through my mind clearly, from the moment of reaching St. Heliers until now. Except for the fact that it is very nice to be with old friends again, I might better have stayed in California where at least there is so much activity that no one can think of herself or indulge in recapitulation. One would have a right to say that *my* past was over and done with long ago, but apparently the years of one's youth make the most profound impression on the mechanism of the memory, and strangely, are not embedded deeply but emerge at the top in old age.[44]

Not long after completing her trip around the world, Stenhouse died April 18, 1904, in Los Angeles, with several of her children (Lorenzo, Minnie, Fanny Maud, and Blanche) surrounding her. The other five surviving children were scattered—Serge in Salt Lake City, Ida in London, T. B. H. Jr. in Philadelphia, George in Canada, and Walter in Arizona.[45] She was praised by the *Salt Lake Tribune*, which noted that although she was known to the general public by the book she had authored, to those who remembered her personally, "she is best known for her kindness of heart, her brilliant social qualities, her unfailing independence of character, and her openness of mind."[46] Her grave in the Angelus-Rosedale Cemetery in Los Angeles has a "modest polished red granite marker, simply inscribed with the word 'Mother', but no other name, two very simple floral designs, and the date of her death."[47]

Over the years of living within Mormonism, Stenhouse's faith would waver—over polygamy or the behavior of church leaders—but again and again she describes pulling herself back to her strong faith in God and her desire to do His will. Take her at her word that she was in earlier years a strong believer in the message of the Mormon gospel, as she learned it and helped teach it in her missionary work. It does not seem credible that she was at heart a disbeliever through all those years of struggle, even though she came to express growing doubts about the wisdom of what she heard from church leaders. Her early profession of faith and dedication to the Mormon church can reasonably be accepted at face value, as can her later, evolving viewpoints about religion.

That she eventually came to a different interpretation of God than she previously believed does not invalidate her faith or belief at any stage of her life. The reader of Stenhouse's "little pamphlet" can note that sometimes warm and active faith turns cold and distant, as hers did, without demeaning the worth of the writer or denying the validity of her experience. Stenhouse's *Exposé* stands on its own, still revealing her as a woman to be reckoned with on her own terms.

His New Wife.—The "Wallflowers."

EXPOSÉ OF POLYGAMY IN UTAH.

A LADY'S LIFE

AMONG THE MORMONS.

A RECORD

OF

PERSONAL EXPERIENCE

AS ONE OF THE WIVES OF A MORMON ELDER

DURING A PERIOD OF MORE THAN TWENTY YEARS.

BY

Mrs. T. B. H. STENHOUSE,

OF SALT LAKE CITY.

ILLUSTRATED BY H. L. STEPHENS.

NEW-YORK

AMERICAN NEWS COMPANY, 119 NASSAU STREET.

1872.

S. W. GREEN, Printer, 16 and 18 Jacob Street, New-York

"HAVE ye not read, that He which made them at the beginning made them male and female, and said, For this cause shall a man leave father and mother, and shall cleave to his wife: and they twain shall be one flesh?"—*MATTHEW 19: 4–5.*

"THERE shall not any man among you have *save it be one wife*, and *concubines he shall have none.*"—*BOOK OF MORMON, p. 118.*

"THOU shalt love thy wife with all thy heart, and shalt cleave unto her *and none else.*"—*BOOK OF COVENANTS, p. 124.*

TO THE READER.

IN presenting this little volume to the public, I trust I may be excused if I give utterance to a few words by way of preface. This I think especially needful, as very probably what I have written will fall into the hands of many who are but imperfectly acquainted with Mormon doctrines and Mormon practice, and who would thus be at a loss to understand much of my story. It is only right that I should explain, among other things—what may appear strange to the reader—that is, the poverty and privations which we endured for so many years. It must be fully understood that this poverty was entirely voluntary. My husband and myself were both zealously devoted to the faith, and when called to missionary labour, we obeyed. We were not only willing to sacrifice cheerfully all the pleasures and comforts of life for the sake of our religion, but we *did* so, and rejoiced that we were counted worthy to suffer.

Again, I must here state that, although I am necessarily compelled to speak of many circumstances of a personal nature, I have studiously avoided all mention of names or details which might reasonably give the least pain to any of my former friends and acquaintances. Even in the case of Brigham Young and his family, with whom I have been on terms of the most intimate acquaintance, although I felt myself at liberty to speak more freely of him as a public man, I have in no instance betrayed the confidence which any of his wives or members of his household have placed in me. This statement I am assured they will willingly confirm.

The following pages are simply what they pretend to be: "What I *know* about Polygamy;" and in order to set the whole matter plainly before the reader, I have given a brief account of my personal experience—what I myself felt, what I saw and knew. Every statement which I make, I can prove to be strictly correct; and if I have erred in any thing, it has been in not giving my subjects so high a colouring, or so sensational a character, as perhaps they had in their reality. The women of Utah will bear me witness that every word which I have written is true, although perhaps only a weak picture of the facts as they occurred.

I do not wish to apologize for any imperfections in what I have written, although perhaps I might, as a woman, claim a little consideration.

This is the first time that I have appeared in print, and probably it will be the last. It had been frequently suggested to me that I should write a short history of my own life as a Mormon, but I never seriously entertained the idea. Only two or three weeks ago, not a single word was written, or a plan even outlined for a work of any kind. Very recent and unforeseen circumstances, although they found me, in every literary sense, unprepared for such an effort, led to a resolution that I would give to the world, and especially to my sisters in Utah, whose sympathy I feel assured I possess, an account of my own trials, which have been, and in many instances still are, their own.

At the end of the volume I give an exact copy of the "Revelation," that any curiosity felt respecting it may be satisfied, and that my readers may see for themselves what the Mormon women are expected to believe and *obey*. The few "choice" extracts which follow it are taken from the writings and discourses of eminent modern Apostles. They will amply corroborate every statement which I have made, and prove to the impartial mind that in no instance have I exaggerated or deviated from the truth—but rather the reverse. I have told *a plain story of facts*, and have endeavoured to present a faithful picture of the terrible realities of Mormon Polygamy. Whether I have succeeded or not, let the reader determine.

FANNY STENHOUSE.

SALT LAKE CITY, UTAH.

CONTENTS.

Vicissitudes of himself and Family—How he was "counselled" to take another Wife—Brigham sends for me—My young Charge— "Not feeling well"—My Husband seeking a second Wife—A "painful" Task!—Striving to submit—My attempts at Friendship with his *Fiancée*—My Heart not quite subdued 93

APPENDIX.

ILLUSTRATIONS

WHAT I KNOW ABOUT POLYGAMY.

CHAPTER I.

Early Life and Experience of the Authoress.

I WAS once a Mormon woman, and for over twenty years I have lived among Mormons. Their faith was once mine as truly as any words can express; their thoughts were the same as mine; their hopes were my hopes; their religious opinions were in sympathy with my own. But that was in the time past. It *seems* long past, and yet it was, as I may say, only a little while ago—a few months, which I might almost count upon my fingers. Yet now all this is changed, and I have learned to see matters in another light.

When I first listened to the preaching of the Mormon elders, I endeavoured to judge impartially of their doctrines. I thought *then* that they were right. To me, *at the time,* they *were* right. But other views, which I now believe to be purer, better, and more truthful, have dawned upon my soul, and I can, I think, fairly say that I am a free woman—free from the bondage of superstition; and as I write this, I feel the pleasure of the captive who shakes himself free from his chains.

It has been suggested to me that I should, from my own personal experience, write the story of a Mormon woman living in the midst of Mormonism. I shall endeavour, in the following pages, to do so impartially and truthfully. But I wish to tell my story as simply as I can. Others, who are but partially informed, may write critically of what they have seen or heard; but I shall give a record of what I myself have *known* and *felt.*

Whatever opinion the reader may form of my life, past or present, is to me of little moment, and to him it can not be of much consequence. Personally, I have no claims to the attention and consideration of the world, nor do I desire that it should be otherwise. But as no woman's experience in Utah, who has been associated with Mormonism and seen its polygamic life, could be very different from my own, the facts set forth in this little work will enable the reader to comprehend the operation of the order of "celestial marriage."

To answer the inquiry, how any woman can submit to the practice of polygamy, I must of necessity give a brief history of my early life. From what I shall there state, the reader will see how I was led on, little by little, from total ignorance of that doctrine, to a firm faith that it was a revelation from God, necessary to salvation.

However strange what I relate may appear to those who are unacquainted with life in Utah, my story is but a shadow of the truth, although my experience was, probably, the same as that of nine tenths of the Mormon women.

My first recollections of life were in St. Helier's, Jersey, one of the islands in the English Channel, where I was born.[1] Through the preferences of my parents, my religious education and associations were with the Baptist denomination, my own disposition and feelings making this connection very agreeable, as I had, probably, for a girl of my age, a more than ordinary interest in religious observances.

When fifteen years of age, I went to Brittany, in France, and entered into a Roman Catholic school as a teacher of English. While there, I had, of course, to conform to the rules of the school, and attend church with the pupils at all times when required to do so. Much as I respected the people with whom I was associated, for their kindness, I could not conscientiously join with them in their devotions. I always took my Bible with me, and read it during the service; and frequently in my loneliness and anxiety for some living religious truth, I would say, "Oh! if there were only a prophet ministering *now* on earth, that I might go to him and ask, 'What shall I do to be saved?' and thus receive an answer which would satisfy the craving of my soul."

I remained in France six years, and then I obtained two months' vacation, for the purpose of visiting my parents, who had now removed from the island of Jersey to Southampton, (England.)

CHAPTER II.

Seeking the Truth—First Acquaintance with Mormonism—
Favourable Impressions—I become the Wife of a Mormon Elder.

On visiting my birthplace, in the summer of 1849,[1] I went to the house of my brother-in-law, who was an "apostate" Mormon. During my stay in his house, he spoke to me about the Mormons in not very flattering terms. At the same time, he told me that my father, mother, and, in fact, all my family, had adopted that faith. As I knew my parents, particularly my mother, to be sincere and devoted Christians, I began to think that Mormonism must be something different from what he represented it to be, or they never would have accepted it. I therefore determined to investigate this religion, for the purpose of exposing its errors to my parents, for whom I entertained the deepest affection.

I attended my first Mormon meeting at St. Helier's, Jersey. With what I heard that afternoon I could find no fault, although I was very much prejudiced against the new religion. On arriving the following week at my father's home in Southampton, I began to observe very closely every thing that was said and done, to see if I could detect any change in the life of my parents and sisters. I could see no difference in my father and mother; but I certainly saw a change in my sisters, who now forsook all amusements suitable to their age, and thought of nothing but going to church and making clothing for the missionaries who were to be sent out "without purse or scrip."

All this interested me very much; and, at my sisters' request, I went one Sunday morning to their place of worship. The sermon that I then heard perfectly fascinated me. It was delivered by an eloquent and enthusiastic young Mormon "Elder," who felt, or thought he felt, that he was "a servant of God," sent to preach deliverance to the people.

He said that "an angel of God had appeared to Joseph Smith, and had revealed to him the everlasting Gospel." "There were now," he said, "living apostles ordained by the angels, the same as in days of old."

At first I thought, "This is indeed glorious news; but can it be true?" The reflection then came that what the Lord had done already He *could* certainly do again. We were urged to be "baptized for the remission of our sins," with the promise that "we should receive the gift of the Holy Ghost, to witness unto us that we had done what the Lord had commanded." I knew that all this was according to Scripture, and I dared not reject it. Indeed, I had no desire to do so. I received it gladly. It was life to my soul. It was that which I had been desiring for years; and I firmly believed that the Lord, in His mercy, had answered my prayers. I concluded to be baptized; and I had no sooner made up my mind to do so, than I wanted it done. Two weeks after my arrival in England, I became formally a member of the Mormon Church.

I felt that I had obeyed the commands of God, and was entitled to His blessing; indeed, I felt that I *was* blessed, for my heart was full of joy and gratitude. This the elders taught me was the Spirit of God. I now believe it was simply the answer of my conscience, which every sincere person enjoys in all religions. I had been taught, and I obeyed.

I felt so happy and satisfied that I was in the right path that I could not make up my mind to return to France and the isolation which I felt there.[2] I therefore determined to resign my position, and make my home among the "Saints."

A few months later, I was married to that same young Mormon Elder;[3] and then, in the joint prosecution of our missionary labours, my troubles began. Some of my friends thought I was risking a great deal by becoming the wife of a man whose life was devoted to the Mormon ministry; while others thought that I was highly honoured in getting a husband who held such a prominent position in the church. I was, however, satisfied, and willingly entered upon my new sphere as a missionary's wife, feeling sure that there were no obstacles so great that I could not overcome them. How little could I imagine then the life that was before me!

CHAPTER III.

My Husband leaves for Italy—Experiences as the Wife of a
Missionary—Privations and Struggles with Poverty in England—
Suspicions of Polygamy—The "Privilege" of "Washing the Elders'
Feet"—Cheerful Words in Time of Trouble.

I HAD been married about four months when my husband was called
to go on a mission to Italy. What terrible news this was to me, for I was to
be left behind! In my grief I exclaimed, "Ah! why could they not have
selected some one else?" Then I remembered how that, in my first joy and
gratitude after being baptized into the church, I had said that I would do
any thing that the Lord required of me; and now I felt that He was going
to put me to the test. Thus it was that, when asked by one of the "Twelve
Apostles" if I were willing that my husband should go, I answered "Yes,"
although even at the time I thought that my very heart would break.

As Mormon elders receive no salary, nor any remuneration whatever, my husband was very much troubled about leaving me dependent
on others, not being sure how I might be provided for, and knowing better than I did what want I should probably be exposed to. At his request,
an old and valued friend was appointed his successor; Mr. S. believing
that in doing so I should be provided for and watched over!

In June, 1850, Mr. S. went on his mission, in company with Lorenzo
Snow, one of the "Twelve Apostles." Though terribly grieved at his departure, I felt some pride in the fact that my husband was the first of the
elders in Britain who was sent on a foreign mission.[1]

For the first few weeks after his departure, my friends gathered
around me and provided me with all that I needed. Before long, however,
most of the "Saints" with whom I had been on intimate terms began to
prepare for emigration to Utah. I soon saw that I should be obliged to
break up my home, and be contented with one room. This I did cheerfully; for, after the great trial of separating from my husband for three
years—as I then thought—this was comparatively nothing.

I got but little assistance from the church, and the question which
now presented itself to my mind most imperatively was, "*What* can I
do?" The reply, mentally returned, was, "Nothing!" I could only teach

39

English. But to whom could I teach English in England? Still, I was not altogether useless or helpless. I could sew very well; but I had as yet no confidence in myself, never having done any thing of the kind before as a matter of business. I was in the greatest trouble. I had neither food nor fire. I could not venture to write to my husband about this, for fear of unfitting him for carrying out fully his mission, which I then believed would be a sin.

I then resolved that I would go round and visit some of my lady acquaintances, who had frequently invited me to come to their houses. I wished, if possible, to see whether, through their influence and introduction, I could do any thing to earn a little money. Besides which I had another reason: I thought that possibly some one would ask me to dine with them. I was hungry enough, but I walked about the city, afraid to carry out my resolution, until I was quite worn out; for I feared in my pride that they might suspect that I came purposely for something to eat. Of this I was perfectly ashamed. No one who has not personally passed through such an ordeal can have any idea of what my feelings were.

The shame I felt was only equalled by my necessities, innocent as I was of any fault which could have placed me in this position. I was utterly miserable, and did not venture to call upon any one, but turned my steps toward my dreary home—only to fast and pray. The fasting, however, was not in my programme at that time. I had no inclination for it, although I was utterly unable to prevent it. I then earnestly prayed to the Lord to help me, and at the same time I thanked Him that I was counted worthy to suffer for His sake.

The time was fast approaching when I knew that I should be compelled to have fire and other necessaries; but where to get them I knew not.

One evening I was asked to dine at the house of a friend where some of the elders from Salt Lake were visiting, and I accepted the invitation with a great deal of pleasure, for more than one reason. It was thought a great privilege at that time to meet with American elders. Some of these gentlemen assumed such authority that they impressed the "Saints" with the idea that they were little gods. *We had not then seen them at home!*

I went to dine with these brethren, and as it is a Mormon woman's "privilege" [?] to sit and "listen" to the "lords of creation," without joining in the conversation at all, I had then, of course, that same privilege of listening while dinner was preparing.

I can not tell the horror of what I then heard. They were talking among themselves about Polygamy, but in such a covert way that it was evident that they thought I could not understand what was said. Neither should I have understood it had it not been that I had heard some whisperings of this kind once, before my husband went away, though then I did not believe it. I had asked him about the new doctrine, and he had reassured me by stating that there was "no truth in it;" that it was a slander, promulgated by some evil-tongued people to injure "the cause." I heard, however, something that day which troubled me very much, and I resolved to ask these "brethren" now present to tell me the honest truth— whether Polygamy really existed in Utah, or did not.

They positively denied its existence, and though I did believe then that what they said was true, I afterwards discovered much which troubled and worried me, and being constantly anxious to learn the truth, there was not much that escaped my notice.

I became wretchedly suspicious. At times, I even fancied that my husband had deceived me; and that thought was to me madness. I said— whatever *other* men may do, *my* husband will not deceive *me*. O dear! no. That I could not believe.

I now felt more inclined for fasting than for praying. In fact, just then it would have been utterly impossible for me to pray, I was so wretched. Doubts and fears had begun to creep into my mind, and it appeared to me (if I may say so) that the Lord, like a hard task-master, was exacting from me more than I had bargained to do or suffer when I embraced Mormonism. These troubled thoughts were not calculated to make me feel happy in my relations with the church, and I tried to overcome my feelings, and attain to a better state of mind, trusting sincerely in God that all would yet be well.

But to return to my difficulty in earning a living.

After some time I finally got a little plain sewing to do. This enabled me to win my daily bread and to pay the rent of my room, as well as to make a few scanty preparations for the little stranger which I now daily expected. The reader may suppose that it was, after all, a very hard struggle.

Now began the arduous task of endeavouring to support myself and my babe. In this dear little one there was to me another strong incentive to exertion. But how and where I was to get work, and what I was to do— and, in fact, what I *could* do—I did not know. There was nothing for me as far as I could see. I was willing to do any work, if only I could get it to do— that was now the difficulty. Yet I determined not to be foiled. I managed to live; but how? Sometimes, for two weeks together, I had nothing but dry bread. I became pale and thin, and so weak that I could scarcely walk.

I now became better acquainted with Mormonism, as I was able to go more among the Saints. But I lost confidence in the missionary brethren when I saw how familiarly they conducted themselves with the young "sisters;" for I knew that the elders I allude to were married men. They taught the "sisters," both married and single, that *it was their privilege to wash the elders' feet, and to comb their hair, and in fact to wait on them in every way imaginable.* This I mean *literally.* There was nothing symbolical about it, and many of our silly girls liked nothing better. I saw even then that this was not right, and it annoyed me greatly.

With the President of the London Conference and his family I was well acquainted, and I knew that this man came down from London to the Southampton Conference about every two or three weeks, to court a young "sister." He supplied her with money, and otherwise acted in a way which appeared to me almost scandalous. His conduct shook the faith of some of the older Saints.[2] In these days the elders would take young girls to the theatres and other places of amusement, while their own wives remained at home. I sincerely believe now that many of these men taught Polygamy to the girls, while they denied it to the public.

I felt lonely, wretched, and disappointed in my religion, though I still believed it. Yet I dared not ask my husband to abandon his mission and come home. I resolved that I would try to endure to the end. Then, too, I knew that even at the worst he would return some time, and all my troubles, I felt, would then be ended; for I believed that he would be able to explain all to me—yes, every thing.

About this time I learned that Lorenzo Snow (the "Apostle" in whose company Mr. S. went to Italy) was on his way to England. This intelligence made me very happy, as may be supposed. I waited anxiously to see him. On his arrival, he came directly to my house. He seemed very much shocked to see the change in my appearance, and said that he would send for my husband to come home immediately.[3]

CHAPTER IV.

Our Mission to Switzerland—Introducing Mormonism—Terrible
Trials of Faith—Geneva—Days without Food—The new Convert—
"The Labourer worthy of his Hire"—Timely Aid.

AFTER about a year's absence, Mr. S. returned to England, and we
were invited to attend a conference of the Saints, which was to be held
in London, in June, 1851. During this conference, the "Apostle" Snow
expressed his great indignation at the manner in which I had been
neglected, and said that I should no longer remain in connection with
the Southampton Conference. It was decided that my husband should
go on a mission to Switzerland; that I should go with him, and that we
should begin our missionary labours in Geneva.[1] One great incentive to
this resolution was, that I could speak the French language fluently. It
was, therefore, thought that I should be of great service in assisting Mr. S.
with his work. I was ready to do any thing that might be required of me, if
only I could be with him.

Mr. S. had once more silenced my fears about Polygamy, and I was
again happy.

We started on our journey—Mr. S., myself, and our dear little Clara,
who was then only six months old.[2] How much I loved that little child, no
tongue can tell! Had she not been my sole companion through so many
weary days and nights of sorrow?

On our arrival at Geneva, we commenced our missionary labours
immediately; but we made very little progress, as Mr. S. was not much
acquainted with the French language, and the Genevese do not readily receive strangers. We had but a small sum of money left when we
reached our destination, and we economized as much as we possibly
could, hoping to make what we had last until some one should join the
church, who might be able to assist the mission. We had full faith and
confidence that the Lord would raise up friends to aid us in the work.
But time rolled on, and we had laboured faithfully for several months
with apparently little success.

My whole soul was in my mission, and I was resolved to fulfil it, as far
as human power, aided by the grace of God, could do so. I sought every

opportunity of introducing among the ladies the Mormon faith; and I tried in every way to live in such a manner as to be an example to those who might be converted and join the church, or who might be inclined to do so. We kept "The Word of Wisdom"* strictly, and never took tea, coffee, wine, or warm drinks of any kind for years.

Mr. S. studied early and late to acquire a knowledge of the French language, hoping soon to be able to make some impression upon the people.

One day he received a letter from an "infidel," who lived in a neighbouring canton, asking him to come and see him, in order that they might talk over Mormonism, for he had heard of us and our doctrine. We were very much pleased at this invitation, for it seemed now that the Lord was about to do something. Mr. S. accordingly went to see this man. He stayed with him several days, convinced him of the truth of the new faith, and, finally, baptized him. He then returned home.

Our money was now nearly gone, and I was very weak from lack of proper nourishment, and dispirited by continual anxiety. I caught a severe cold, and was confined to my bed for a time. My courage at last entirely failed me. Weak and sick as I was, not a soul came to my room. In fact, *who* should come? I had no friend there. The very knowledge that we had come to set forth a strange and unpopular religion, made every one avoid me.

My husband was sad and very anxious. Nor need this excite wonder when it is considered that there was nothing to make life pleasant to either of us, except the thought that we were both the servants of God, and had dedicated our lives to His service.

About a month after the return of Mr. S. from the house of the gentleman whom he had baptized, we received a letter from him. As it was opened, a piece of gold fell on the table. It afterward appeared that this new convert, although he "suspected it might be useful," did not like to offer money to Mr. S. But when he had gone, he determined to send a trifle, saying, at the same time, that "the labourer is worthy of his hire." Never was a Scripture phrase more truthful and welcome in its application. We were very grateful indeed for this timely help, small as it was, for it seemed to us like a recognition of our work. How great are trifles to the hopeful mind!

There were dark clouds on every side, and in moments of despondency we almost feared that they would never clear away. Yet in all this trouble, our faith remained unshaken; and even in the darkest hour of trial, we felt happy in the belief in the divinity of Mormonism.

With all our faith, one question was, perforce, ever uppermost in our minds, how to obtain the necessary means of subsistence? This was an unanswerable difficulty. With the very greatest economy, the time came

* A "Revelation" of Joseph Smith, which all good Mormons observed.

at last when our money was all gone. We had not a coin, or any representative of money, and we had no reason to hope for any. We were in a strange country, among strangers, and in the depth of winter, without fire and without food. What was to be done? In the anguish of my soul, I exclaimed, with bitter tears, "Look down, O God! in Thy mercy, upon my innocent little one, who is now suffering from cold and hunger, while we, her parents, are devoting our lives, our all, to Thy service."

In this trying hour we were speechless. We both felt our helplessness, but neither dared to speak to the other about that which weighed so heavily upon our hearts. It was only our belief in the divinity of our mission that sustained us. Incredible as it may appear, for nearly one week all that we had to exist upon was about a pint of corn flour or maize, and that was principally reserved for our child.

Up to this time, but two persons had joined the church in Geneva. They were poor men, and their wives were very much opposed to the step which they had taken in embracing Mormonism, and thus there was very little to expect from them. We were living in a furnished room, and my little daughter was a great favourite with the family in whose house we were. I was not sorry for this; for in the time of our greatest distress, I used often quietly to open my door at their meal times, and the child would make her way to the dining-room, and get something to eat. Humiliating as this was to me, I felt satisfied for a while, at least, that she was not suffering from hunger as much as we ourselves were.

At the end of that week, when it seemed that we could not exist another day without some nourishment, Mr. S. went to the house of one of the newly converted brethren, whom I have mentioned, with the intention of telling him of our peculiarly distressing circumstances; but when he arrived there, he really had not courage to do so, and he returned again without saying any thing of the matter. My heart sank within me, for I entered into his thoughts, although he did not speak. My little one was then reposing in my arms. She had cried herself to sleep, hungry and cold.

I could not say any thing to my husband when he came home; for I felt instinctively that he had been unsuccessful, and I was almost choking with emotion, which I attempted to suppress. As we sat there silently in the twilight, neither of us venturing to speak to the other, I mentally prayed to the Lord, (if it was His will,) that rather than see my darling wake up again to hunger and suffering, she might quietly sleep her sweet young life away. As I now write, the recollection of that time comes back so vividly that my eyes fill with tears.

While sitting in this fearful gloom, which afterward seemed to me the most solemn hour of my life, I heard a step in the hall, and something whispered to me, "Help is coming." A moment after, the brother whom Mr. Stenhouse had called upon entered the room with some provisions, and he slipped a five-franc piece into my hand. Mr. S. had said nothing to him; but after he had left the house, this brother said that from my husband's manner, he felt convinced that we were suffering, as he knew that as missionaries we had no means of subsistence, and that according to the usual custom among the Mormons, we had to preach "without purse or scrip."

The assistance thus received was a relief from present want, but the future seemed like a dark cloud to hang over my path. I was now in worse circumstances than I had been at the birth of my first child; for I was among strangers, and had absolutely nothing but what the few brethren were kind enough to bring to us from time to time.

I again found, as I had previously experienced at many other periods of my life, the truth of the old verse:

> "Behind a frowning providence,
> God hides a smiling face."

The "smiling face" this time took once more the form of the "Apostle" Snow. Oh! how glad I was to see him. He had, as I have related, brought me joy and gladness once before when I was in great trouble, and I almost looked upon him as my good genius. After all, I was not so very much mistaken; for he gave me a little money to provide for our present necessities, and told Mr. Stenhouse that after a while he should return to England, and raise whatever funds might be needful to enable us to carry out our mission; for he plainly saw that, however enduring faith might be, no one could live without money. In fact, the American elders, as I afterward discovered, did not themselves try, under similar circumstances, to work unaided, although they had no objection to the British elders doing so.

After the birth of my second child,[3] we went to Lausanne, Canton de Vaud; for Mr. Stenhouse thought it would be better for me to remain there during his absence in England, as he had, in addition to this "infidel," whom he had baptized, made the acquaintance of a very good man of very excellent family. In this gentleman's house I engaged apartments, expecting to pay for them, but he never permitted me to do so; and from that day, I never suffered in Switzerland from want of the necessaries of life.

I lived very quietly and comfortably for three months, during the absence of Mr. S. in England. I had not much, it is true; but then a very little sufficed for my wants. I had that, and I was satisfied and happy; for this Mr. B. and his family were very kind indeed to me, and even now, as I review the past, I can say, with all truthfulness, that from the commencement of my missionary life—now over twenty years ago—till I left Mormonism, that brief period in Switzerland was the only happy time I ever knew.[4]

CHAPTER V.

The "Revelation" on Polygamy—How I received it—Left without
Hope—The Doctrine first taught—"Beauties" of the System—My
first Convert to Polygamy—A Scene—How Work progressed—Disaster to Swiss emigration.

Mr. S. returned from England, and, after a while, began in conversation to introduce—gently and enigmatically, I thought—the subject of
Polygamy, at the same time telling me that he "*did not know*" that it was
true, but that he had heard that there had been a revelation given about
it. He dreaded to tell me the truth; but I had heard enough, and determined not to accept the doctrine. Still, at times, I tried to hide my feelings from him; for I hoped that, after all, the intelligence might even now
not prove true. Vain hope! for very soon the "revelation" was sent from
"Zion," with instructions to make no secret of it.

A printed copy of the "revelation" was given to me to read.[1] I was just
about to sit down to the breakfast-table. There were present a Protestant
minister, whom Mr. S. had baptized, and two Mormon elders. The minister knew nothing of the "revelation;" but my husband and the two elders
looked at me, to watch the effect produced upon my mind by its perusal,
with an interest and solemnity as if they were breaking to me cautiously
the news of my mother's death.

I immediately left the room and sought the retirement of my own
apartment, where, after locking the door, I began to read the document;
but before I had got through one half I threw it aside, feeling altogether
rebellious against God. I now began to feel perfectly reckless, and even
willing to throw aside my religion, and take "my chance of salvation,"
rather than submit to Polygamy; for I felt that that new doctrine was a
degradation to womankind. I asked myself, "Why did the Lord wish to
humiliate my sex in this manner?" though at the same time I believed, as I
was told, that the "revelation" was indeed sent from God. Perhaps if I had
kept calm, and had I read it through very carefully and allowed my own
judgment to be exercised upon it, I might have detected there and then
that there was no divinity in it, as I afterwards discovered, to my satisfaction, when I read it a second time, after the lapse of many years.

47

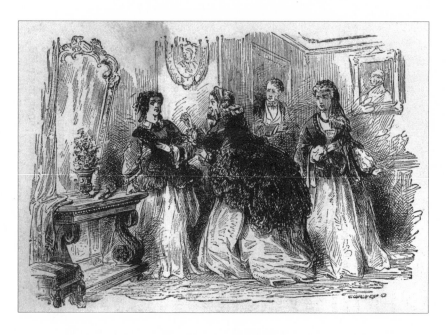

"I could tear you to pieces!"

After some time I began to feel a little more calm, and was able to reason with myself about Polygamy. If, said I, this "revelation" is of God, (and of course it is,) then I ought not to oppose it. It never once entered my mind that any man would dare to give a revelation to the world as coming from God except it was true. Then, I thought, if the Lord requires me to submit, it must be for some good purpose; for "He doeth all things well." I must, therefore, try to subdue this wicked and rebellious nature of mine, and submit to His divine will, and surely He will aid and bless me. After these reflections and constant prayer, I managed to subdue my disobedient heart sufficiently to make my appearance again among the brethren in the breakfast-room. But, oh! that was indeed a wretched day for me; and every day after was more wretched than the previous one. Polygamy was the last thing I thought of at night, and the first thing in the morning. It was with me in my waking hours and in the dead of the night. It haunted me like a spectre. It was like a fearful blight that had fallen upon me and was withering my soul. One thought was ever present in my mind—that thought, Polygamy!

How should I be ever able to bear it? In a moment, every thing in life appeared to have lost its charm for me, except my darling children, and they seemed now to be dearer than ever; for I felt that *they* were indeed *my own*, and that no one could take them away from me. But how I mourned over my little daughter; for I felt that she, perhaps, would some day suffer as I did. Oh! I exclaimed, may heaven forbid it! She is to-day a polygamic wife, and the mother of two children![2]

I would not have my readers think that I bore all my troubles in the introduction of Polygamy meekly, like a saint. Indeed I did not; and I firmly believe that I was a sore trial to my husband. I was wicked and rebellious at times, and said very bitter things of "the Prophet of the Lord," and all his sex, my husband included; for I began to hate the very name of "man." I am afraid that Mr. S. was very much shocked indeed, for he was then a devoted Mormon. He often told me that I was a great clog to him, and more than once he said he could not enjoy the Spirit of God and live with me.

But I was not always so rebellious. There were days when I was full of sorrow and regret for what I deemed my wicked thoughts about "celestial marriage," and then I would fast and pray, and seek forgiveness from the Lord and from my husband. But even in my best moments, I could never bear to hear him speak about Polygamy; and whenever the elders came to our house, the painful topic was sure to be discussed. As soon as I heard it, all my angry excitement returned, and I instantly felt a spirit of rebellion stirring within me. I could not help it. I felt that womankind was insulted whenever the subject was mentioned, and I never got over the feeling. Oh! I thought, how shall I ever "get salvation" with such an offending heart as mine?

It was necessary, however, for me to do something; for I was told by my husband, and the other elders who were present at the time, that it devolved on me to teach the hateful doctrine to the women of Switzerland. That was to be my mission, and I, poor, deluded thing that I was, believed it to be so. I concealed my feelings as best I could, for I was obliged to nerve myself to the task, and prepare to perform my duty, trusting in God to assist me. How fearful a task this was!

My sorrow concerning the introduction of Polygamy was not like any other grief, for it was utterly without hope. Had its teachings been for this life only, I could have borne it with more fortitude, and should have endeavoured to resign myself to my fate. But we were taught that it was to be "for time and for eternity." When I thought that some time my life must end, and that then earthly sorrows would cease, this brought me no comfort; for the cause of my grief was still to exist beyond the grave. Polygamy was to be practised in heaven as well as on the earth. The only possible hope that remained to me was that there—in another world—I might perhaps be so changed as not to know myself or any one else; or that my feelings might be so greatly altered from what they were in this world that I should not realize any pain from what we were taught were the matrimonial arrangements in heaven.

Feeling, as I did, so acutely myself, how was I to break the intelligence of this new and terrible "revelation" to those honest, loving women with whom I was acquainted? I shrank from the task of inflicting so much pain. Their own husbands had not courage to tell them, and I am sure that I had not. But I had already been instructed in the manner in which I was to endeavour to impart to them a knowledge of the doctrine. I had also myself been taught respecting the *beauties* of the "system," so that I might be able to introduce it in a proper manner. It is needless to say that I failed to see those "beauties."

It was soon settled which of the sisters was to be the first victim. She was one whom we all dreaded most, although for rather peculiar reasons. She was a good woman; but, like myself, possessed the weakness of being too fond of her husband. She was possessed also of a very high spirit, and was indeed a completely spoiled child.[3]

It was told her that I had some new principle to communicate to her from "Zion," and she was sent to my apartment to hear it.

"No, I have nothing to tell you," I said.

"Yes, you have," she replied; "for your husband and mine said so."

"No," I answered; "if there was any thing, I can not now remember what it might be." The truth was, my courage had all left me.

I stood there, pale and trembling, even though she was my intimate friend. She noticed it, and feared that I was ill. I *was* ill—worse than she thought or could yet imagine.

However, I presently regained composure enough to commence telling her, and she listened quietly for a while, when suddenly she sprang up, and, with great emotion, cried, "*O mon Dieu! Qu'elle religion des animaux!* And your husband to come to us Swiss with such a religion as that!" She perfectly scared me. She nearly annihilated me with her looks. What a commencement to my mission!

I did not attempt to stop her or get away, say what she liked, for I knew from my own experience what she suffered. I believed, however, that there was no other way for her to "obtain salvation," and my heart ached for her. After she had spent her wrath, she came and sat by me and said, "Does my husband believe this?"

"Yes," I replied, "he does."

Then followed another outburst of grief and rage fearful to witness. I tried to soothe her, but it was useless. She was one of those gushing, impulsive women, who give way to passions of grief, and I saw that it was best to leave her alone. When she became more calm, we talked over it and wept together, and together knelt and prayed. I was almost going to add, we *swore* together in the same breath! This, of course, we did not do. It was something else! Finally, we came to the conclusion that we would both of us fight against the doctrine, and that we would likewise teach all the sisters to do so.

This was certainly a pretty state of affairs!

After she had left the room, I began to feel ashamed of myself, that I, a missionary's wife, should have thus given way. Here, I thought, is all my work to do over again. However, she repented, and I repented; and we now agreed to talk to the other sisters about it, and see how they would take it. I felt a little better, now that I had a companion in misery who could sympathize with me; and we consoled each other, neither of us believing that *our* husbands would ever *practically* adopt the doctrine, or, at least, not for a long time to come.

We taught it to the other sisters; but it was the same sad story over and over again. Some rebelled, and some even fell sick over it. They all lost their joyous, happy looks; and now understood why, for some time past, I had appeared so unhappy and miserable.

At every council of the missionary brethren, the sisters became suspicious of their husbands and what teaching they might be listening to. It was very evident that Polygamy was not going to contribute in any way to our peace of mind or happiness. We could not see how it was possible that any good could result from it. The missionary elders, on the contrary, seemed deeply interested in the new doctrine, and saw "glories" and "beauties" in it that had never been dreamed of before. They could see far away into the eternal world the "exaltation" that awaited the women who would "give wives to their husbands."

The teaching of the doctrine of plural wives, in Switzerland, was fortunately limited. The Protestant minister, of whom I before spoke, received at first the announcement of "celestial marriage" with unfeigned pleasure. He had no son to transmit his name to posterity, and he flattered himself with hope. But his wife, who was not very young, attacked him so violently that he soon abandoned not only the ideas of patriarchal marriage, but also Mormonism itself.

A sister of the lady to whom I had first taught the doctrine of Polygamy, as soon as she discovered that I had converted her sister, called to see me, in company with another lady. She was a tall, angular woman. As she entered the room, she asked me if I were Mrs. Stenhouse. I answered affirmatively; and, before I had time to ask her to be seated, she caught hold of me by the shoulders, like a maniac, and shook me violently, quite taking away my breath. I was like a child in her hands, and could offer no resistance. I had not been accustomed to such violence as this. She then began to declaim wildly against me, and declared that she hated me for teaching her sister such an abominable religion. Her passion rising again, she seized me a second time, and, forcing me into a corner, stood nervously clutching her hands and making for my face, screaming violently that she felt as if she "could tear me to pieces." All this time her friend stood by, with an amused expression on her countenance, as if she quite enjoyed the sight. But to me it was no joke; and I do not know what the enraged woman would have done to me, had not a gentleman, who was a friend of Mr. S., happened to come in at the moment, and, hearing the uproar, hastened to my rescue. The reader may well suppose that I shall not easily forget my experiences in introducing Polygamy among the Swiss.

The first emigration from Switzerland had a sad history. The emigrants were a good people, of the class *bourgeoisie*, who for the Mormon faith left all that was dear to them in fatherland, and, in many cases, gave up the homesteads which had been theirs and their ancestors' for many generations.

Once, when Mr. S. returned from visiting several cantons where he had been for the purpose of counselling the Saints to emigrate, he told me it took all the courage he could muster to tell people in such comfortable circumstances to sell all and to gather to the deserts of Utah. The thought was painful; but faith prevailed, and those among the simple people of the Helvetian Republic who had embraced the Mormon faith, set out, regarding little the perils of the ocean or the privations of the prairie, believing only that every weary step they took led them nearer to the "Zion" of their hopes.

The story of that emigrant band is very sad. Faith had been the actuating principle which induced each one of the company to leave all that was dear on earth and set out for the City of the Saints. But privation and misery shook the faith of some, and in many instances banished even the shadow of hope.

On their way to "Zion," some of the emigrants became dissatisfied, and separated from the general company. They were overtaken between St. Louis and the frontiers by the dreadful cholera of 1853, and almost totally perished. When the news reached Switzerland, the friends of those who were thus lost were very naturally enraged with the Mormon missionary who had "led them into all their trouble and to death." This demonstration of anger was somewhat unreasonable, for every emigrant must himself have known that his way to Utah was not over a path strewn with roses; and the missionaries who advised the journey, being only human, could not possibly foresee the visitation of the cholera, which proved so fatal to the pilgrims.

These facts, however, no one seemed to take into consideration; and it was with difficulty that Mr. S. escaped from personal violence in Lausanne. Though his friends counselled his instant departure from the place, with his usual "confidence in God," he stopped over night; but the morning's reflections suggested discretion and an early departure.

Those of the Swiss pilgrims who escaped the scourge of the cholera were only spared to realize that other scourge—Polygamy.

Many a time, amidst the horrors of polygamous "Zion," have faithful wives, who passed unscathed through that terrible plague, wished that it might have been their own fate to have perished with their countrywomen on the desert wilds.

We remained in Switzerland about three years and a half. The mission, notwithstanding its dark beginning, had been very successful. Mormonism had been introduced into seven cantons; a paper, in the French language, was published by Mr. S., in the interests of that faith, in Geneva, as well as books and *brochures* in the French, German, and Italian languages, almost entirely supported at the expense of the converted Swiss. By the time that we left, there were several missionaries from Utah, and about the same number from England, labouring in Helvetia.

Mr. S. requested to be released from his presidency of the Swiss and Italian missions; and, with the means which some of the more wealthy of the emigrating Swiss had generously furnished, we were provided with what was necessary for our journey to Utah.

CHAPTER VI.

We return to England—How Polygamy was taught there—
The Girls happy—The Wives miserable—General Effects of the
Doctrine—A Runaway Wife—How she acted in Haste and repented
at Leisure—A Mother leaves her Babes—A Lady is "counselled"
to emigrate without her Husband—Follies of certain Elders—
Polygamic "Poetry!"

WE returned to England in November, 1854, with the intention of
leaving for Utah in the following spring. Until the period of emigration
arrived, we went to reside in the house of the President of the London
Conference,[1] and it was at that time that I first began seriously to doubt
the truth of Mormonism. I gradually became convinced, though I could
scarcely explain how, that there was *something wrong*, something that I did
not understand, underlying the whole system. I began to realize that there
was more of frail humanity about it than of the pure and holy religion
that I had believed it to be; for the reader must remember that, however
much I was opposed to Polygamy, it never once entered my thoughts to
question that it was a pure and religious principle.

I believed that my opposition to Polygamy in Switzerland was the
result of my own "depraved nature," and not the fault of my religion. But
soon after our arrival in London, I began to hear things about the authorities of the church in Utah that I was convinced could not be right.

On the continent we had only seen and heard ourselves and our
own converts on the new revelation. On our arrival in England, I was
somewhat anxious to learn how others had received it.

The young girls were pleased with it, for it extended their chances
of marriage, and they were the recipients of many attentions from the
elders. It was natural for them to be gratified with the assurance that it
was their "privilege" to tell any man of their love, and that it was his duty
to marry them. But during a year's residence in London, I never met a
happily married woman in the Mormon Church who did not abhor it.
They were submissive to its teachings, as it had no immediate results
there; but it troubled them terribly and rendered them miserable when
they thought of going to Utah.

Married women had, however, the same favorable attentions and compliments paid them as the young girls, for the Gentile marriage never stood in the way. It could at any time be broken, if the lady had only the inclination or nerve to do it. No married missionary could take another wife in Europe without special permission from Brigham Young; but they could, and did, teach married women that in "Zion" the "Gentile chain was broken," and that the ladies could choose for husbands, "whom they would in the Lord," when they got there, hinting, at the same time, that they, themselves, would be in the market. That teaching was not listened to by some; but it was by others, and many homes in England have been blighted by it, and broken up.

Women who were ill-mated, or imagined that they were, saw an easy way of settling their difficulties when Polygamic teaching instructed them that all marital covenants and obligations, before entering into the church, were unrecognized by the Lord. All that they had to do was to induce their husbands to take them to Utah, and if the husband refused to go, the wife could go alone. "Get away pleasantly and quietly if you can; if you cannot—get away any how." This was frequently the counsel given, and not infrequently acted upon. A pretty face or attractive person never lacked facilities for getting away.

Husbands who were dissatisfied with their wives could leave them and their families, also, and go to "Zion" alone, if the wife and family refused to accompany them. The husband was the head of the wife, and should do his own duty, whether his wife and children did theirs or not. If his family did not follow him, he could take a young wife or wives there, and "lay the foundation anew" for another family; and in his experience he believed that the promise was singularly fulfilled, that "he who forsaketh wife or child for my sake shall have a hundred fold." That run-a-way husband was, of course, entitled to a hundred young girls, if he could only get them and keep them.

Such things were not taught to ignorant men and women only, but also to people in very much better positions. I know one gentleman in Liverpool who separated from his family because of their unbelief in Mormonism, and made great sacrifices in order to go to Utah. He married an accomplished young lady in Salt Lake City, and lived long enough in Zion to wish that he had never been there. The last marriage was happy enough; but the gentleman and lady outlived their faith, and concluded to separate and leave the country. The young lady returned to London, the gentleman to Liverpool—a poorer, but a wiser man.

There was also an old couple with whom I was well acquainted in Portsmouth. They were engaged in business, and doing very well. The wife joined the Mormon Church, and the husband, being a good-natured old gentleman, allowed her to do just what she liked, and she was very liberal to the missionaries. She heard so much of the glories of "Zion" that she began to tease her husband to emigrate, although he did not wish to do so. But as he discovered that she was growing dissatisfied and unhappy about it, he consented to let her go alone, believing that she would return again. She went to Utah provided with abundance of every thing and plenty of money. Soon after her arrival there, she was married to an old Mormon elder, who built a house with her money and otherwise made himself very comfortable. Then he took a young wife, and then another; and among them they led the old lady such a life that she was glad to leave the house and labour for her support as best she could. She frequently heard from her husband in England, who had fretted until he fell sick. He had to get a nurse or housekeeper, and as he was well to do, this person contrived to get him to marry her. After a year or two, he died, leaving all his property to her; while the poor old lady was living in Utah in poverty, very unhappy and bitterly repenting her folly in leaving so good a husband as he had been to her. While the old gentleman was sick, I saw the old lady in deep distress of mind, as she could not get money to take her back to England. Had she got there while the old gentleman was still alive, she would doubtless have inherited all his property; but now she is poor and homeless.

Some years later, while living in New York, I saw other illustrations of the baneful teachings in England. One of the Mormon elders, on his return from a mission to Europe, came to my house accompanied by a "sister," who, he said, had just arrived with other emigrants from England. He told me that she was feeling dull, and he would like her to be with some family of the Saints where she would feel at home for about two weeks. At the end of that time, they intended to go to Salt Lake.

She took one of my little ones in her arms, and seemed, for a stranger, to fondle it with great affection. I soon noticed that she was in tears, and my sympathy was instantly enlisted for her. I saw she had trouble on her mind, and I tried to discover the cause of her sorrow. She told me that she had left two little children at home, and was pining to see them. I asked her why she had left them, and she told me that she had been "counselled" to leave a good husband, a good home, and two darling little ones, and go to "Zion." She was perfectly wretched. She had nothing to complain of in her husband's conduct towards her, only he did not believe in Mormonism, and would not allow her to attend the meetings of the Saints. She had come off stealthily with the assurance from "the servants of God" that she should have her children soon.

I told her that I did not believe she would ever see them again, nor did I think that she deserved to, unless she returned to her husband immediately and sought his forgiveness. She had been taught, she said, that it was necessary for her salvation that she should "gather with the

Saints to Salt Lake." Her husband opposed her going, and as she had to leave unknown to him, she could not manage to get her children away.

I used every means in my power to get her to return, and tried to picture to her that once happy home now made desolate through her desertion; but she felt that her religion required her to make the sacrifice, believing as she had been taught, that if she "sought first *the kingdom* of God and His righteousness," all other things should be added unto her. She was, after all, very much to be pitied; for she was a victim to the teachings of the elders, and she firmly believed that whatever they told her was the revelation of heaven to her.

She left me, and I feared that she would still pursue her journey in despite of all that I had said to her; but in about two months from that time, I was one morning told that a lady wished to see me. I was agreeably surprised to find that it was the runaway mother. She told me that after our conversation she could not go to Salt Lake, but had remained in St. Louis, had written to her husband and had made every thing right with him, and she was now on her way back again to her home in England. She was very happy, and I rejoiced with her.

This circumstance is given to illustrate the power of the teachings of the elders. To all appearances it could not have been a love affair, for there was nothing in the look of the man that could captivate any woman. To be sure, there is no accounting for taste in matters of love, and she might have seen qualities in him that every one else had failed to perceive.

Another circumstance somewhat similar to this came directly under my personal notice. In this instance the lady, whom I knew, was married very happily. Her husband held a very lucrative position, but who was at times obliged to be absent from home for several months together, on one occasion found it necessary to leave his family for nearly a year. He went; but not wishing to be separated from his family for so long a time, he wrote to her, requesting that she would come out to him with her children, sending her at the same time funds necessary for that purpose. The brethren heard of this, and "counselled" her to go to "Zion" instead, telling her that if she did not go then she might not have another opportunity for a long time, as the country would be involved in war. She obeyed the "counsel," and without replying to her husband, left for Utah, and crossed the plains with her four little children, and arrived in "Zion" almost dead with the trials and difficulties she had had to encounter, not having a protector, and being so entirely ignorant of the nature of the journey. Her husband, who was a very excellent man, followed her, some time subsequently; but of course he felt that he had been very badly treated, and it was with difficulty that he could be reconciled.

All the missionaries, before they leave Utah, are instructed to make no selections from the lambs of the flock; and though many of them have no doubt honoured these instructions, many others have seemed to do little more than preach on Sundays, attend one or two meetings during the week, and devote the rest of their leisure to the "sisters"—taking them to theatres, public entertainments, and wherever they themselves were invited to visit.

If any family invited a Utah elder to dine with them on any given day, if he was at all familiar with them, he was almost certain to bring "a sister" with him. This was frequently a great annoyance; for instead of imparting instruction to the family, or entertaining them with information about "Zion," his chair after dinner was almost certain to travel with that of the lady visitor to the neighbourhood of a window, or to a quiet corner, where they could entertain each other with soft nonsense.

The follies of such missionaries, (though they doubtless preserved themselves free from immorality,) their silly talk, childish amusements, nonsense, flirting, and extravagance with girls as silly as themselves, was a great stumbling-block to many a married woman at the introduction of the principles of Polygamy in England.

At the time of my sojourn in London, there was a feeling of great uncertainty among the Saints about every thing connected with domestic relations. Ignorant men preaching the doctrine of Polygamy to a public audience might be expected to talk a great deal of nonsense upon such a delicate subject, and that was bad enough; but when to this was added the fanatical feeling about the glory of "Zion," and the destruction of the Gentile world within a few years, it was worse still. There was much anxiety and excitement among the Saints. It was one continued stream of prediction that the world was to be devastated by wars that would destroy the greater portion of the men, and thus bring about a fulfilment of the prophecy which says that "Seven women shall take hold of one man." The women were to become so urgent in their importunities for marriage, that they would gladly promise to "eat their own bread and wear their own apparel;" and all they would ask would be the privilege of being called by some man's name, to "take away their reproach."

With such preaching, Sunday after Sunday, it is not to be wondered at that the Saints became bewildered, scarcely knowing what to do. One thing alone they knew: that they were to "flee to Zion," and get all their marital relations settled in the "Endowment House," so that every woman should have a husband who could "save her," and every man have all the wives and children that he could gather round him, before the "great day of wrath, and the coming of the Lord."

One of the most popular axioms of the elders at that time was, "It is better to be the mate of a ship of war than the captain of a schooner." This was well understood by the sisters to mean that it was better to be *one* of the wives of a *great* man in "the kingdom," than to be the *only* wife of a little man. It was of no consequence how kind a husband might be to his wife and family; if he was not also abounding with zeal, and full of talk in the meetings, he was very little esteemed. Many a silly woman has been carried away by such nonsense till she scarcely knew what she was doing or wanted to do. She probably loved her husband, but mourned to think that he could not take his stand among the favoured of the Lord. In the course of time, her regrets would grow into discontent; and when some raving, enthusiastic preacher came along, she was ready to form the conclusion that she ought to hasten to Zion; and thus, from one step to the other, she was soon on her way to Utah, with her children, if she could, or without them if she could do no better.

This was the period when Polygamy was introduced, and that was the spirit of the times when I made my visit to London, preparatory to going to "Zion."

The following are one or two of about a dozen verses of Mormon "poetry," once extremely popular among the "Saints," and which certainly express very truly their sentiments at the time of which I speak:

"The time the prophet saw is on the wing,
When seven women to one man shall cling.

"Not for the lack of clothing or of bread,
But for a husband—a man—a head!
To obviate reproach and share his name,
As to be single then will be a shame;

"For war will strew its victims o'er the plain,
And maddened men rush heedless to be slain;
A man shall be more precious in the land
Than golden wedges from the Ophir strand.

"If you perchance among the worthies stand,
And seven women claim your saving hand,
Do not reject the six and save the one,
And boast of magnanimity when done."

Doggerel, no better than this, and much of it a great deal worse, might be heard in almost every meeting of the "Saints."

CHAPTER VII.

Mormon Life in London—"Counselled" to go to Salt Lake
Valley—Sickness and Annoyances—Doubts and Fears—Faith
wavering—Loneliness in the Great City—"The dear American
Brethren"—Preparations for leaving England.

MR. M., the Mormon President in London, was constantly in
receipt of letters from Salt Lake during the time of our residence in his
house; and I observed that he acted in a very mysterious manner with
them. He would read them to my husband when he thought that they
were alone, and conceal them when I came into the room. This made
me resolve to see these letters, if possible. I mentioned this to Mrs. M.,
and she volunteered to get them for me. What I discovered I have no
right to reveal now, just as I had then no right (although through the
kindness of this lady they had been placed in my hands) to pry into
them. Suffice it, however, to say that they set me thinking, and the more
I thought the worse I felt. I was bewildered and wretched, losing confidence in myself and in every thing. In fact, I had not enough experience to rely upon my own judgment, and my husband was a slave to
Mormonism; but from what I had read in those letters about the teachings in Utah, and from my observation of the conduct of the American
brethren, I began to feel the greatest horror of going out to Salt Lake.
I knew it was decided that we should go in the spring, and the thought
made me very melancholy.

At this time—Christmas Day, 1854—my fourth child was born. When
he was three weeks old, my second daughter was taken very ill. I mention
these things for reasons which will soon be apparent to the reader.[1]

I had now another—a real and tangible trouble added to the grief
caused by my previous forebodings respecting the future, which I have
already described. My child was very ill indeed. Her life was even despaired
of, and in my then weak state I felt this additional trial all the more.

When the time arrived for us to prepare for emigration, it seemed
to me impossible for us even to think of such a thing. The reader will
understand this when I remind him that we had four little children—the
youngest only a month old—and one dangerously ill. The Utah brethren

60

knew my state of mind, for I had talked with them very freely about the matter. It was therefore suspected that I was not willing to emigrate, and perhaps might even refuse to do so. This was an entire mistake; for I had not yet arrived at the feeling that I could reject Mormonism altogether and throw off my connexion with that faith. How often, afterwards, I wished it had been so!

Had I then been as devoted a Mormon as I was a few months previously, I know that I should have made a greater effort to go. But, although I still clung to that religion, my faith was already undermined; I was soulless and dispirited.

One day Mr. M. came home and said to me, "Mrs. Stenhouse, it has been decided to 'counsel' your husband to emigrate without you if you will not immediately get ready. I thought I would let you know this much, although it is not right for me to relate what takes place in council. But," he continued, "I think it is villainous with this sick child on your hands and a young babe, to require you to do so. Yet, what can be done? Their plan is this: Your husband, if he finds you will not go, is to get ready and leave for Liverpool; and, as soon as he is gone, I shall be instructed to tell you that I need the rooms you now occupy, and that you must leave directly. You will be puzzled in the midst of your trouble to know what to do. Then some of the brethren will be at hand to send you after your husband, and you will be very glad to go; for you will have no choice, and will be ready to do any thing to get out of your troubles."

Oh! I can not tell how indignant I was when I heard this. I utterly loathed and detested every one of them; and I walked about the room so full of contending emotions that it was some time before I could utter a word. At last I was able to speak, and I said:— "Mr. M——, *would* you send me away?"

"If they 'counsel' me to do so," he replied, "I shall have to do it."

"Can you not, or have you not enough courage to oppose a thing you *know* to be wrong?" I enquired.

"If I did so," said he, "I should get into trouble."

He knew me too well to suppose that I should repeat what he said while it could harm him; nor would I now have written so much had he remained a Mormon.

"Now," said I, "I shall tell them that I will not go in my present condition; nor will I! If my husband wishes to take their counsel and go, he may go alone; and they shall see that I will not follow him now or ever after." I was greatly excited as I said this.

When Mr. S. returned home, I told him what had been said; but, as he agreed with me in believing that it was impossible for me to go with our sick child, that settled it for the present. The elders visited me and talked with me until I was nearly worried to death. They made Mr. M.

give us notice to leave his apartments purely on that account; and I had to move our sick child in cold, damp weather, just as she was getting better. As might be expected, she caught cold and had a relapse, and we despaired of her ever recovering.

I was now so worn out with care and anxiety and watching my sick child that my health began to fail, and I grew weaker and weaker. My little one was, however, now becoming better. She had been sick for more than two months; and I myself alone had carefully tended her during all that period, at the same time having the charge and nursing of my young babe. All the help I had was the assistance of a girl, a mere child, only twelve years of age.

My husband having frequently to preach at a distance, was now a great deal from home, and I led a lonely life. I was, in fact, buried alive in the vast wilderness of London; and nothing can be more desolate than the feeling of loneliness in the midst of a great city. Left to my own melancholy thoughts about Polygamy and the reported teachings in Utah, my confidence in the authorities of the church was most terribly shaken, and I dreaded worse than death going to Salt Lake City. This so preyed upon my mind that my health was fast failing, and I was unable to walk across the room or hold my infant in my arms.

My physician told me that he did not know what was the matter with me; and twice, when visiting me, he urged me to confide in him, that he might be able to benefit me. He said that I had no disease, yet I was failing fast. I could not tell him of the sorrow that was eating my life away. I never knew what he said to my husband; but, immediately after consultation, I was sent to the West End of London with a nurse, hoping by this slight change to recruit my health, and a kind friend took charge of my children. I did not care much what was done with me, for I fully believed that I was going to die.

I had not been away more than a week when Mr. S. came to tell me that he had been notified that a ship would sail from Liverpool in the course of two weeks from that time, and that it was expected that we should sail in her.

I did not feel that this was possible; but the fact of Mr. S. speaking to me about it, showed me that he particularly wished to go, and I resolved to make the attempt. We ordered a carriage and I went to my apartment, leaving my babe with the nurse. Mr. S., after taking me to the house, left me, and I began to pack a trunk. Before I had been busy ten minutes, I fainted; but how long I remained in that condition I cannot tell. When Mr. S. returned and found that I was so very ill, he telegraphed to Liverpool to say that I was not well enough to make the journey. A telegram was returned:—"Bring her along, and she will get better." But Mr. S. had a little independence left, and we did not go.

The summer passed very drearily, as Mr. S. was away from home nearly all the time, lecturing in different places. My children were too young to be companions, and the Mormons rather shunned me, because of my weakness in the faith. The young sisters did not like to hear me talk about those "dear American Brethren," and therefore they stayed away. I had, however, a few particular friends, and I felt that that was sufficient. And yet it was my husband's society that I yearned for, and this fearful Mormonism always deprived me of that. I could not, therefore, feel happy; for when he was away from me, I was always imagining some dreadful thing, which afterwards proved to have had no foundation in truth. I was doubtful of every thing now. This was the beautiful result of my religion!

I fear that by this time the reader may begin to think that I must be of a very unhappy temperament. But this is not exactly the truth. Until the time when the horrors of apprehension respecting the doctrine of Polygamy began to weigh upon my mind, I had always been looked upon as a cheerful, lighthearted, and hopeful girl. But there was a canker-worm gnawing continually at my heart *now*. Hope had died out. I felt that I was doomed for time and for eternity, and sometimes it seemed to me impossible that I should pray to a God who could make such unjust laws. How could I teach my little ones to love Him?

How different to me were these ideas of God and of His truth, from the feelings and sentiments which were mine when a girl! Then I could look around upon the beauties of nature and see the hand of God in every thing, while my soul would be filled with joy and gladness; my only anxiety being to know what I should do to become acceptable in His sight. But now I saw no beauty in any thing. Nothing had power to divert me from my sad thoughts.

Mormonism to me at that time was a melancholy fact.

"Labouring" with a Rebellious Wife.

CHAPTER VIII.

We emigrate to America—New York—The Mormon—An
"Apostle," two "High-Priests," and a "Seventy," and what they did—
Polygamy in New York—Disarrangement of Plans—We set out for
"Zion"—The Utah Elders choose other Wives—Three Months on
the Plains—First Glimpse of "The City of Saints."

ABOUT the middle of November, 1855, we sailed from Liverpool,
with several hundred Mormons, for New York, where we landed on the
last day of the year.[1]

Before we left England, Mr. Stenhouse concluded that ten years'
constant missionary service, without fee or reward, and living in the
dependent condition that I have related, was all that the church had any
right to expect of him, especially as his family was growing up, and would
soon demand more than daily bread. It was his purpose to seek in the
New World any occupation for which he might be fitted.

He regretted that the vessel we were to sail in was to land us at New
York; but in emigration, as in every thing else in Mormonism, the priesthood dictate; and to have sailed in any other vessel would have been evidence of want of faith and a good spirit. He would have preferred almost
any other seaport, as he wished to avoid the *Mormon* newspaper office; for
he had an idea that he might possibly be called to associate himself with
it in some way, and that again would be a renewal of missionary life. The
very thing he dreaded came upon him.

Our residence in New York, while Mr. S. was associate editor of the
Mormon, was characterized by extreme poverty. But, with all the luxuries
in the world around me, my spectre—Polygamy—would have spoiled
them all.

There were four brethren from Utah at that time in New York—an
"Apostle," two "High-Priests," and a "Seventy." The last was much like
myself in faith; and, on his return to Utah, he settled up his affairs, and,
with his family, left the country. The High-Priests picked up each a young
lady, to whom they were married after they returned to the mountains;
but the Apostle was favoured with a special dispensation from Brigham
Young, and took his sixth wife—a very amiable young lady, then living in

Connecticut. They occupied a pleasant house in East-Brooklyn, and had all the comforts and endearments of home while on mission.

The "Apostle" was well used to the polygamic business, and suffered no inconvenience on returning home with his youngest bride; but the High-Priests realized the truth of the adage, that the course of true love does not always run smooth. The first wife of one of them kept him at a respectful distance from her "bed and board," and the first wife of the other kept her younger rival at an equally respectful distance from herself. The first "High Priest" has "gone to heaven," and the second High Priest had, in course of time, to give a bill of divorce to his young wife. They were all three good girls, and accepted their copartnership in matrimony as purely for the sake of their faith as ever women could do. What happiness they have had in it they best know; but the young widow seems the most contented of the three.[2]

The difficulty in Utah in 1857 brought the *Mormon* to a close, and, with its expiration, my poverty vanished. Mr. S. was now at liberty to do as he pleased, and his pen found ready remuneration on the staff of the New-York *Herald*.

The settlement of the "Utah Difficulty" in 1858 threatened another change in our life. Mr. S. was appointed by Brigham Young to preside over the Saints in the Eastern States; but he had got a taste of freedom, and he never afterwards was wholly engaged in the propagation of Mormonism.

In the following year, Elder George Q. Cannon, now the prominent Apostle in Utah, was appointed to succeed Mr. Stenhouse; and, at the end of the emigration season of that year, we were permitted to go to "Zion."

Our journey across the plains occupied three months, and we experienced the same vicissitudes of travel as other emigrants who have already told their tale.[3]

It was the month of September—the commencement of our beautiful Indian summer—when we emerged from the cañon and caught sight of Salt Lake City. Every thing looked green and lovely; and, in spite of all the sad forebodings which troubled me in crossing the plains, I involuntarily exclaimed, "Ah! what a glorious spot!" It looked like a beautiful garden—another Eden—in the midst of a desert valley. We had a glimpse of the Great Salt Lake, far away in the distance, stretching out like a placid sheet of molten silver, while everywhere were the lofty and lonely-looking snow-capped mountains, which entirely encircled us, like mighty prison walls.

It would be impossible for me to describe my feelings at that time. Even while I was enchanted with the glorious prospect before me, there arose again in my mind that haunting spectre of my existence—Polygamy! I remembered that this little earthly paradise would probably be to me a prison-house; and with a mother's instinct, I dreaded what my daughters might be destined to suffer there. Lovely as the scene was, there was yet a fatal shadow overhanging it all.

If the sad forebodings of my heart were realized, I could see no prospect of ever getting away. As to having a railroad across those plains—that seemed to me utterly impossible. Even if I had ever thought for a moment that such a work could be carried out, I never should have believed that it could be accomplished in my own lifetime. No! there was no help for me—even if it came to the worst.

I felt that my doom was sealed; and many another woman in the company was troubled at heart with thoughts as sad as mine.

What living contradictions we were!—singing the songs of Zion night and morning in a circle, and listening to prayers of thankfulness for being permitted to gather out of Babylon; and during the day, as we trudged along over the plains, in twos and threes, we were expressing to each other the bitterness of our thoughts. How little, sometimes, do the songs of gladness reflect the sentiments of the heart! Have I not heard many a woman sing, to the tune of the "Bonnie Breast-knots," the sweet though untruthful song, "Hey, the merry Mormons!"

"I never knew what joy was
Till I became a Mormon!"

My edition of the song was slightly changed. I substituted *sorrow* for "joy," and then the words seemed more applicable to my own case.

We were kindly received in Salt Lake City. Having been missionaries for so many years, we were known by name; and we also had a wide circle of personal acquaintances among the chief Elders and emigrants. It was now that the fearful Polygamy, which I so much dreaded, was to be brought before my eyes in practice.

Almost all the elders with whom I had formerly become acquainted had more than one wife. Some of these brethren called on me, and kindly insisted that I should visit their families, which I, in many instances, refused, for fear that what I might see would make me feel worse, and that was not at all necessary.

Shortly after our arrival, we visited President Young, who received us very graciously, and appointed an early day after that for us to dine with him. On that occasion, he invited some of the apostles and leading elders, with their families, to meet us at his table; and we passed an exceedingly pleasant afternoon and evening, Brigham making himself very affable. His wives, I found, were all, as far as I could judge, amiable and kind-hearted ladies, making every effort to render our visit agreeable. I was much pleased with the manner and appearance of Brigham Young, and felt greatly reassured; and I began to hope that there was no truth in the reports which I had heard of him while in London. I was thankful to feel this, for it gave me encouragement to think that, after all, things might not be so bad as I had anticipated. Brigham *to-day* does not seem the same man! I have no doubt that if he were to deign to read this little work, he would say, "It is Sister Stenhouse who has changed, not me." I would give much to believe that some of the facts of Utah history were but an idle dream!

During that visit, Brigham hinted to Mr. S. something about another mission; and when we got home, Mr. S. asked me how I should feel if he were sent away again. After all that we had gone through for Mormonism, I thought that this would be exacting too much; but Mr. S. was ready, and really began to plan how he could secure bread for us during his absence—the butter I should have had to provide myself, or go without; but he soon became very useful with his pen, and, therefore, was not sent away.

CHAPTER IX.

Life in Utah—Polygamy in Practice—The first Wife to be
"Destroyed," unless she "consents"—Deceptive Teaching about tak-
ing a second Wife—The Mormon Plan—"Labouring" with refractory
Wives—Elderly Ladies assisting in Courtship—A first Wife's Trials—
Anomalies of Polygamic Life.

I was now in the chief city of "Zion"—the dwelling-place of the
Prophet and the principal Saints, which every good Mormon longed
so earnestly to see. I had suffered very much, as I anticipated the time
when we should arrive in Utah, and my fears of the future had long
banished all peace from my mind. Now I had an opportunity of learning
whether the evils which I dreaded really existed, or whether I had too
credulously listened to scandalous reports, and the promptings of my
own womanly apprehensions.

I had the daily and hourly cares of a young and dependent family
devolving upon me, and, of course, had not much leisure for any thing
else. At the same time I had abundant opportunities of observation, and
thus my experience of Mormonism and Polygamy in Utah is much the
same as that which any woman of ordinary sense could tell, if she had the
inclination and opportunity.

When Polygamy was first taught in Europe and in the United States,
great stress was laid upon *the assertion* that in no case would any man be
allowed to take a second or third wife without (as they wished it to be
supposed) the entire consent and approval of the first. This statement,
though false and deceptive, naturally silenced the fears of many women
who would otherwise have opposed the doctrine; for they were deceived
into thinking that, as their husbands could not take another wife without
first consulting them and obtaining their permission to do so, it would
always be in their power to refuse; and thus they supposed they would
not themselves be practically affected by Polygamy until their own faith
prompted them to consent. I need not say how greatly they were deceived.
The elders have been often accused of deception in thus explaining away
the doctrine to the women. But it seems to me that, although they were
not right in doing so, it is very probable that they were influenced by good

and kind motives. The fact is, many of the elders were much better men than their religion taught them to be; and when the "revelations" which they had to teach were harsh or unjust, they would try to adapt them to the weakness of their hearers, and put them in as pleasant a way as possible. Such was the case when the revelation on Polygamy was introduced.

The *theory* of plural marriages in Utah is this:

When a Mormon husband desires to take another wife, the prescribed formula requires (1) that the Lord give a revelation to Brigham Young that He approves of the proposed extension of the man's family; next, (2) that the would-be patriarch obtain the "consent" of the first wife to take another; then (3) he is to obtain the consent of the parents or guardians of the selected damsel, so that he can address her in loving terms respecting his devotion to God, His kingdom, and herself personally; and (4) he must secure the acquiescence of the damsel. Should "the Lord"* veto the proposition, the suit is ended. Should "the Lord" approve and the wife disapprove, no further advance can be made. Should the parents withhold consent, "the Lord" and the wife are held in check. Finally, if they are all agreed and the maiden objects, then the approval of all the other consenting parties is set aside. That is the *theory*.

But there is no truth in all these statements—not a particle. Without the consent and approval of Brigham Young, no patriarchal marriage can be consummated; with his approval, that of the wife, the parents, and the girl herself can all be dispensed with.

Cases are not few to sustain these assertions. Many a maiden has been married without the consent of her parents; and others have "obeyed counsel," when they had no heart in the matter—then or ever after.

The "Revelation on Polygamy" was written by the scribe of Joseph Smith, from the prophet's dictation, after he had already taken other "wives." It is worded so as to have at one moment the appearance of a fair and proper understanding between the husband and wife whenever the former entertained the idea of taking to himself another bride; and yet, when viewed in another light, it has quite an opposite sense, and tries to terrify the first wife, if disobedient, with threats of the wrath of God.[1]

When a woman's "consent" is asked, she knows very well that she will have to give it—if she is not prepared to live in open warfare with her husband. She knows, too, that he will take that other wife independently of her, and she is powerless to prevent it. She may as well consent.

---

* On one occasion, when a Mormon gentleman from Liverpool was expressing to one of the Apostles his dissatisfaction about something, he remarked, "Surely the Lord would not sanction this!" Whereupon the Apostle, touching him on the arm, pointed to the White House, where Brigham Young resided, and emphatically remarked, "Your '*Lord*' resides up there!"

But some brave women have never given their consent, and have never allowed the second wife to enter their homes. Some refined ladies, with excellent families, have had the happiest of homes destroyed by withholding their consent; and where peace and warm affection were proverbial, the bitterest strife ensued.

The men who have acted in this way are not the gross and ignorant brethren, but more often the particularly "pious" men, who make long prayers in their families, who preach in the ward meetings, and in the Tabernacle; men of smooth words, with the name of the Lord always upon their lips. These are the men who have mercilessly wrung the hearts of the wives of Utah. What to such men are a wife's tears and sorrows? Nothing.

If the wife shows "temper," it makes it only worse. He wants peace, so he says; and if he can not find it there, it furnishes him with the better excuse for going back again to his younger wife—just where he wants to go!

Aiding and abetting these brethren, and encouraging them in multiplying their wives, there is a class of good-meaning sisters who are always dabbling in other people's affairs, and making love-matches. These go round from one unhappy victim to another, and talk to the poor, broken-hearted women, to soothe and comfort them; and before they go away they give them the very pleasing assurance that woman was cursed in the Garden of Eden, and that

"We've all got the cross for to bear."*

They are "laboured with" in the interest of the husband till they are, in most cases, entirely subdued.

If a woman gets "broken in," or "tamed," the husband rejoices, and the "sisters" "join in prayer," relating in the subjugated woman's ears all the blessings of "obedience," the great glory that awaiteth all who live in the holy order of "celestial marriage." When their work is complete, it is fortunate for all parties; but a dose of that kind generally only lasts till the first wife gets a glimpse again of the second wife, or hears about her and her husband going together to the theatre or to the dance. Then "the devil," who was only scotched, is "raised" again; and before he can

---

* The following is from the New-York *World*, November 14th, 1871:—

Reporter—What is really the position of the women on the question of Polygamy?

Mr. Perris—They are generally subject to what may be called a forced lead, by the older women—those who are childless, and the others who seem to be entirely without maternal instincts. These go about among the mass of better women, talk to them, impress upon them the practice as a religious duty, even necessary to their salvation; get them to sign papers in its favour, and, if they hesitate, threaten to expose them as having become dangerously weak in the faith. That is the way an appearance of unanimity in favour of Polygamy is maintained.

be finally "laid," the whole affair has to be repeated from the beginning, and in many cases the experiment has to be tried again and again before the desired results are produced, and not infrequently this labour of love is a total failure, when a bitterness ensues which is unknown outside of polygamic households.

When kindness fails to "soften down" the rebellious wife, then wrath is poured into her ears, and she learns from the revelation that "If any man have a wife who hold the keys of this power, and he teaches her the law of my priesthood, as pertaining to these things, then *she shall believe*, and administer unto him, or *she shall be destroyed*, saith the Lord your God, for *I will destroy her*."

This is a beautiful position for any loving wife to be placed in! Her husband is to teach her Polygamy, and she *must* believe; for it is distinctly said, "She *shall* believe." But should she lack evidence of the truth of the revelation, and can not believe in its divinity, then "*She shall be destroyed;*" and the Lord, like a kind and loving father, adds, "*I will destroy her*." What language to place in the mouth of a kind and loving God and Father! How opposite is this to the teachings of Jesus Christ! But it is in keeping with the other teachings of the Mormon Church. Mormonism taught me to look upon the great Ruler of the Universe as a "God of vengeance," while every thing in nature has taught me that He is a "God of love."

So repugnant has this teaching of the Lord's vengeance been to the women in Utah, who oppose Polygamy, that many of them have the utmost disgust for religion, and care as little about "the Lord" as they do about their husbands.

How little do the Mormon men of Utah know what it is, in the truest sense, to have *a wife*, though they have so many "wives," after their own fashion. Almost imperceptibly to the husband, and even to the wife herself, a barrier rises between them from the very day that he marries another woman. It matters not how much she believes in the doctrine of plural marriages, or how willing she may be to submit to it; the fact remains the same. The estrangement begins by her trying to hide from him all her secret sorrow; for she feels that what has been done can not be undone now, and she says, "I can not change it; neither would I if I could, because it is the will of God, and I must bear it; besides, what good will it do to worry my husband with all my feelings? He can not help me, and is he not another woman's husband?"

Then comes the painful feeling, "I have no longer any desire to confide in him."

Perhaps, too, she may detect some familiarity between her husband and the other wife. Then she would feel full of anger and bitterness toward them both, and, strive as she may, human nature would prevail.

His presence becomes irksome to her; even his touch would make her shudder. And yet she might hide all this; but with what anguish of soul! She might keep up a calm exterior, and when spoken to about plural marriages, might lead persons to believe that all was pleasant; and even her own husband might think that his wife had become "used to it." Don't you believe it, men of Utah! Your wives *never* get "used to it" until they have, in a great measure, or perhaps *entirely*, lost their love for you.

When this little book falls into the hands of some of the women of Utah, they will, I know, acknowledge in their hearts, if not in words, how true my statements are. A man may have a dozen wives; but from the whole of them combined he will not receive as much real love and devotion as he might from one alone, if he had made her feel that she had his undivided affection and confidence. How terribly these men deceive themselves! When peace, or rather quiet, reigns in their homes, they think that the spirit of God is there. But it is *not* so! It is a calm, not like the gentle silence of sleep, but as the horrible stillness of death— the death of the heart's best affections, and all that is worth calling love. All *true* love has fled, and indifference has taken its place. The very children feel it. What do they—what *can* they care about their fathers? They seldom see them. I am writing now of polygamists in general. Of course there are exceptions to this rule.

When a man has more than one wife, his affections must certainly be divided; and he really has no particular home, for his homes are simply boarding-houses. Should he have all his wives in one house, as is often the case, then they are all slaves; for they know that each one is watching the others, and in many instances trying to discover something that they can secretly tell their husband, to draw away his affections from the rest, and secure them to themselves.

There are again other women, frequently the first and second wives, who become friendly to each other. When this is the case, they care very little for the husband. They set their faces against the third, and the others who come after. The poor girl is to be pitied, and the husband too, who ventures to bring her home; for the two friendly wives are sure to lead her and him a terrible life. The man who enters this most delightful order of marriage ought not to allow his wives to become too intimate, for they will certainly plot mischief, and destroy his power and peace. The more they hate each other, the more secure he is.

But what a state of mind is this for mothers to be in! And if children partake of the nature and feelings of their mothers, what kind of dispositions can these poor children inherit, whose mothers have been the victims of these strong and fearful emotions? Oh! it is a cruel wrong to womankind; it is a terrible wrong to innocent children! It is a most wicked wrong, in every sense of the word!

Mother and Daughter Wives to the same Husband.

CHAPTER X.

Shocking Effects of Polygamy—Marrying a Half-Sister—A
Mother and Daughter married to one Man—Marrying three Sisters
in one Day—"Covenants of Marriage"—A deluded "Sister"—Her
Persecutor—Influence of Elders—Mistaken Ideas of Duty—Another
"Sister" betrayed—Men unhappy in Polygamy.

THE PRACTICE of Polygamy in some instances results in alliances
which among all civilized peoples would be considered equally unnatu-
ral, immoral, and opposed to the dictates of religion.

It is quite a common thing in Utah for a man to marry two, and
even three sisters. I was very well acquainted with one man who married
his half-sister; and I know of several who have married mother and daughter. I know also another man who married a widow with several children;
and when one of the girls had grown into her teens, he insisted on marrying her, having first by some means won her affections. The lady, however, was, I am pleased to say, very much opposed to this marriage, and
finally gave up her husband entirely to her daughter; but to this very day
this daughter bears children to her stepfather, living in the same house
with her mother! These things are so revolting to me that I have scarcely
patience to write about them.

I will, however, mention another instance which is nearly as bad. A
rather prominent man in Salt Lake City, who has several wives and married daughters, only a few weeks ago married a young girl about fifteen
years of age—a child that his first wife had adopted and brought up as
her own. It is said to be a source of great sorrow to his first wife. Such men
deserve punishment; for there is no shadow of religious obligation in the
transaction. I know that he has next to no faith in Brigham Young.

But there is a pleasing change noticeable in the plural marriages
in Salt Lake. There are not nearly so many marriages of this kind among
the actual citizens of Salt Lake City as there were three or four years ago.
The girls, although they will tell you that they believe it is right, will also
say that they would rather do with "a little less glory" hereafter and take
a little more comfort here. Many at the same time do not hesitate to say
that they are altogether doubtful about the propriety of such marriages,

for the doctrine and practice of Polygamy have made such bad men of their fathers and such victims of their mothers.

It is not our city girls who maintain so much the plural marriages; but it is chiefly the newly arrived English and country girls who supply the Patriarchs.

The American Elders have derived a rich harvest from Britain for many years past. Soon after the introduction of Polygamy, an elder was seldom known to return from his mission to England without arranging there for one, sometimes two, and I have known as many as three girls—and these own sisters also—brought out at one time and all married by the same man. I personally know several men who have done so, but, on account of their families, I do not wish to mention their names.

The elders are not permitted to marry these extra wives while engaged on their missions in foreign countries, but are counselled to wait till they return "home." Some of these weak brothers, however, have not been able to wait for the ceremonies of the "Endowment House." It is but just to add that they do marry them when they get to "Zion."

Some elders have bound the foreign girls by solemn vows or covenants to become their wives when they get to Utah; and the poor girls, believing that these men, because they were missionaries, were justified in all they did, have many times, to their great injury, kept those "covenants" and married them. One young lady, on her arrival in Salt Lake City, came to my house to live, and after she had been with me about a week, I noticed that a married man came very frequently to see her. As I took a great interest in her, I questioned her, and advised her not to enter rashly into any marriage. She was a very handsome and a good girl, and she assented to the propriety of what I said. But the visitor still continued to come, and I observed that the girl became very much depressed and unhappy, and I frequently found her in tears. I then determined to inquire into the matter, for I had heard so much of the elders binding women by these covenants; and I found that in this case the man had persecuted her with his attentions and protestations of undying love, and his power to "exalt" her in the kingdom of God, until he had exacted from her a promise to become his wife. Not contented with her simple promise, for he knew that she did not really love him, he framed an oath and made her repeat it after him. She would not tell me the nature of the oath, for she said it was too dreadful to repeat. She said that since she had taken this vow she had become perfectly wretched, and could not tell what to do.

I advised her to go to President Young about it; for I knew that he had publicly told the Elders that they were not to make these covenants, and I thought that he was too honourable a man to see a helpless girl imposed upon. She did not like to go and see him, and said that she was ashamed of having made such a covenant; "besides," she added, "no matter what the President might say, I know that the Lord would curse me if I were to break that covenant." As she did not lodge at my house, I could not keep her out of this man's company as much as I wished; and he, knowing that delays are dangerous, lost no time in accomplishing his wishes. She had no relations, and was therefore entirely in his power.

One Friday evening I asked Mr. Stenhouse to invite her to accompany us to a ball, and she gladly accepted, as she had refused to go with her tormenter, and she hoped that it would offend him. Next day she did not make her appearance as usual, and I became alarmed, for Saturday is the day on which they marry at the "Endowment House." I sent to her friend's house where she slept, and they replied that she had gone to be married.

In the afternoon she came to me looking the picture of wretchedness, and said, "Mrs. Stenhouse, last night at the ball, that man —— brought President —— to me and told him that I had promised to marry him, and now would not do so. President —— said, 'If you have promised, keep your covenant.' I have fulfilled my covenant, but I have wrecked my happiness, for I cannot bear the man I have married. I have told him so," she continued, "but he does not care about it." I even then begged of her to let me see President Young, and consult with him, that if possible something might be done to assist her out of her trouble. But she would not let me do so; and it was evident that the man had acquired such a terrifying influence over her that she really believed she would be lost for ever if she did not literally fulfil the covenant which she had made. This was one case that came particularly under my notice. But I have frequently heard of such follies and dastardly impositions upon young and inexperienced girls.[1]

Another young lady, a very near and dear friend, was crossing the plains to Utah, when she met with one of the elders, who had been on a mission and was returning. They became quite intimate, as people did at that time when taking so long a journey together; and he proposed marriage to her. At the same time he used all his eloquence to show her how much better it would be to marry a man who held such a high position in the church as he held. He managed to convince her, and then persuaded her to enter into a covenant with him by which she would be bound to marry him.

Upon their arrival in Utah, he took her straight to his home, fearing, I suppose, that some one else might get her; for at that time young girls did not long remain single, and she was a very fine-looking girl and very clever with her needle. She would, therefore, have made a desirable addition to any man's family; but when she saw the home he took her to, she was horrified, and made up her mind to escape. But he had got her there, and as she knew no one in the country, she felt that there was no possibility of escape.

When I arrived in Salt Lake City, I made enquiry about all this, as I had a right to, and found that he had actually frightened her into marrying him by making her believe that the curse of heaven would rest upon her if she were to break that covenant; and she passed a most wretched life, raising a family in abject poverty.

I would not have my readers think that I wish to say unkind things of the men of Utah, for I do not feel unkindly towards them. I once felt as if I perfectly hated the whole of the male sex, so great was my indignation. But now it is different; for I am a free woman, and therefore happy. How delightful is the sense of liberty! Oh! that all the women of Utah could feel as I do this day. My object is not to decry or speak evil of individuals. I simply want to show what men will do when under the influence of superstition, and how it will destroy the finest feelings of their natures.

People upon whom I could rely have told me of men who have unexpectedly married other wives and brought them home before their first wives knew any thing about it; and this, simply because they had not courage to introduce the subject, and thought, as they say, that it would be best to "take a deep plunge and struggle out." Who can conceive the feelings of a wife who has been thus treated; and what does a man know of woman's nature, who can dare to treat her so; thinking and saying that "bye-and-bye she will be all right, and will get over it!"

Men of Utah! don't you believe it! Women *never* do get over such treatment. They may *appear* calm; they may appear to forget; but all the while the remembrance of their wrongs is rankling in their hearts against you, and is never, *never* forgotten. The more devotedly a woman loves her husband, the more keenly she feels any thing that is calculated to destroy her confidence in the man she has looked upon as superior to all others, and when once that confidence is destroyed, how is it to be renewed?

O men of Utah! if you only knew the secret heart-aches of those you have vowed to love and protect, (and I believe that many of you would guard and protect them from sorrow, if you could,) sift this matter, and know for yourselves how more than foolish it is for you to cast away the true and undivided love of one devoted heart. Pay no attention to your wives when they tell you that they are happy, that they are satisfied. They may *tell* you this when their very hearts are breaking, simply because they wish to please their husbands, and, above all, to do the will of God. If you had the least discernment, you would discover by the changed manner, the almost cold indifference of the loved ones, who once were gushing with affection, whose winning and endearing ways captivated your hearts, that something must be wrong. I can never believe that the great God created our natures, such as they are, and then gave us laws that would outrage them.

I know that the Mormons would answer—"But you must bring your natures into subjection to the laws of God." I know that no human being ever tried harder than I did to bring my own nature into subjection to this so-called "law of God;" but the more I saw of it, the more I loathed it, until I became perfectly disgusted and humiliated at being obliged to live in accordance with it.

"Are these all you have got?"

CHAPTER XI.

Illustrations of practical Polygamy—A "Sister" in deep
Affliction—A Husband's Cruelty—A sad End—Various and fearful
Results of Polygamy—Broken Hearts and Lunacy—Men "spark-
ing" in the Ball-Room—Women sitting as "Wall-flowers"—Painful
Memories—Introduced to five Wives—"Are these *all* you have
got?"—Matrimonial Felicities.

Soon after my arrival in Salt Lake City, I visited a family where there
were five wives, three of whom I met on my first visit. They were all three
intelligent women; but it pained me very much to see the sorrow depicted
on the face of the first wife. She appeared to me to be suffering intensely
while I was there; for the last wife, who seemed to be a thoughtless, lively
girl, was jesting with her husband, toying with his hair, and fussing with
him in general, in a manner which I felt at the time was quite out of place,
even had she been his only wife. Under the circumstances, it was to me
terribly offensive; and I felt that, if I had been the first wife, I should have
annihilated her, could I have done so.

My sympathies then were all with the first wife. In fact, they have
been always so, to a very great extent. But I also feel deeply for young
girls, who contract such marriages from a sincere conviction that they are
doing what is right, and what will be most pleasing in the sight of God.
Then there are women who ignore religion, and every thing else, in the
matter; all they think about is getting the man they want. These women
are devoid of principle, and invariably cause trouble.

My whole soul was drawn out toward the lady whom I have just mentioned, when I saw how deeply she was suffering. I felt as if I wanted to
throw my arms around her and speak words of comfort, if one in misery
could console another; and I resolved to become better acquainted with
her. I did so, and we became very friendly. She told me of her sorrows.
She thought it was very wicked of her to feel as she did, but she could not
help it; and she told me that when she saw her husband so happy with the
other wives, it was then that she felt most miserable, and could not hide
her feelings from him. At those times, he would "sulk" with her, coming in and out of the house for days together without noticing her, and

showing more than ever his fondness for the other one. She said, "I bear it as long as I can, and then I beg of him not to treat me so, as I can not live without his love."

I asked her how she could continue to love him when he treated her so?

"O Mrs. Stenhouse!" she said, "when he treats me at all kindly, I am satisfied. When he smiles on me, I am only too happy. When I cease to love him, then I must be dead; and even then," she added, "I think I should love him still!"

I felt all this very much; and, after a few words of sympathy to the neglected wife, I left her. But what I had heard made a great impression on my mind. "Thank God," I said, *my* husband will *never* act like this!" In fact, I did not at that time believe that he would even wish to take another wife; but I was soon to be undeceived. I saw this lady many times after the occasion which I have mentioned, and I became very much attached to her. She was a very sweet, intelligent little woman; and she would often say to me, "I think I should like to die when my babe is born; for I feel that they could do without me, and I am only a trouble to them here. I am always sick, because I am always unhappy."

I tried to rally her out of these sad feelings, but my efforts availed but little. I was myself sick a few weeks after; and, when I recovered, I heard that she was dead, and her babe also. I said, "Thank God, she is now at rest!"

This is only one sad story out of many equally as sad.

Some wives have gone crazy, and died in this condition, all through their sad experience in Polygamy. Not long since, the fifth or sixth wife of one of the leading men of Salt Lake City died bereft of reason. Her husband was about marrying a young girl at the same time, and refused to go and see his dying wife. That man's name would astonish my readers, did I publish it, for he is universally respected as one of the best men in Mormonism; and I can only account for his inhumanity by considering the poverty and debasement into which Polygamy had plunged him.[1]

Several cases of lunacy have come under my own personal notice; and two young women, of very respectable families, with whom I am acquainted, narrowly escaped from the effects of poison, which, in their misery, they had taken as a last resource. I have heard of many more cases of desperate attempts at suicide.

To say that there are no men who try to be just in the practice of Polygamy would be very wrong, for there are men in Utah who try their best to act rightly to all their wives. These men are generally those who care very little about religion; and I have often said of them, (of one in particular,) if they are good with Mormonism, how much better would they be without it. It is my firm belief that Mormonism has perverted some of the best of natures.

On the other hand, I have known men who were reputed good husbands and fathers before they went to Utah, and, after they had been there a few years, they did not seem like the same beings. They became harsh and cold in their natures, and so cruel to their wives and neglectful of their children, that it seemed as if they thought of nothing but getting wives and pleasing themselves, regardless of whether they could support their families or not. These were generally the most religious men.

We had not been long in Salt Lake City before the ball season commenced. These balls afford splendid opportunities to the men for flirting with the girls. No matter how old and homely a man is, he thinks that he has as much right to flirt and dance with the girls as the youngest boy; for they all look upon themselves and each other as boys and single men, even if they have a dozen wives. There is no limit to their "privileges." They are always in the market. Brigham, in his public discourses, has said that the brethren "are all young men under a hundred years of age." With such an extended privilege, it is here in Utah that hoary Winter and smiling May can be seen galloping forth in the dance together. A thoughtful subject for the artist's pencil.

It is of no consequence how much a man may flirt in the presence of his wife or wives. They must not presume to say one word to him about it; for the husband is free to do whatever he likes. He is one of the lords of creation. He is master of his wives, of his children. Then, how can one of his own dare to call in question any thing he may think fit to do? She *may*, it is true, do so; but she must take the consequences of that rash act.

Oh! how I loathe even the very remembrance of those hateful ball-rooms, where I have seen so many unhappy wives, and have heard so many tales of sorrow. For, while the wives would be sitting as "wall-flowers," along the sides of the hall, after having danced the first dance with their husbands, as a matter of form, I have heard them many times telling each other about what they had seen their husbands doing during the evening; and how they had been compelled to pay attention to some jabbering little girl that their husbands chanced to fancy; and they had to do it also for peace' sake, and appear to be satisfied.

I do not mean to say that I did not like these social amusements myself, for I did; and could, under other circumstances, have enjoyed them very much. But I had been told so many things of the unpleasantnesses of a ball-room in Salt Lake City—at least, to married women—that my apprehensions were aroused. But all that was ever told me never half came up to the truth; nor can I possibly myself give the reader any correct idea of the heart-aches and sorrows which these scenes bring to the wives of Mormons.

It is quite a common thing for married men to go with young girls to these balls. The majority of the men, however, prefer to take their first wives with them at the same time; but it is not infrequent to hear a lady say, in the ball-room, "My husband has brought his girl here to-night; but I have not spoken one word to her, nor will I do so." Yet if any one were to ask these same ladies if they believed that Polygamy was right, they would say, "Certainly, I do; but I do not like *her*,"—and this simply because their husbands had paid *her* attentions. This seems like inconsistency; but it serves to show what conflicting feelings Mormon women have to contend with.

The men should hear what their wives say about them in the ball-rooms, and the hatred they feel for them. I have seen some women sitting quietly eyeing their husbands, as they danced or flirted with their younger loves, till their cup of indignation was full. Then they would make for the dressing-rooms, where their anger would burst upon the ears of a group of eager listeners, who were seemingly pleased to learn that some one else was suffering as well as themselves. A half-repressed threat, "I will be equal with him," has escaped the lips of those who, before that, had passed for being happily situated.

Where new matrimonial alliances are continually taking place, the arrival of a gentleman, with his wife, wives, or a maiden, in the ball-room, is never remarked; and, not infrequently, different wives arrive at different hours during the evening, as it suits their convenience; and thus it would be difficult to say who came with their "lord." Besides, no observation is made if a lady thus enters the ball-room alone, though it is expected that her husband is aware of her coming. This coming alone, however, is not a common habit; but, as it is admissible, it does occasionally happen that a husband is dancing or enjoying himself in the ball-room with his last *fiancée*, when a vigilant pair of eyes searches over the room and lights upon the happy "lord." When eyes like these encounter the eyes they seek, a change is seen, and the youthful airiness of the gentleman vanishes, and sober looks follow the gaiety of the earlier hour.

It is a very difficult thing for a woman, after passing through such scenes over and over again, and knowing them to be true, to have much respect left for the Mormon men who *practice* Polygamy. Though they consider themselves to be benefactors, they act like oppressors of womankind. I am not alone in this opinion. I know scores of ladies in Utah, both married and single, who feel and speak exactly as I do on this subject.

I met President Heber C. Kimball at one of these balls, soon after my arrival. He said that he would introduce me to *his wife*. Every one liked Heber for his outspoken, honest bluntness. He took me up the hall and introduced me to five wives in succession! "Now," said he, "I think I'll quit; for I fancy you are not over strong in the faith."

I asked, "Are these all you have got?"

"O dear! no," he said; "I have *a few more at home,* and *about fifty more* scattered over the earth somewhere. I have never seen them since they were sealed to me in Nauvoo, and I hope I never shall again."

I thought this was terrible; but it was only the beginning of worse things.

After this winter, I had very little peace; for the women were constantly talking to me about my husband getting another wife. He held out, however, for five years,[2] but at last he "felt it was his duty to do so," and I was silly enough to allow that "he was not living up to his religion" unless he took an extra wife.

I shall never forget those ball-room scenes. Even to this day, when I chance to listen to tunes which I used to hear played in those times, they grate so terribly upon my ear, and bring back so many sad recollections, that I want to get away from the sound of them as quickly as possible, for they are more than I can endure. Bygone recollections are often recalled by trifles such as this.

A few months ago, I attended a ball in Salt Lake City. It was the first I had been to since I withdrew from the church; and of course it was got up by the "Liberal Party." I felt free and happy, for there was nothing to annoy or disturb me. Suddenly the band struck up a tune which I had heard while attending the Mormon balls. It sounded like the death knell of all my pleasant feelings, and aroused memories of the past which were so intensely painful that I could not rally from the depression that I felt for the rest of the evening. I had heard that tune before, and many like it, and had even danced to it, while my heart was breaking. Can it excite wonder that I should feel thus? I knew too much of those assemblies, which to some are heaven, to others purgatory!

Let me ask my lady readers—those, I mean, who have never been in Utah—Ladies, how do you think you would feel if *you* were kept waiting long after the hour of midnight, far away into the morning, until your husbands had got through with their dancing and flirting, while your own hearts were breaking? I think I hear you say, "I would not stand it." You do not know, I assure you, *what* you would do under the circumstances. What can you know—you, American women, who are petted and indulged to such an extent that you do not really know what sorrow is? How can you possibly judge what the feelings of a Mormon woman are, who has been taught to believe that "her desire shall be unto her husband, *and he shall rule over her.*"

This is no imaginary "rule," but a stern fact. Woman in Utah is only a chattel!

CHAPTER XII.

Going to the "Endowment House"—Wives cruel to other Wives—
The Story of a young second Wife—How she came to Marry—How
she was treated—Her Husband's neglect—Cruelty of the first
Wife—Goes to the "Bishop"—How young Girls in Polygamy value
the Attentions of their Husbands—The Ways of Mormon Men.

ONE day my husband came home, apparently very much pleased
about something, and said to me, "What do you think?—we have the privilege of receiving our 'Endowments'* next Saturday." This, he added, was
really a great favor, as many had been there a much longer time and had
not received them. I made no answer, and finally he asked—"Are you not
pleased with the invitation?"

I answered—"No, I do not want to have my Endowments."

"And why not?" he enquired.

"Because," I said, "I have heard so much about it, that I have not
only no desire, but I have a great repugnance to 'going through the
Endowments.'"

This surprised him. We had, as might be expected, a little very pleasant (?) conversation on the subject; and finally Mr. S., dissatisfied with my
opposition, left the house. When he returned, he told me that it was not
absolutely needful for us to go on the ensuing Saturday, but we could go
on the Saturday following, and that would give me time to think of it. In
my own mind I said—I shall not go at all! But, after quietly reflecting about
the matter, I saw that my husband was willing to concede somewhat, and it
only seemed fair that I should do as much; particularly as I knew that when
he was told to go there, he was obliged to do so. For if he had said that he
could not go to receive the Endowments because wife did not wish to, he
would have made himself an object of ridicule. He would probably have
been "counselled" to take another wife and go through the Endowments
with her, (as he could not go alone,) and I should have been baffled and
humiliated. I, therefore, thought it was best for me to submit; but I did not
do so by any means with a good feeling. I simply "stooped to conquer."

* Secret rites of the Priesthood.

I went through that "Endowment House" with the very worst feelings that any woman could have, and scarcely noticed what was passing around me. In justice to the Mormons, I feel bound to state that the accounts which I have frequently read, professing to give a description of the "Endowments" given in Salt Lake City, are almost altogether exaggerated, and have generally been written either by the enemies of the Saints, or by those who knew nothing at all about the matter. I myself saw nothing indelicate; though I had been led to believe that improper things did take place there, and I was determined not to submit to any thing of the kind.

When we had got through, I thought—"If there is really any good in these ceremonies, or any blessing to be derived from them, I certainly shall never get it." It did not, however, trouble me very much; for I was beginning in real earnest to feel tired of serving "the Lord" after the fashion taught by the Mormon elders, and that I should have to give up the whole religion. It was a one-sided affair altogether, and it was rarely that I could get so much as a good feeling to help me along.[1]

There was scarcely a day passed without something unpleasant, or something calculated to shake my faith, occurring before my eyes. Either some woman was suffering from neglect, while her husband was living with a young wife and spending all his time and money with her; or some young girl was abused and persecuted by the first wife; or it might be that there was nothing but quarrelling, hatred, and complaints among them all. Then I would ask myself—"Where is the Spirit of God in all this? Surely this is none of His work!" The injustice and cruelty of men to their wives, the hardness of women towards each other, and the dejected, timid, cringing women who were afraid to call their lives their own, were sights so painful to behold that I could scarcely continue to believe that the Lord had any thing to do with the Mormon faith.

These are things that I have seen, and that I know to be true. Were I at liberty to do so, and were it not a betrayal of confidence, I could give the names of women in Salt Lake City who are now residing there, and who have suffered and are suffering this oppression as much now as then.

I could tell the reader tales of such cruelty in the case of one woman towards another—wives of the same man—that he would hardly believe it could be true, and I should be ashamed to relate the story. I will, however, give one short account which will perhaps afford an insight into the whole system, when illustrated by bad men.

I knew a young woman who was a second wife, and she had two children. She came to me one day in great distress, and asked me if I would allow her to come and work for me. I saw she was in trouble; and, as I had seen her several times before, and knew that she was a second wife to a man who lived only a short distance from us, I asked her to tell me what her trouble was. At first she hesitated, and then she told me that she had nothing to eat and nothing for her little ones. I was surprised at this, for I knew that her husband was in good circumstances; and I asked her where he was. She said, "He is away just now, but it makes no difference when he is at home; it is all the same. I live," she added, "in the garret, and the wind blows through the roof, and it is so cold that we are nearly frozen; and, when I have asked for a stove, he has told me to go and earn one. I can cook at their kitchen stove; but, if I stay there too long, his first wife and children do not like it. I have not been out to work since I have been confined." Her babe was then only one month old.

Presently she continued—"I am out of every thing, and the other wife says that she won't give me any thing; that I must go and work for it."

"But," I said, "you can not work yet; you are not strong enough."

"Oh! yes, I can," said she. "My husband made me work in the yard when I had only been confined two weeks."

Reader, would you believe that this man (if I may call such a creature a "man") was an American? Now, I have always thought that the American husbands spoiled their wives; but I do not think *this* man was guilty of doing so.

The poor girl told me that during her confinement she had been left alone in that garret. They would bring her, once a day, something to eat of whatever chanced to be at hand, but she had no light or warmth, and she added—"I have neither food nor proper clothing for my children, and I must go to work; I must try to get a place to live in, as my husband will not give me one."

I told her that she might come and work for me, and she had to bring her two little children with her. How I pitied her! She was a really good-looking Danish girl; and, before she had married this man, she had worked in his family as a servant, and had helped in the field. I believe that he married her only to retain her services; for she said that both he and his wife ill-treated her because she would not work in the field all the time.

Another case I think I may mention as confirmatory of what I have stated. It is that of a young woman who was a sempstress. The first wife had induced her to marry her husband; and, as soon as they were married, she (the first wife) discovered that she could not endure Polygamy. Then began a series of persecutions. She managed to make her do all the sewing for the family, which consisted of boys; and, when that was done, she insisted on her going out to work by the day, and giving *her* the money that she earned; saying that she knew best how to spend it. This poor silly girl did as she was told; all the home that was allotted to her being a miserable little room scarcely furnished.

She worked as long as she could, trudging through all kinds of weather to go to her every-day labor, until the very day that her first child was born. The first three days after the birth of her child, the first wife procured some help for her; but after that she would just open the door and put in something for her to eat, on a tin-plate. This she did, not because she had no other plates, but because she wanted to show her contempt for the young mother; and if her husband went into the room for ten minutes to see her, there would be a tremendous fuss. As soon as she was able, she was made to go to work again. This was a house where the first wife ruled.

The poor creature (the second wife) went to the Bishop, and asked what she should do. He told her to bear it, and "the Lord" would make it all right some day. "The Lord," however, failed to do so. After she had borne her weary trials for four years, and after a long illness, in which she was shamefully neglected, she concluded very wisely that she would endure it no longer, and she left them. It is hardly possible to believe what the poor girl suffered in that illness. Weak and sick as she was, she had to get out of bed and *crawl* to the fire-place, (for she was far too weak to walk,) and then prepare a fire as well as she could, in order to make herself a little tea, or any thing she might require. This was when her second child was born. But this is nothing, compared with what I might write. I pass over such very painful details. This is the kind of treatment that one woman will sometimes give to another under Polygamy; and it is those women who, from religious zeal, are most anxious to "get wives for their husbands," who thus misconduct themselves, when their religion is put into practice. Thank God that such women are comparatively few!

There is another class of men in Polygamy who are deserving of notice. These are honest, good men, untiring in their efforts to make their wives comfortable and happy—were that possible. If they could pro-vide a palace for each wife, they would do so. Such men, it may well be said, are slaves to their families; but, with their best efforts, they can not chase away from their homes this skeleton—Polygamy.

With their several wives these men try to be scrupulously just, never showing partiality in look, word, or deed. I know quite a number of such.

But a short time since I met with one of them while spending the evening with some of my friends. His fourth wife—a young lady—was present with him. He was very attentive and kind to her; and, had she been his only wife, he could not have been more so. My attention was attracted by her manner towards him. A stranger would probably never have noticed what I then observed. There was a certain sarcastic bitter-ness of tone while accepting his attentions, as if she felt that they were simply hers by right. I looked at her and thought—"Is it possible that you have arrived at that condition already?" She was a young lady scarcely out of her teens, only a few months married, and surrounded with every comfort. I knew how she felt, for I had passed through a similar experience myself. It recalled vividly to my mind scenes that had passed in my own home, when my husband had perhaps taken particular pains to show me some attention, or speak kind words to me; and I had met him with that same half-concealed bitter tone, believing that he was only acting a part with me.

I was pained to think that one so young, whom I had seen only a few months before a gay and happy girl, should feel like this; and yet I knew that it was the fate of every woman who lives in Polygamy. It can not be otherwise. She felt, I know, that all these attentions and loving words would be given to another—perhaps an hour after leaving her—and then to another and another still; and thus they lost their value to her. Thence the cold and thankless tones with which she responded to her husband.

A gentleman of my acquaintance who has lived many years in Polygamy, a good, kind husband and father, recently said to me that one of his wives suffered terribly from Polygamy. He always avoided any mention of the word in her presence. He told me that he had often seen her happy and gay, with everything pleasant and agreeable around her, when, by some unforeseen fatality, some one present would allude to Polygamy. In an instant a deep gloom would come over her face; and, strive as he might to drive it away, it was impossible. It would haunt her even for days.

Such men as these lose no opportunity of showing their wives every kind attention. If they are affluent and keep a carriage, they may be seen driving out with one of the wives on every occasion. Their sleighs are the first out in the season. They are to be seen at nearly every public amusement. They attend all the balls, and dance only with their wives and other married ladies, except when compelled to do otherwise with their intimate acquaintances.

All this they do to try to make their wives happy and divert their thoughts from their secret sorrow. These poor men do not know that the very means which they take to destroy that feeling only excites it the more. A woman, as she receives these kindnesses, only loves her husband the better and wishes that she had *all* his love.

There is no possible happiness in Polygamy, even with such men. There *can be none!* And, therefore, the less love there is, the better are women able to bear it. Brigham knew it when he said in the Bowery some years ago that there should be no love; it was only a weakness. He understood the case perfectly.

It was once remarked to me by a visitor to Salt Lake City, in speaking of a lady friend of mine—"How beautiful she is when she smiles, but what a difficult thing it is to get her to smile; she looks so sad and mournful."

I had known that lady for many years and how deep her sorrow was. Her husband had been away for a long time on a mission; and on his return, when he had been home only a week or two, he married two young girls. It is said that his father "counselled" him to do so; and from that day, now many years ago, she has mourned in deep affliction, to which has been added the troubles which her two lovely daughters have experienced.

Some men, feeling that they have got to practice Polygamy or else lose their hopes for futurity, set themselves to work to discover in what way the task can be most easily accomplished to spare their wives' feelings, and make as little change as possible in their households. On the arrival of the emigrants, they will visit the camp; and, if they see a young girl who takes their fancy, (it may be that they have met before in another country; if not, it makes no difference,) they will offer to take her home until she can "look around and see what she can do." Or, if it should be the fall when they arrive, (and it always was so before the railroad was in operation,) they would offer them a home for the winter, which was generally accepted with gratitude, as a great many of them had no relatives to go to.

Then they had an opportunity of becoming well acquainted with each other and with the first wife; and many a wife consents to this addition, believing that, as she has got to pass through the ordeal at some time, this will be the best way. I know an indulgent husband who has taken half a dozen girls, one after the other, into his house for this purpose; but not one of them seemed to suit his wife exactly, and he has seemingly given it up in despair. I hope his sweet little wife may never be suited!

Wife at Home.—Husband Abroad.

CHAPTER XIII.

Fears realized—Meeting an old Friend from Switzerland—The
Vicissitudes of himself and Family—How he was "counselled" to take
another Wife—Brigham sends for me—My young Charge—"Not
feeling well"—My Husband seeks a second Wife—A "Painful" Task—
Striving to submit—My Attempts at Friendship with his Fiancée—My
Heart not quite subdued.

Upon our arrival in Utah, I longed to see the converts who had pre-
ceded us from Switzerland. But it was some time before I had the mingled
pleasure and pain that that meeting afforded me.

One day a countryman called to see us. It was Mr. ——. I was surprised at the difference in the appearance of this gentleman. I hardly
knew him. He was changed from the fine-looking, well-to-do *bourgeois* to a
hard-working, labouring man, poorly clad, sun-burnt, wrinkled, and old.
I could have wept over him when I saw the change; and when I inquired
about his family, he told me how they were, and that he had married the
young servant-girl who had come with them from Switzerland. I was very
much surprised at this, but dared not ask him how it had occurred. I
thought I would wait till I could see his wife; but as they lived about eighty
miles from the city, I was not enabled to do so till several months after.

He told me of his difficulties and struggles to obtain even a bare
livelihood. His story was that of many others going to a new country. But
he did not complain. When he arrived in Utah, he did not know what
to turn his attention to, and, after some hesitation, went to farming. As
he was entirely ignorant of agriculture, he could not, of course, succeed.
Then the grasshoppers came and destroyed their crops; and one reverse
after another followed, until they were reduced to miserable poverty, and
utterly broken down. Still, though weak in body, he was firm and robust
in his faith in Mormonism. He was a sterling man.[1]

As soon as I had opportunity I went to see his wife. She was the
lady to whom I had first preached Polygamy in Switzerland. I found her
in a little log-cabin of two rooms, and of course no carpet on the floors.
In this abode of poverty lived my two kind friends whom I had known
under such different circumstances, and with them were their five little

children.[2] But this was not all. The other wife was also living there, and she, poor girl, was certainly not to blame; and under the same roof were also her two children.[3]

What a change was this! When I first knew them in their own country, this lady (the first wife) was a gay, light-hearted, happy woman. Now she was care-worn, dull, and broken-spirited.

I asked her how her husband came to marry.

She answered me:—"If you had been here during 'the Reformation,'* you would not need to ask that question." Then she added—"You ought to thank God that you were not. The men were all crazy here, and were marrying every woman they could get. The Bishop came to my husband one day and told him that he had not 'kept the commandments,' and that he must get another wife within a week. The teachers also went to the servant-girl and told her that she must get married, and that, if she had no one in view, they would select some one for her.

"Those were fearful times. No one dared refuse to listen to 'counsel.' What *could* we do?

"My husband talked to me about the matter. He said that he had never before thought of it, and therefore he did not know whom to ask to be his second wife. We began to consider the whole affair in a practical light. If they made this girl marry and leave us, what should I do with all my family without her assistance? Only one solution of the difficulty presented itself, and we came to the conclusion that my husband had better ask her to be his second wife. As she also was 'under counsel,' she accepted him, and it made no great change in our household. She has been a good girl, and although, of course, I feel all this, I try to bear it— but *I hate the Mormons!*"

No one could see at that time how they could escape over these vast, dreary plains, and, therefore, they had to submit to their fate.

It is a matter of surprise to many persons that intelligent people can be influenced by the Mormon teachers to this extent. But it must be remembered that, when once the disciples of any faith can be brought to believe in present revelation, they think it is wicked to question what they are taught, and they do not allow their own judgments to influence them in the least.

I had been in Salt Lake City about two years, and had been working during that time at millinery in order to assist in supporting my family,[4] when one day Brigham Young sent me word that he wished to see me. I went to him, and he told me that there was a young girl, in whom he took an interest, and he wished me to see her. He said she "was not feeling

---

* 1855–6.—A period of great and almost incredible excitement in Utah, when the wildest doctrines were urged by the teachers and elders, producing the most fearful results.

well," (which I discovered afterwards meant that she was almost ready to apostatize,) and he wanted me to have her with me every day, and try to make her "feel well." If she wished it, I was to teach her my business; if not, I was to let her do just what she pleased, so that she was with me every day. Her parents, he stated, were both dead.[5]

I listened to all that President Young said, and acepted [sic] the trust in good faith, for I was very unsuspecting at that time. I called upon the young lady and made arrangements with her. She came to my house, and I found her to be a particularly sweet girl, but very unhappy and also very delicate.

Several of my friends, who were old residents in Salt Lake City, said to me, "Mrs. Stenhouse, there is some design in all this. Be on your guard." Some women in Salt Lake are always ready with their painful advice. In this instance, however, they were not far from the truth. I did not suspect any thing; I soon formed, however, an attachment for the young girl, as she did also for me, and I may add—my husband had also for her; although I had no suspicion of it then. She remained with me many months, until her health became so poor that she was obliged to stay at home. During this time, ladies would frequently tell me that my husband visited her regularly, and that it was supposed he would marry her. As may be supposed, I was very much shocked at this intelligence, and asked him about it. He told me that there was no truth in what I had heard, and I tried to believe him. However, he spent much less time at home than he used to while she was with me, and although I did not know certainly where he was when absent, I felt sure that he was engaged in something which interested him very much.

I may here mention that it is not customary for a Mormon wife to ask her husband where he is going when he leaves home in the evening after arranging his toilet very carefully. If she feels that she must say something to give vent to her overwrought feelings, it is simply to ask him when he will be home; and in many instances to wish in her secret heart that he might say—"Never!"

I sometimes am almost inclined to think that the baneful effects of this fearful religion will not only pursue us through life, but will also go with us to our graves. To this day, although every thing is so greatly changed, and my husband is now "all my own," I cannot entirely forget the past, and often I feel like a guilty thing if I venture to ask him where he is going, or where he has been. The reader who knows what the varied experience of life is, will understand what I mean, but which words fail me to tell.

I have lived a separate life so long, hiding my sorrows in my own breast, that now it has become almost impossible to restore that long-lost confidence which constitutes the true pleasure of married life, without which no woman is really happy. I cannot forget the past. It was fraught with a perpetual fear which my mind can never entirely shake off—a fear which even now makes me think that the teachings of that religion can never be utterly effaced from our hearts, and which reminds me sadly of the words which the poet has put into the mouth of one of those sympathizing angels who are said to watch over the interests of mankind:—

> "Poor race of men, said the pitying spirit,
>   Dearly ye pay for your primal fall;
> Some traces of Eden ye still inherit,
>   But the trail of the serpent is over them all."

But there was no poetry to soothe my mind in the hour of my trial. There was no music then that could lull the storm which gathered in my breast. The only word which could then depict my feelings was—*weariness!*—weariness of mind and body, a longing to die, that I might be at rest. If the reader never felt thus, let him not judge me. If he has known troubles such as mine, he will, out of his own experience, sympathize with me.

But I return to my story.

I began at last to think, as some of my friends had told me, that Brigham Young had some design when he sent the young girl to my house. Possibly he never thought of it.

However, I saw no more to trouble me at that time, and as my husband persisted in denying the truth of the rumours which I had heard, I tried to believe that they were false. But at the same time, I was so troubled and agitated by these things that I found it impossible to make up my mind to go and see *her.*

From this time my husband (apparently) began to feel seriously that it was his "duty to take another wife."

Some years later, when I had more experience in the ways of men, I discovered several never-failing signs by which one might know when a man wished to take another wife. He would suddenly awaken to a sense of his duties, and would have great fears that "the Lord" would not pardon him for any neglect. He would become very religious, attend to his "meetings"—testimony meetings—singing meetings, and various *other* meetings! In fact, he would show a great determination to leave nothing undone which ought to be done. My husband, being a good and conscientious Mormon, experienced all these feelings. Of course he did; and his kind brethren, knowing just how he felt, sympathized, urged, and even aided him in his noble efforts to carry out the "commands of God."

The young lady was at last selected.[6] She was very pretty, and very *youthful.* The last qualification is very necessary in a Mormon's wife, for then it is expected that she will have more time to bear children to the glory of the kingdom. It must not be supposed that any other consideration influences a Mormon mind. O dear! no. They are such very pure-minded men.

Then commenced the task, the painful task of paying his addresses to her. It is a "painful task" I know, for my husband told me it was, and of course I, as a dutiful wife, believed him. He seemed, however, to bear it remarkably well, and went at it with a zeal that was perfectly astonishing to me, who knew, from what he said, how painful it was to him.

I had really to restrain him a little for the benefit of his health; for when the duties of the day were over, and evening came, he would scarcely take time to eat his supper, so anxious was he to continue this labour of love.

But deeply as I sympathized with my husband in the "painful duty" which he had to perform, there were times when I felt that my *real* sorrow was greater than his fancied difficulties. I was in fact now truly overwhelmed with trouble. It seemed to me as if affliction was right at my door. I would sometimes almost rave with anger. Then I would pray, then cry. Such were the days and nights that I spent, not once only, but constantly, and without ceasing. I may truly say that I never knew at that time what it was to smile. I never knew in any sense what it was to be happy. I was pale, thin, and nervous, and I was often asked by my friends, who only judged from appearance, if I were consumptive. Yes, I might have answered, there is a consuming sorrow at my heart that is gnawing my life away. There was no possibility of evading my trouble. I had to face it, and though I felt that I had not courage to endure it, yet I lived!

I knew the very hours that my husband was with *her.* Mentally I was myself with him, and saw all. O the anguish that I felt in those times! No tongue can describe it, no one is capable of imagining it, but a woman who truly loves her husband and has endured the same anguish as that which I then felt. Had my husband been in any sense a bad man, I dare say, like many other women, I would have hardened my heart and have tried to forget that I ever cared for him. But this was not the case. He was a really good man in every respect. I knew how fondly he had once loved me, and in my heart I believed that he would even now be unchanged but for the influence of his religion, which he still thought was "the way, the truth, and the life."

If I had for one moment supposed what he did was from any other than the purest motives, I should have cast his love from me; but even up to that time I feared, and almost believed, that all this might be right; although I saw so much wrong connected with it.

I knew very well that if it was the law of God, as I had been led to believe it was, I must endure it, though it should cost me my life. Besides which, Brigham Young and all the authorities used to say that it was "a cross that we all had got to bear," though I used to think that the heaviest portion of the cross was put on woman's shoulders. They have all told me frequently and positively that there was no salvation or *"exaltation in the heavens"* without it. The thought of it was, nevertheless, so revolting to me that, had I been left to my own choice, I would rather have gone to some other place than the kind of heaven they spoke of, without it, than have gone to glory with it. But I was a wife, and had to consult my husband's interests as well as my own. No matter how weak I was in the faith, if my husband felt condemned by not practising the doctrine of Polygamy, it became my duty to submit, or at least I thought so.

With these convictions and feelings, I would sometimes nerve myself to the task of enduring; but if I happened to get a glimpse of the girl that my husband was going to marry, all my good resolutions would vanish like chaff before the wind, and I would feel sick and nervous, and entirely unfitted to attend to my duties.

I had often heard it said that the Lord gave strength according to our day, but I certainly felt that it was not true in my case. My day had come, but I had very little strength.

About this time my husband left the city to go to the Eastern States, and his marriage was put off to some indefinite period on account of the extreme youthfulness of the bride-elect. I felt in a measure relieved; for now they could not meet, and I thought that it would be a good opportunity for me to try to show her some attention, which I felt it was my duty to do. I thought that I would invite her to my house, now that there was no danger of my husband meeting her, and I did so. She came, and I had one or two other ladies present, for I was not like my husband in this particular—*I* could not endure to be alone with her.

I don't think that she enjoyed herself very much, for I could not at this time take to her. I longed for the time to come for her to go home, and when she had gone, I did not feel very satisfied, but thought that I would try it again. I did so, but this time it was an entire failure; for before she came, I had been brooding over the matter, and so hated the sight of her that I feigned sickness and kindly asked her to go home. After that, I gave up my attempt at friendliness as a bad job, and thought she must take her chances of any attention from me. She was a very nice girl, and under any other circumstances I think I could have liked her very well.

During my husband's absence, the young lady that I mentioned before as having lived with me, had not recovered from her illness, but was growing worse all the time. She had been out of the city, and I had not seen her for some months. She now sent for me, and I went to see her every day; for I saw that she was failing fast, and I felt assured that she could not live long.

She told me that she had left my house because she would not do any thing to make me suffer. She said that my husband had hinted at marriage to her, and that she liked him, but had avoided him for my sake. This was an instance of such self-denial as I had never expected to find in Utah, and I looked on her as almost an angel. I told her that my husband had denied it, and she said that he did so to spare my feelings, as it was not likely to result in any thing.[7] This I did not appreciate at all. I only felt that I had been deceived. But Polygamic Mormonism is full of deceptions. They deceive each other, and are at the same time often themselves the most deceived.

I knew well enough that my husband was not happy. It was not in his nature to have deceived me; but he was compelled to do so from the very circumstances of the case; and, as I said before, for peace' sake. He knew that there were times when I was perfectly wild with despair, and was reckless of consequences; and I was prepared to cast aside my hope of salvation, my life, and every thing, rather than endure another day what I then was suffering.

At these times I would say the most bitter things that I could think of, of Joseph Smith, Brigham Young, and all the leading men of the church. My husband was perfectly awe-stricken at the attacks I would make upon those whom he then believed were the servants of God. I know that there were times when he felt that it was the greatest sin that I could commit to speak thus.

In my calmer moments, seeing my husband so terribly in earnest, and having confidence in his superior judgment, I would come back to the old feeling that the wrong was in myself, and I would earnestly pray to the Lord to be forgiven.

I do not think that I should ever make a very good saint, for in all this that I have related there was one thing that consoled me—I felt that my husband's intended would some day learn that *she* was *not* his *first and only love* after myself. I am almost ashamed to own that this should be any gratification to me, but the young girls at that time frequently got the idea that the men had never really loved until they met with them. How far the men were to blame for this I do not know; but it is a fact, and I have little doubt that they had a pretty good share in the deception.

CHAPTER XIV.

The Sacrifice of my Life—I give another Wife to my Husband—
The Scene in the "Endowment House"—My Day of Trial—"It was
all over now"—Bitter Miseries of Polygamy—Rebellious Thoughts—
Retrospect of that Time—The first Wife not alone unhappy—
Watchful Eyes—A Ludicrous Picture—Want of Sympathy—Seeking
another "Jewel" for his "Crown"—Enlarging the "Kingdom"—"Stolen
Waters"—Love-Letters read in Secret—Reading the "Revelation" a
Second Time.

I WAS now expecting soon to be called upon to undergo the most
fearful ordeal that any woman can possibly be required to pass through—
that of giving my husband another wife. The thought of doing this was
even worse than death. It would have been fearful to have followed my
husband to his grave; but to live and see him the husband of another
woman seemed to me like exacting more than human nature was capable
of enduring. With all my faith in Mormonism, doubts would arise, and in
my bitterest moments of anguish I would exclaim, "This is more like the
work of cruel man than of God. Why should man have this power over
woman, and she so helpless? Surely, a just and impartial God can have
nothing to do with this!" Then, again, I would come to the conclusion, as
I had many times before, that "the ways of the Lord are past finding out,"
and, therefore, I must submit.

As the time approached for me to do this, I felt like a condemned
felon in his cell, waiting in agony the day of his execution. I knew that my
husband suffered also, now that it was so near; for he necessarily saw that
it would make a great change in his future life. His freedom was gone.

The dreaded day at length arrived. As may well be supposed, I had
passed a very wakeful and unhappy night, and I felt very sick and nervous; for I was soon to become a mother, and it seemed to me that I had
not courage to go through that day.[1] However, I nerved myself to the task,
and silently made my preparations for going to the "Endowment House."
The morning was bright and lovely, and calculated to inspire joyous hopes
and happy feelings. To me it brought nothing but fear and trembling. I
could not even trust myself to speak to my children, for I was choking

with suppressed emotion; and they, not knowing how deeply I was suffer-ing, looked at me with wonder in their innocent eyes. "Oh!" I thought, "surely my husband will at last understand the depth of the love I bear him; for, were it not that he believes the doctrine to be true, I would even now dash this bitter cup from my lips!" There was a darkness before my eyes, and, struggle as I might, I could see no ray of light, no glimmering of hope. I was utterly cast down and broken-hearted, and felt almost as if the Lord had forsaken me. I could not go to my husband for sympathy; for I felt that his thoughts were with his young bride, and that my sorrows would only worry him at a time when he must desire to be at peace.

The time at length arrived for us to go to the "Endowment House," and there at the altar the first wife is expected to give proof of her faith in her religion by placing the hand of the new wife in that of her husband. She is asked the question by Brigham Young, "Are you willing to give this woman to your husband, to be his lawful and wedded wife, for time and for all eternity? If you are, you will manifest it by placing her right hand within the right hand of your husband." I did so. But what words can describe my feelings? The anguish of a whole lifetime was crowded into that one single moment. When it was done, I felt that I had laid every thing upon the altar, and that there was no more to sacrifice. I had given away my husband. What more could the Lord require of me that I could not do? Nothing![2]

I was bewildered and almost beside myself, and yet I had to hide my feelings; for to whom should I turn for sympathy among those who were around me? My husband was there, it is true; but he was now the husband of another woman, and a newly-made bridegroom. I felt that I stood alone, our union was severed. I had given away my husband, and he no longer belonged only to me! The thought was madness. I could not think it possible that there *ever* could be any copartnership between that other wife and myself. From that day, I began to hide all my sorrows from my husband; and it was only when I was compelled, as I might say, to give vent to my highly-wrought feelings, that I ever uttered a word of discontent. Then, when I spoke or expressed what I felt, it was in anger; but never in sorrow, seeking sympathy.

I remember well that when I returned home—that "home" which was now to become hateful to me, for his young wife was to live there— my husband said to me, "You have been very brave; but it is not so hard to do, after all, is it?" He had seen me bear it so well, that he even supposed I was indifferent. So much for the penetration of men!

During the remainder of that day, how I watched their looks and noted their every word. To me, their tender tones were like daggers, piercing me to the heart. One moment I yearned for my husband's undivided love; the next moment I hated even the very sight of him, and vowed that he never again should have a place in my heart. Then I would feel that there was no justice in heaven, or this great sorrow would not have come upon me.

Why did the Lord implant this love in my nature? If it is wrong, He could have created me without it. Or was it for the pleasure of torturing His daughters that this was done? I could not but feel that the Lord whom I served was partial; for He allowed His sons to indulge in their love, while His daughters, who by man are considered the weaker vessels, were expected to be strong enough to crush out from their natures all love and all weakness.

I felt that day that if I could not soon get away by myself, in privacy, and give vent to my overcharged feelings, I should certainly go mad.

It was only in the dead of night, in my own chamber, that I gave way to the terrible anguish that was consuming me. God and my own soul can alone bear witness to that time of woe. That night was to me such that even the most God-forsaken might pray never to know; and morning dawned without my having for a moment closed my eyes.

It was all over now. Nothing remained but for me to face the fearful reality day after day and hour after hour. I do indeed believe that a man, if he could have felt as I did then, would have sunk beneath the trial. Who but a woman could endure such things and yet live?

I had been married then about fifteen years.[3]

When I look back to those days, I feel that all ill-feeling, all those manifold causes of sorrow, have fully died away; for the cause is now removed. I can *now* afford to think as kindly of the second as well as of the first wife; for those young women who marry into Polygamy very often—in fact, I may say, generally—do so from a sincere belief that it is their duty; and I know that they also have their trials. What can they know of happiness—*real* happiness? If they are sensitive, intelligent girls, they must feel almost as intruders in the home of another woman, never daring to show their affection for their husbands, and knowing as they do that keen eyes are always watching them.

If their sorrow is even less than that of the first wife, they certainly can know no joy. And if the husband has the whole of his family in one house, as is often the case, where is *his* happiness? One might truly say that then he is nothing but a slave in the midst of his slaves—his own wives. This can be readily understood. His every look and action will be closely watched and criticised. If he should chance to give a new dress to one, he must also give a dress to the other, no matter whether she needs it or not. Every thing is noticed. Nothing is overlooked. When a woman's heart is anxious, her eye is never weary.

This state of affairs, painful as it must be to all who are themselves personally interested in such things, not infrequently presents a ludicrous picture to those who are only lookers-on. In fact, sometimes these things are even grotesque in their results. I have more than once seen sights of this kind which were most laughably ridiculous. Let the reader imagine a very old wife, and a very young one, dressed alike! Yet this is not infrequently the case. The poor old lady sometimes thinks that if she can only make herself look a little juvenile she will be quite as attractive to her husband as his young wife is. All women would prefer to be young; but women in Utah have a perfect dread of growing old, for they do not like the idea of being set aside to make room for younger ones, which is very often their fate. In fact, this is so common, that it is seen daily.

I had lived in Polygamy for about three years, and nearly one year of that time it was brought home to me most painfully, for it was right before my eyes, under my own roof, day after day. To attempt to describe to the reader the contending feelings that continually and without ceasing tortured my very soul, would be impossible. In my struggles to hide them I thought they would send me mad. I felt that it required more courage to live than to die, but the thought of my little ones restrained me; and I thought that, although my life seemed so utterly worthless to me, it was of the utmost value to them, and to them it should be devoted. I would not die. I would live for their sake.

All this time my husband was kind to me. What would it have been had he been otherwise? But this perpetual conflict of feelings unfitted me for my duties. Even the prattle of my children, which had always been as music to my ear, was now almost a discordant sound. Their little questionings, too, were irksome; for I wanted to be alone. I had no sympathy; for there was none that knew of all these sorrows and trials, or who could feel with me in my affliction; no, not one. Besides, whom *could* I tell them to if not to my husband; and I certainly could not tell him *now*. Then, too, what good would it do me to tell him of my grief? The thing was done, and I must endure it; or, as I have heard some men say to their wives, "You must round up your shoulders and bear it; it is as much your duty as mine." Besides, I thought, how do I know but what he may tell his other wife of my feelings? and that would be too great a humiliation for me, should she think that I am jealous.

I am not naturally a jealous woman. But, I contend that where there is no jealousy there is very little love; and, in the trying situation in which Mormon women are placed, they must be more than human not to feel it. Besides, I did not think that what I felt was jealousy. Even if it was so, it was mingled with feelings of indignation and humiliation.

I was indeed indignant at seeing another woman under my roof, bearing my husband's name, and treated as his wife. Oh! this seemed sometimes really more than I could endure. I was ready to say, She is not his wife! dare to call her by his name! Then I would feel humiliation at the position which I occupied, when I fully realized it in all its bearings.

If any one had then told my husband that those were my feelings, he would not have believed it; for when we had assembled in our little parlour of an evening, (men generally spend their evenings at home after taking a new wife, at least for a while,) I would so far have subdued my feelings as at least to be calm, if not entertaining. But how I watched their looks! how I weighed every word, and often put a meaning to many things where there probably was none.

My husband would frequently say to me, "You do not feel bad now, do you? You have got used to it." I am proud to say, *I never got used to it.*

I had lived in Polygamy about three years when Mr. S. thought it was about time that he should add another jewel to his crown. I raised no objection to this; for I felt that he might just as well have twenty more as the one already too many, particularly as we had been taught to believe, the more wives the more glory. He told me who the favoured damsel was, and I had no objection to her.[4] The only promise I tried to exact from him was that there should be no long courtship. This he did not object to. But I was doomed to be disappointed, although there seemed to be no obstacle in the way this time; for her mother declared to me soon after that "no man had ever moved her daughter's heart to love" but my husband; "he was her *first* and *only* love"—pleasant communication to make to a wife! Her daughter confirmed this; and I myself had little doubt that she spoke the truth, when I saw letters constantly coming to my house, brought by persons who I knew came from her, and I perceived how much care was taken that they should not fall into my hands. It had always been represented to me, as to every woman, that I was a partner in the affair, and I thought that it was nothing but right and just that I should see and understand for myself how the courtship was progressing. I did not wish to be guilty of any thing that was mean; but as my partner in the business did not seem inclined to show me those letters, I thought that I would just take a glance at them without leave. Accordingly, while he was sweetly and unconsciously slumbering, night after night I extracted those charming epistles from his pocket. When I opened them, I found that one glance at them only gave me a taste for more, and I was not satisfied till I had read them through. I do not wish to justify myself for acting thus. But let the reader remember what cause of provocation I had, and how desperate I felt, before he too hastily judges me or condemns what I did.

To my great astonishment, I found from those midnight readings that the affair had progressed far beyond my utmost anticipations, and when I saw the intensity of the love depicted in those letters, I began to think that *I* had before known nothing about that tender sentiment.

The young lady became most terribly exacting during fifteen long and dreary months, so fraught with misery to me that it would be impossible to tell truly a thousandth part of what I felt. Even the recollection of those times I wish to banish. What I endured through this love affair was simply what many a woman has had to pass through before me in Utah, but which I then *firmly resolved I never* would endure *again.* I had come to the conclusion that if the Lord would not give me "salvation" without *that,* I would do without it. I had striven hard to do His will; but I had failed in every single instance to see, in what I was called upon to suffer, any indication of a God of justice. "How," said I, "could the humiliation, abasement, and misery of thousands of women contribute to the glory of God?"[5]

I now determined that I would satisfy myself concerning the true origin of Mormonism, and of that extraordinary "revelation" which first established Polygamy.

I had through all these years seen many, *many* things that, even after making every allowance, and taking them at their best, I knew were wrong. At least they appeared so to me, and, according to my views, the teachings of the church abounded with inconsistencies which considerably weakened my confidence in its authority.

I procured a copy of "The Revelation on Marriage," and read it carefully and calmly. I had not seen it since I had partially read it in Switzerland seventeen years before.[6] Then I had cast it aside in grief, with disgust and indignation. But I now perused it with anxious care, desiring only to learn the truth. I saw plainly from its own wording that *if* ever it had been given to Joseph Smith, no matter by whom, it was given after he had practiced Polygamy, or something worse, and to sanction what he had done. I began to make careful inquiry into all these things; and I found that evidence was not wanting to prove, at least to me, that this doctrine of plural marriages was *not* of divine origin.[7]

To doubt one doctrine was to begin to doubt all, and I soon felt that my religion was rapidly crumbling away before my eyes, and that I was losing confidence in every thing and every body. I was like a ship at sea without a compass, not knowing where to go or what to do.

At that moment, I believe I would sooner have proved my religion true than false, much as it had caused me to suffer. But the more I tried to prove it true, the more I proved it false; until in disgust I gave up the idea of solving my difficulties, resolving that I would have nothing more to do with the matter. I had noticed, for some time past, with no small degree of pleasure, that my husband's faith in the divine mission of Brigham Young was shaken. He would not confess as much to me; but the way I discovered it was very simple. My ears were opened, and my eyes were ever watchfully bent upon him, and I observed that in his prayers with his family when he would ask that Brigham Young might have the Spirit of God to enable him to judge justly of the actions of his brethren, and that he might comprehend the situation of the people, I thought I detected in his peculiar earnestness a foreshadowing of doubt creeping over him, and I rejoiced to think that at last there was a probability that he would yet use his own brains and experience, upon which I placed great reliance, and be no longer a slave to others.

CHAPTER XV.

Trouble with the Church—Implicit Obedience demanded—Confidence in the Church Authorities declining—Clinging to Faith—Attempts to suppress Doubts—How Inquiry was suggested—Brigham angry—"A Prophet might be mistaken"—Day dawning at last—"Obeying Counsel," and what it cost—An Article on "Progress"—A Scene—We withdraw from the Church—A brutal and scandalous Outrage upon my Husband and myself—Strange Police!—Without Redress—Popular Anger—Private Sympathy.

MR. STENHOUSE has been a member of the church since 1845. He had, to the very best of his ability, lectured, preached, written, and published in Great Britain, and various parts of the Continent, as well as in the United States, in support of the Mormon faith. He was a most *earnest* advocate of Mormonism, laying aside his own interests, and those of his family, all the time.

Personally, he was devotedly attached to Brigham Young for many years. While the members of the church have unshaken confidence in the faith of the new revelation, they very naturally acquire a regard for the Prophet, and render him unquestioning obedience. When Brigham spoke, he was ready to obey; and at any time during twenty years he would joyfully have given up his own life to save the life of the Prophet, had it been endangered. Whatever he might have seen or heard of Brigham's disregard of the rights of the working poor, and his ridiculous counsellings and teachings to the brethren on business affairs, he was ready to excuse it all, on the plea that "Brigham was the servant of the Lord," and, therefore, knew more than all the rest, and doubtless had inspiration to direct him in all that he did.

While he was in this condition of mind, I was almost without hope that the change I had so long desired would ever come. When I would bring before him things which I frequently heard of Brigham, and his oppression of any one, he would answer me that I could not righteously judge; for I only partially knew the facts, and that if I knew more, I would probably think otherwise. This was his answer to every thing; and probably many women in Utah have had something like this experience with

The Wealthy Polygamist.

husbands devoted to the Prophet's interests and reputation. He was not, however, so satisfied with every thing as his answers indicated. From the conversations that I listened to between him and influential men in the church, I clearly saw that many of the most devoted brethren around Brigham did not approve of much that he said and did; but their observations were always tempered with a fear of "meddling with the servant of the Lord." There is, indeed, a dread in the soul of every good Mormon of entertaining any doubts about their leaders, or criticising in any way whatever they might think proper to do or say.

Brigham Young, in one of his sermons, says, "*In the days of Joseph, the first thing manifested in the case of apostasy was the idea that Joseph was liable to be mistaken; and when a man admits that in his feelings, and sets it down as a fact, it is a step toward apostasy; and he only needs to take one step more, and he is cut off from the church.*" It is this kind of teaching that binds every man in Mormonism. I was, fortunately, not a man; and as women will sometimes persist in thinking for themselves, I kept on thinking and admitting that Joseph Smith was liable to be mistaken, and that Brigham Young even excelled him in this particular. In fact, he was not only "liable," but I knew that he *had* been mistaken many times. My thinking very often seriously troubled Mr. S.

The frequent visits we had from strangers passing through Salt Lake City, and Mr. S.'s own frequent travels in the States, contributed much to undermine his confidence in the teachings of the church. In their isolation, and the infrequency with which the Saints had any intercourse with others than themselves, it afforded the teachers an opportunity to represent the Gentiles in the worst possible manner; and in harmony with their faith, they believed the world was corrupt, and fit only to be destroyed. When visitors had retired from our house, the remark would frequently be made, "What a pity these persons are not in the church!" Instinctively there would follow that expression, the suggestion that surely they would not be damned because they did not accept the mission of Joseph Smith, the founder of Mormonism. The more we had of that intercourse, the less confidence we had in the Tabernacle faith. The malignant and abusive language, too, so frequently used in the sermons, was a puzzle that did not tend to confirm confidence. It seemed that the inspiration of "the Lord" was continually at war with good sense and experience. The more we knew of Christian institutions, and of persons outside of the Mormon Church, the less we believed in the priesthood's declarations of damnation, and there was a gradual returning to reason. The Mormon leaders had always counselled the people to avoid intercourse with the rest of the world; and in that they were right, for there are few persons who have much intercourse and acquaintance with the world, who are strong in the Mormon faith. With a better knowledge of mankind, the less they believe in the revelations of Joseph Smith, and of the world coming to an end within the next twenty years. If they grow at all, they outgrow the Mormon faith.

How I prayed in secret that Brigham would some day attack Mr. S.! and how glad was my heart when that time came!

Brigham had been to the country for a few days, and during his absence some contention had arisen among the brethren at an election, which dreadfully annoyed him. On the morning after his return to the city, the police reported to him that the Gentiles were mingling freely with the Mormon girls, and skating on the same ice, on the Hot Spring Lake, north of the city. He was furious, and was "mad" with every thing and every body.

Mr. S. called upon him, and without perceiving his sweet temper, introduced some newspaper business on the very subject that had made the Prophet angry. Brigham accused him of publishing a favourable notice in his paper of (to him) a very objectionable Gentile store; and added to that personal charges about matters that had been published in his paper during Mr. S.'s absence in the Eastern States. Mr. S. angrily replied to him that what was personal to him "was not true;" and as Brigham was on the eve of leaving, he asked for a conference with him in the evening.

"After all these years of labour and devotion," said Mr. S. to me in the afternoon, "for Brigham Young to speak to me and of me with such bitterness, without a particle of foundation! where was his divine inspiration?" He suddenly checked himself; but the truth was out, and I saw he had reached the conclusion that indeed "a prophet might be mistaken" in ordinary matters of life.

When he returned home in the evening, he told me that Brigham had received him very kindly, and had apologized, in his way, for the morning scene. The reconciliation made no change in my mind; for I knew that, however frankly Mr. S. would forgive Brigham, there was too much of the Scotchman in his nature to allow him ever to forget it. But to get him to avow that Brigham was simply human, was a great step in the direction of future freedom.

One circumstance followed another, and I saw growing upon Mr. S. a disposition to listen to and weigh what he heard; and at the same time his confidence in divine inspiration began to dwindle gently away. I was contented, and believed that the day which I had long looked for was dawning at last.

The strength of Mormonism consists in the "blind obedience" of its disciples. Let them once question what they hear from the Prophet, and they are gone! The quotation I have already given from Brigham's sermon illustrates this. He knew what he spoke. Instead of rebelling against Polygamy, had I only read the revelation carefully, and doubted its divine origin, I would have been saved a life of misery. It was only when I came to the conclusion that Joseph Smith never had this revelation *from God* that I was delivered from my former faith, and became once more happy.

When I saw Mr. S. looking upon Brigham Young and his teachings and actions as he looked upon other men, I knew instinctively that he would finally conclude that Brigham was not only fallible, but even very liable to make mistakes.

Mr. S. had been so long engaged in the defence of Mormonism, that it was deeply grounded in him. Its teachings and observances seemed to him beyond a doubt, and were strongly riveted in his mind. Its weak and doubtful points fled before his faith. When I heard him with others bringing up some of the questionable teachings of the church, criticising Brigham's "counsellings," and doubting some of his measures, and speaking of him as they would of any other of the brethren, I was satisfied that he could not long remain such as he once had been.

Long years of submission, and the receiving, without question, a prophet's teaching as divine inspiration, necessarily benumbs the soul and withers its life, till unconsciously the victim becomes an abject slave— a mere automaton.

With Mr. S., Mormonism had been every thing for a score of years and more. It had grown with his years, until it had become a part of himself. A trifling incident might possibly awaken doubts, but it required time to effect a perfect change.

The measures adopted by Brigham in the spring of 1869, for the purpose of controlling the commerce of Utah, as well as the faith of the people, caused great discontent. The teachings of the Tabernacle were wild and arrogant; Brigham assuming that it was his right to dictate in every thing, "even to the setting up of a stocking," (so he said,) or "to the ribbons that a woman should wear." What Brigham said, and the fanaticism that it created, aroused many of the people to opposition, and the more he observed the signs of the opposition, the more fierce he became in his denunciations, and harsh in his measures.

One Sunday evening, which I shall never forget, my husband came home and said to me, "President Young wants me to move the *Telegraph*," (a daily paper, of which Mr. S. was editor and proprietor,) "to Ogden."

With the vividness of lightning, a glimpse of what was in store for us flashed across my mind, and I exclaimed,

"What is that you say?"

He repeated, "President Young wants me to go to Ogden."

"With the *Telegraph?*" I inquired.

"Yes," he replied.

"Does he mean," I asked, "that you should leave all you have accomplished during these past years of labour, and begin again at Ogden?"

"He does," answered Mr. S.

"Surely, you must be deceived," I suggested.

"No," he replied, "I am not deceived."

"But who had told you this?" I asked.

"One of the Apostles," said he.

"But," I questioned, "*will* you go?"

"What can I do?" he replied.

"Do!" I exclaimed; "why, I would tell him at once that I would not go."

"Then," said he, "I shall be charged with rebellion."

"But," I responded, "will you quietly and submissively lose the business that you have created by these years of struggle, without telling him what you think?"

"If I object to go," he replied, "Brigham will charge me with want of faith in the Lord, and I may as well close up my business and leave the church."

"But surely, " I questioned, "you will not yield to this despotism?"

"I don't know," he said, "I do not see very clearly yet, but I shall know better after he has spoken to me."

That night, little as I then thought it, and little as I then guessed what it would cost us, was the dawning of the day of liberty to me.

The following evening, my husband came home very sorrowful. I knew at once that he was unhappy; and the more he tried to conceal his trouble, the more I observed the depression under which he was labouring.

"Have you seen the President?" I inquired.

"Yes, I have," he briefly replied.

"And *are* you going to Ogden?" I said.

"Yes," he answered, "I am going."

"You *are!*" I exclaimed.

"What can I do else?" he asked.

"Do!" said I; "why, do what your own experience dictates."

"You speak," said he, "like a woman."

"And I am a woman," I replied, with warmth; "but if you submit to this, you are only a slave!"

"Oh! be quiet," he said; "let me at least have a little peace here."

In the face of the most certain ruin, and with the urgent remonstrances of his best friends ringing in his ears, Mr. Stenhouse yielded to Brigham's order to "pull up the *Telegraph,* root and branch, and go to Ogden."

As soon as my husband told me that he had been told to "pull up the *Telegraph,* root and branch, and go," I knew what that meant. It was like going into a desert and giving up all, simply to prove faith and obedience.

"But surely, after all, you will not go?"

He replied, "I have always obeyed 'counsel,' and I am not prepared now to disobey it. What can I do? I *must* go."

"Well," I answered, "you must do as you think best; but if you would take my advice, you would tell Brigham Young plainly that you would not go. Tell him that you are the best judge of your own affairs, and that you can see clearly how obeying his instructions will bring ruin to your family."

I felt that this would certainly be the case. I had always had a thorough contempt for what was called "asking counsel," although occasionally I had been obliged to submit to it. I really could not understand why people should have brains at all if they were not to use them; and I am sure I utterly failed to see the superiority of those who set themselves up as "counsellors" to the men whom they attempted to "counsel." Besides, I had often discovered that the counsel thus given was not always for the benefit of the person counselled.

My husband carefully thought over the matter. I saw he was much troubled, but he came to the conclusion that he would unreservedly accept the order, "obey," and go.

It was of no use to resist, and so I held my tongue. Very often since, it has occurred to me that probably this was the best thing, after all, that he could do; for it was, in a measure, the means of bringing him to realize his dependent position upon the will of Brigham Young.

He went to visit Ogden, and on his return he said to me, "President Young might as well have sent me into a desert. He may perhaps not know it, for probably he does not comprehend the expenses of a daily paper; but it will ruin me."

I, of course, did not exult over this unpleasant fulfilment of my anticipations, for I knew too well how greatly it would affect both my family and myself. It had, however, as I hoped, the desired effect of adding to his growing convictions about Brigham and the priesthood, and with this I was satisfied.

Since then I have often asked Mr. S. if he had not better have taken my advice, and he has answered me, "There is a period in every man's life in Mormonism when he must show his obedience; my time was *then*. I gave evidence of my obedience, and it brought ruin, as I expected. Henceforth I will follow the best experience of my life."

Much as the trial had cost us, I rejoiced; for I saw in this a renewal of his own manhood.

Shortly after Mr. S. returned to Salt Lake City with the *Telegraph*, the *Utah Magazine* began to question Brigham's measures, and the editors assumed to speak to the people of their position. This was at once pronounced rebellion and apostasy. The *Telegraph* took no part against the rebels, and that was construed to be "aid and comfort" to the enemy. Mr. S. could not oppose a movement that he felt was destined to shake the unchallenged power of the priesthood.

I well remember Mr. S. writing an article upon "Progress," for the *Telegraph*. He wrote it at home, and read it to me, paragraph by paragraph, as he wrote it. I thought he was "inspired;" the reasoning was so just, and the words came so freely from his pen. When it was finished, and he read it to me entire, we looked at each other. I thought his look was asking my opinion, and I quickly replied, "Publish it; it is true." He said, "It is true, but it will bring trouble if published." "Never mind," I added, "if it brings us to the door; let us be true to the truth."

It was published on the 2d of October, 1869.[1]

The semi-annual conference of the church was held that week, and continued in session five days. At the close of the session, on the Sunday afternoon, the Apostle Amasa Lyman, and Mr. William S. Godbe, soon after prominent men in the reform movement, came to dine with us, by previous appointment. Mr. S. had gone to the post-office, but soon joined them in the parlour, carrying a small newspaper open in his hand as he entered.

After the usual greetings he said, "Brethren, the ball is open; hear this." In that little paper there was a letter reviewing the article upon "Progress," and with it the correspondent professed to reveal that there was a "movement" on foot in Salt Lake City to attack Brigham's assumptions, and make a strike for "civil and religious liberty;" and that the article on "Progress," while it professed to treat of France under Louis Napoleon, meant Utah under Brigham Young. The article had just only been read a few minutes, and the gentlemen named, Mr. S., and myself, were looking with that vacant, thinking, meditative stare which showed that each one was fully absorbed with the idea that there was something to come of it. At that very instant, Mr. Joseph A. Young, President Young's eldest son, entered the parlour.

After friendly salutations, Mr. Young excused himself from joining us at dinner; and as we entered the dining-room, we instinctively turned to each other and remarked how singular it was that he should drop in upon us while his father was the subject of conversation and meditation. That, however, was all right.[2]

On the following Tuesday evening, I made Mr. Joseph A. Young acquainted with the feeling in opposition to his father, and avowed that Mr. S. was in the hostile camp.[3] On Saturday, seven elders, of which number Mr. S. was one, were attacked in "the School of the Prophets," and summoned to appear on the following Saturday.

This was looked for; but Brigham, in his anger, had gone too far, and "disfellowshipped them from the church of Jesus Christ, for irregular attendance at the school."[4] Brigham's assumption of the right to disfellowship men from Christ because of irregular attendance at a school, brought Mr. S. to a conclusion. He said to me, "With such an assumption of authority, what will he not do next? To submit to it is to acknowledge him absolute and me a slave. There is but one choice now—slavery or freedom. Cost me what it may, I shall be free." From that day we never attended a meeting of the Saints. In August of the following year, 1870, Mr. S. sent a respectful, kindly letter to the bishop of our Ward, stating that he had not faith in Brigham's claim to an Infallible Priesthood, and that he ought to be cut off from the church. I added a postscript, stating that I wished to share his fate,[5] although I little dreamed that in three days after that my request should have such a malignant fulfilment.

We were going home on the Saturday night succeeding our withdrawal from the church, a few minutes past ten o'clock. The night was very dark. Our residence is in the suburbs of the city, north of the Temple block, and the road is very quiet. As we went along we suddenly and dimly saw four men come out from under some trees a little distance from us. They separated, and two of them came forward and stumbled up against us, and two passed by the side of us. I thought for a moment that they were intoxicated, but it was soon clear that they were acting from design.

As soon as they approached, they, one on each side, seized hold of my husband's arms, and he, although by no means deficient in strength, was thus rendered powerless. The men, I should state, were masked so that we could not distinguish their features. I imagine that they supposed I should be frightened and run away. But in this they had calculated wrongly. I still clung to my husband's arm, but with my left hand caught hold of one of the ruffians by the collar of his coat; for I apprehended the worst, well knowing of what atrocities these men were capable. This considerably impeded their movements. The other two, who were likewise masked, stood a few feet distant, and seemed to hesitate for a moment. One of the men who held my husband's arm exclaimed, "Brethren, do your duty!" The voice was in an instant recognized as that of one of the policemen, whom Mr. S. and myself had patted on the head when a child in England.

Instantly I saw them raise their arms. It was too dark to distinguish any thing definitely, and I thought they were about to kill us. We had both the same thought, and this probably *would* have been Mr. Stenhouse's fate had he been alone; but I think that my presence somewhat disarranged their plans. A much less noble fate was reserved for us. I am ashamed to tell what they did. * * * Even now I shudder, as I recall the scenes of that night. I was nearly insane with rage and indignation. I felt at the moment that life was nothing to me, and I called to them to come and kill us. It would have been an honour and even pleasant to have been shot or killed by the assassin's knife, rather than endure such an indignity as this.[6]

Although the men who attacked us were masked, there is no question in our minds that they were two of the regular, and two of the special police. I have every reason to believe that their original intention was to kill Mr. S. About ten minutes before, they had seen him alone, and they did not believe that I should be with him. Had I run away and left him with them, I believe they would have beaten him to death. Men who would commit such an assault were capable of committing murder.

When they had perpetrated this disgusting and brutal outrage, they turned and fled. We ran after them for some little distance; but we had no arms or any thing to defend ourselves, and as there was another man lurking about a little distance in the direction in which they ran, we thought best not to go any further; for we knew that they would not shrink from murder, if that would conceal what they had done.

I declared in my anger that if there yet remained one solitary link which bound me to Mormonism, it should be severed that night. Not that I blame the mass of the Mormon people; for I know the honest hearts of that community, and that as a body they revolted at the atrocious wrong that was done us; and although not one of them came openly to express that feeling to me, hundreds of them did so in private. I was sick for three days after, so that it was impossible to attend to business. I could not calm my agitated feelings or stifle my indignation. Probably I was wrong in giving way to anger; but it seemed to me that nothing except revenge upon those horrible men could satisfy me. My husband and I felt sure that we knew who they were, but how could we swear to masked men? Some time after, a wife of one of these men, whom we suspected, came to see me, and told me that she believed her husband had been engaged in the affair. It seems perhaps strange that any wife should do this; but she had a great respect for me, and none at all for her husband, as he was very brutal to her.

When I had sufficiently recovered to return to business, I went down to the city with my husband. In passing the house of D. H. Wells, the Mayor of the city, we saw him standing at a short distance from us; but he made no attempt to come forward and express any regret. This I considered it was his place, as mayor of the city, to do; and as an old friend I fully expected as much from him. No Mormon, as I before intimated, came purposely to sympathize with me; but the whole of that day my store was filled with Gentiles,* and for several days after they kept coming to tell me how disgusted and indignant they were at such an abominable

---

* The Mormons use the term "Gentiles" to designate *all* outside of the church, whether Christians, Jews, or any other religion, and in this sense it is used in this volume. When a man forsakes Mormonism, he does not become a "Gentile" again, but an "Apostate," which is a still more odious and opprobrious appellation among the Saints.

outrage. I received also many letters from different parts of the country, both within the Territory of Utah and outside of it.

Mr. Joseph A. Young offered a reward to the chief of police on the night of the attack for the apprehension of the ruffians, and a few "Gentile" friends offered a reward of $500 for evidence that would lead to their identification, but there was no response. A Mormon paper, in order to direct attention away from the guilty parties, tried to insinuate that it was caused by some "personal difficulty." This course was not a new one. When Dr. Robinson, a few years before, was murdered in Salt Lake City, the *Tabernacle* insinuated that he had met his death in gambling. That gentleman was utterly innocent of gambling, and was not known to have an enemy.[7]

CHAPTER XVI.

Recent Conclusions on Polygamy—Faith in the Doctrine declining—How Women in Utah feel—False Notions and Statements—
Sophistries about Want of Faith—Opinions of Young Girls—Better
Chances now—Changes operating in Utah—Brigham becomes
fashionable; he abandons his own Teachings—How a Man with
two Wives cleverly escaped from Polygamy and Utah—Difficulties
of Husbands when they leave the Faith—Effects of the Law of
1862—Domestic Sympathies—Evil Effects of Example upon Boys.

I HAVE watched the whole system of Polygamy closely, and have tried
earnestly to discover wherein it was productive of any good; but in not
one single instance could I find, after the most diligent observation, any
but the very worst results. On the contrary, it was the same story again
and again repeated—evil—evil—evil!

That some men have practised Polygamy with honest intentions and
a desire to "keep the commandments of God," I know well to be true.
I respect such men even while they do so. They err in blindness, and I
believe they suffer while they are willing to make the sacrifice, (for to
such men it *is* a sacrifice;) but it is only the first step that troubles them.
They soon get over it. I know others in whom I had not this confidence—
men who seem always ready and anxious to "live up to their privileges," as
they call it, without regard to any sacred obligations.

It has been frequently said to me in my travels, both in the Eastern
and Western States, that gentlemen from Utah had been asked how the
ladies submitted to Polygamy, and that they had made answer, "Oh! very
well: they are perfectly happy, for they look upon its practice as a religious
duty, and are satisfied and contented with it."

Those women (if there be any?) who prefer this state of things are
few and far between, and wherever such a woman may be found, I am certain that it will be discovered that the husband is some worthless fellow,
or else so disagreeable in his family that the wives have no affection for
him, and they therefore seek the companionship of each other.

Why gentlemen should make statements so very likely to mislead
the public, I do not know. Possibly some of them really believe it; for, as I

before stated, where a man has more than one wife his wives are careful to conceal their real feelings from him, for fear of creating a prejudice against themselves and in favour of the other wife; for whether a woman loves her husband or not, she does not like it to be said that she has been cast off for another; and I know from experience that Mormon husbands are the very last to learn of their wives' feelings.

Women who tell the world that they are happy and contented, if they would only express themselves freely would tell of their heart-aches, of their sleepless nights, and of their loneliness. Others could tell that, in spite of their husband's kindness to them, their hearts knew no joy or happiness. If a woman in this condition of mind were asked if she did not love her husband as formerly, very probably she would answer, "O dear! no; if I did, I could not live. The greatest trouble I had was to withdraw my affections from my husband and fix them on my children. If I had not done this, where would my children be?—with their mother in the grave." Oh! how true this is! I know it—I feel it!

Heaven help these poor women! If they could only know for themselves that this continued sacrifice was not necessary, their very hearts would sing for joy.

I once said to a lady holding a high position in the church,[1] when she was persuading me to give another wife to my husband, "What good will it do me to give him another wife? I cannot do it with a good feeling. I know that I should loathe both him and her; and how could I expect to get any blessing from God by so doing?" She answered, "If you had a loaf of bread to make, what would it matter how you felt while making it, so long as you did make it?" That is just what the church authorities have thought: no matter how many women were crushed, or how many were sent to their graves, in the effort to establish Polygamy, if only they could establish it.

The young girls in Utah feel about Polygamy much as their mothers do. They like it so little that when one of the city girls marries a man who has already a wife or wives, it is generally supposed that she does so because he can keep her better than a younger man could. Until very recently, the young men in Utah were not generally very attractive to any sensible girl. They seemed to be destitute of ambition, but perhaps, after all, they were not so much to blame for that. Poor boys! There was really but little else for them to do but to haul wood for their fathers' different families, and hunt stray cattle.

It is now greatly different in Salt Lake City; as young men can get remunerative employment, and are very willing to engage in useful work; while a corresponding change is effected in their favour with the girls. There are very few sensible, educated girls in Salt Lake City, who would to-day prefer Polygamy to monogamy: I doubt whether there is really ONE.

The sermons, newspapers, and songs at one time were full of "the glory of the old man and the maiden going forth in the dance together," but the rapid change that is coming over the country and people is fast dispelling all this. In a few years more, the anxiety to fulfil ancient Hebrew predictions at the cruel sacrifice of youth, beauty, and honourable maidenly ambition, will disappear and be looked back upon by the Mormons themselves as follies of the past. When the Mormons lived in log huts and "dug-outs," wore coarse, homespun garments, drank "coffee" made of roasted barley and wheat, and their women and children wore shakers and sun-bonnets in summer, and covered their heads in winter with cravats and shawls, an extra wife, or an extra half-dozen wives, could be very easily provided for. In that condition of poverty and isolation, the women did truly "eat their own bread and wear their own apparel." The commercial development of the country has changed every thing and every body; and in no one has the change been more observed than on Brigham Young himself. Accordingly, Polygamy is becoming unpopular, and a natural desire for a higher condition in life is taking its place.

Aware of the *marked* difference in his own appearance, and in the comforts and luxuries with which himself and family are surrounded, Brigham tries to excuse himself for wearing broadcloth by pleading the old-fashioned weakness of Eden, "The woman tempted me"—"My wives insist that I shall wear better clothes." This is the only instance wherein Brigham Young was ever known to be ruled by his wives!

While his family was confined to his first fifteen or sixteen wives, good women of faith and hard labour, he was plain, home-clad "Brother Brigham;" but with the later additions of vanity and fashion to his household, he found his Delilah. And if he lives long enough, at the rate he has been going on of late years, he will soon rival Solomon in more ways than one. He has apostatized further from his first teachings of faith and on Polygamy than any man in Mormonism.

When once a Mormon has entered into that order of marriage, he is no longer a free man; he is bound and cannot help himself, and this the authorities know. Where could a man go to outside of Utah with more than one wife? He must remain where he is, or give up his family.

That many a man has been counselled to add wives to his first with the intention of binding him to the church and hindering him from either apostatizing or leaving the country, is a commonly understood fact; and many a man has keenly felt the wrong to himself as well as to his wife, when neither of them desired to disturb the peaceful harmony of their family happiness by the experiment of imitating the domestic life of the Jewish Patriarchs.

One man only of my acquaintance has been successful in breaking his polygamic relations and in leaving the country. He was in business as a merchant, and apparently tied up, so that he could not leave; but as his wives were as anxious as he was to break up the relationship, their movements were so well concealed that none of the authorities of the church had the slightest idea of his intended departure. His family had gone a few miles into the country on a visit, and he left his store with his coat off, and rode out of the town in a grain-wagon as if he were going to the gristmill. The overland mail-stage picked him up a few miles from Salt Lake City, and a few miles further, the family were taken into the stage, and they were off to California. The second wife, who had no children, acquiesced in the right of the first wife to remain with the husband. She got a satisfactory portion of his property, became a "Miss" again, and is to-day in California, rejoicing in her deliverance.

I know a gentleman in Salt Lake City who was urgently and constantly "counselled" to take a second wife. For years he resisted, but finally gave in to the importunities of counsel, as he saw that he must do so or rebel. As he could not do the latter conscientiously, he took a pure and beautiful girl for his second wife. Now, when he is no longer under the same religious obligations, he realizes that he is bound to protect and support her; yet he knows that in living with her, he is violating the laws of the land. In obeying "counsel," he felt that he had done right in a religious sense; but, as a man and citizen, he knows that he is not acting as he should, and that is one of the intended difficulties in leaving the church.

It is related of Joseph Smith that when he got Brigham Young and Heber C. Kimball to take other wives he was perfectly delighted, because, as he expressed it, he had got them "as much in the mud as he was in the mire." He was liable to indictment for bigamy in Illinois when he took other wives, and they were then in the same predicament. Many men of faith in Utah have become polygamists, not from any personal desire on their part to assume either its obligations or possess its glory, but purely to share in the risks and penalties of violated law with their brethren. Such appeals to the patriotism and devotion of men to their religion, accounts for much that has been done. They obeyed in haste, and repented at leisure.

Brigham Young's first violation of the law against Polygamy was regarded by the Saints, whether he intended it or not, as an expression of his confidence in God and his defiance of Congress. The faithful and believing brethren could not do less than follow the example of their leader. The law of 1862 against Polygamy has made very many more polygamists in Utah than existed there before. This opposition was not confined to the men only: the women in many instances partook of the same spirit; and in their moments of enthusiasm have seconded their husbands, but have afterwards had bitter cause to repent.

The greatest enemy to Polygamy is found in almost every polygamic family. It may be concealed; but it nevertheless is there, and only requires time to accomplish its overthrow. This enemy is the great dislike or repugnance that many children born in Polygamy have to that system. It can have no foe more powerful than this. If the husband is neglectful of his wife, the son comes to the aid and protection of his mother; while the gentle, loving daughter consoles her with sweet sympathy.

Between mother and children there exists a bond of union in which the father has no part. They counsel with each other; and the result of their communings is unfavourable to Polygamy. This is indeed the leaven which will eventually permeate the whole system of Mormonism.

It is painful to witness among the rising generation of boys in Utah the contempt which many evince for every thing that a woman says or does, looking upon her as an inferior being. But this is not to be wondered at, when it is remembered what kind of teaching they have had in the Tabernacle, and the example of some of their own fathers. The sermons abound with allusions to woman's dependence upon men. Even her salvation through Jesus Christ has to be obtained through her husband! How much greater, then, must man be, with his numerous wives, than either of the wives is individually.

Polygamy in Poverty.

CHAPTER XVII.

An Interesting Courtship—Brigham Young seeks another
Wife—Martha Brotherton tells her Story of the Wooing—Abstract
of her History—"Tricks that are Vain"—"Are you ready to
take Counsel?"—Joseph Smith's little Room—"Positively No
Admittance"—Joseph comes in—He assists Brigham's Courtship—
The Prophet a Proxy Lover—"A few Questions"—"Lawful and
Right"—The best Man in the World, but me!—"*I will have a kiss,
anyhow!*"—"Don't you believe in me?"—"If you accept Brigham, you
shall be blessed"—"If he turns you off, I will take you on"—"Not
exactly, sir."

As I have written so much of the troubles of the sisters, perhaps
it will be as well to give the reader an idea of the trials and difficulties
which the brethren had to contend with when they first attempted the
introduction of Polygamy. To do this, I shall give the correspondence of
Miss Martha Brotherton,[1] relating a very interesting courtship between
herself and Brigham Young. I would have the reader remark that this correspondence distinctly proves that Polygamy was taught by the heads of
the Church *before* the Prophet received the professed revelation.

This account was published just a year—lacking one day—before
the revelation on Polygamy was given to Joseph Smith. It was published in
Boston, in book form, in 1842.[2] The revelation was given at Nauvoo, on
the 12th of July, 1843.

I do not vouch for the facts stated by Miss Brotherton; but those
who were acquainted with Elder Heber C. Kimball, and those who know
Brigham Young and the style of address of the Mormon elders when
Polygamy first was presented to the Saints, will very readily accept the
lady's statements as more than probable. The language is familiar to
the Mormons. What a high and exalted idea Joseph Smith must have
had of the sacredness of marriage when he told the young lady that "if
Brigham turned her off" he "would take her on." And how immaculate
was Brigham Young's morality, when he suggested a clandestine marriage
there and then, without the knowledge of her parents.

The following is the letter referred to:

124

*"ST. LOUIS, Missouri, July 13th, A.D. 1842.[3]

* * * * *

"DEAR SIR: I left Warsaw a short time since for this city, and having been called upon by you, through the *Sangamo Journal,* to come out and disclose to the world the facts of the case in relation to certain propositions made to me, at Nauvoo, by some of the Mormon leaders, I now proceed to respond to the call, and discharge what I consider to be a duty devolving upon me as an innocent, but insulted and abused female. I had been at Nauvoo nearly three weeks, during which time my father's family received frequent visits from Elders Brigham Young and Heber C. Kimball, two of the Mormon Apostles; when, early one morning, they both came to my brother-in-law's (John McIlwrick's) house, at which place I was then on a visit, and particularly requested me to go and spend a few days with them. I told them I could not at that time, as my brother-in-law was not at home; however, they urged me to go the next day and spend one day with them. The day being fine, I accordingly went. When I arrived at the foot of the hill, Young and Kimball were standing conversing together. They both came to me, and, after several flattering compliments, Kimball wished me to go to his house first. I said it was immaterial to me, and went accordingly. We had not, however, gone many steps when Young suddenly stopped and said he would go to that brother's, (pointing to a little log hut a few yards distant,) and tell him that you (speaking to Kimball) and Brother Glover, or Grover, (I do not remember which,) will value his land. When he had gone, Kimball turned to me and said, 'Martha, I want you to say to my wife, when you go to my house, that you want to buy some things at Joseph's store, (Joseph Smith's,) and I will say I am going with you to show you the way. You know you want to see the Prophet, and you will then have an opportunity.' I made no reply. Young again made his appearance, and the subject was dropped. We soon reached Kimball's house, when Young took his leave, saying, 'I shall see you again, Martha.' I remained at Kimball's nearly an hour; when Kimball, seeing I would not tell the lies he wished me to, told them to his wife himself. He then went and whispered in her ear, and asked if that would please her. 'Yes,' said she, 'or I can go along with you and Martha.' 'No,' said he, 'I have some business to do, and I will call for you afterwards to go with me to the debate,' meaning the debate between yourself and Joseph. To this she consented. So Kimball and I went to the store together. As we were going along, he said, 'Sister Martha, are you willing to do all that the Prophet requires you to do?' I said, I believed I was—thinking, of course, he would require nothing wrong. 'Then,' said he, 'are you ready to take counsel?' I answered in the affirmative, thinking of the great and

* *Mormonism Exposed,* p. 236.

glorious blessings that had been pronounced upon my head if I adhered to the counsel of those placed over me in the Lord. 'Well,' said he 'there are many things revealed in these last days that the world would laugh and scoff at; but unto us is given to know the mysteries of the kingdom.' He further observed, 'Martha, you must learn to hold your tongue, and it will be well with you. You will see Joseph, and very likely will have some conversation with him, and he will tell you what you shall do.' When we reached the building, he led me up some stairs to a small room, the door of which was locked, and on it the following inscription, 'Positively no admittance.' He observed, 'Ah! Brother Joseph must be sick, for, strange to say, he is not here. Come down into the tithing-office, Martha.' He then left me in the tithing-office, and went out, I know not where. In this office were two men writing, one of whom, William Clayton, I had seen in England; the other I did not know. Young came in and seated himself before me, and asked where Kimball was. I said he had gone out. He said it was all right. Soon after, Joseph came in and spoke to one of the clerks, and then went up-stairs, followed by Young. Immediately after, Kimball came in. 'Now, Martha,' said he, 'the Prophet has come; come up-stairs.' I went, and we found Young and the Prophet alone. I was introduced to the Prophet by Young. Joseph offered me his seat, and, to my astonishment, the moment I was seated, Joseph and Kimball walked out of the room, and left me with Young, who arose, locked the door, closed the window, and drew the curtain. He then came and sat before me and said, 'This is our private room, Martha.' 'Indeed, sir,' said I; 'I must be highly honoured to be permitted to enter it.' He smiled, and then proceeded, 'Sister Martha, I want to ask you a few questions; will you answer them?' 'Yes, sir,' said I. 'And will you promise not to mention them to any one?' 'If it is your desire, sir,' said I, 'I will not.' 'And you will not think any the worse of me for it; will you, Martha?' said he. 'No, sir,' I replied. 'Well,' said he, 'what are your feelings toward me?' I replied, 'My feelings are just the same toward you that they ever were, sir.' 'But, to come to the point more closely,' said he, 'have not you an affection for me, that, were it lawful and right, you would accept of me for your husband and companion?' My feelings at this moment were indescribable. God only knows them. What, thought I, are these men, that I thought almost perfection itself, deceivers? and is all my fancied happiness but a dream? 'Twas even so; but my next thought was, which is the best way for me to act at this time? If I say *No,* they may do as they think proper; and to say *Yes,* I never would. So I considered it best to ask for time to think and pray about it. I therefore said, 'If it was lawful and right, perhaps I might; but you know, sir, it is not.' 'Well, but,' said he, 'Brother Joseph has had a revelation from God that it is lawful and right for a man to have two wives; for, as it was in the days of Abraham, so it shall be in these last days, and whoever is the first that is willing to take up the cross will receive the greatest blessings; and, if you will accept of me, I will take you straight to the celestial kingdom; and, if you will have me in this world, I will have you in that which is to come, and Brother Joseph will marry us here to-day, and you can go home this evening, and your parents will not know any thing about it.' 'Sir,' said I, 'I should not like to do any thing of the kind without the permission of my parents.' 'Well, but,' said he, 'you are of age, are you not?' 'No, sir,' said I; 'I shall not be until the 24th of May.' 'Well,' said he, 'that does not make any difference. You will be of age before they know, and you need not fear. If you will take my counsel, it will be well with you, for I know it to be right before God; and if there is any sin in it, I will answer for it. But Brother Joseph wishes to have some talk with you on the subject; he will explain things; will you hear him?' 'I do not mind,' said I. 'Well, but I want you to say something,' said he. 'I want to think about it,' said I. 'Well,' said he, 'I will have a kiss, anyhow,' and then rose, and said he would bring Joseph. He then unlocked the door, and took the key, and locked me up alone. He was absent about ten minutes, and then returned with Joseph. 'Well,' said Young, 'Sister Martha would be willing, if she knew it was lawful and right before God.' 'Well, Martha,' said Joseph, 'it is lawful and right before God—I *know* it is. Look here, sis; don't you believe in me.' I did not answer. 'Well, Martha,' said Joseph, 'just go ahead, and do as Brigham wants you to; he is the best man in the world, except me.' 'Oh!' said Brigham, 'then you are as good.' 'Yes,' said Joseph. 'Well,' said Young, 'we believe Joseph to be a Prophet. I have known him near eight years, and have always found him the same.' 'Yes,' said Joseph, 'and I know that this is lawful and right before God, and if there is any sin in it, I will answer for it before God; and I have the keys of the kingdom, and whatever I bind on earth is bound in heaven, and whatever I loose on earth is loosed in heaven; and if you will accept of Brigham, you shall be blessed—God shall bless you, and my blessing shall rest upon you; and, if you will be led by him, you will do well; for I know that Brigham will do well by you, and if he don't do his duty to you, come to me, and I will make him; and if you do not like it in a month or two, come to me and I will make you free again; and if he turns you off, I will take you on.' 'Sir,' said I, rather warmly, 'it will be too late to think in a month or two after. I want time to think first.' 'Well, but,' said he, 'the old proverb is, "Nothing ventured, nothing gained;" and it would be the greatest blessing that was ever bestowed upon you.' 'Yes,' said Young, 'and you will never have reason to repent it—that is, if I do not turn from righteousness, and that, I trust, I never shall; for I believe God, who has kept me so long, will continue to keep me faithful. Did you ever see me act in any way wrong in England, Martha?' 'No, sir,' said I. 'No,' said he; 'neither can any one else lay any thing to my charge.' 'Well, then,' said Joseph, 'what are you afraid of, sis? Come, let me do the business for you.' 'Sir,' said I, 'do let me have a little time to think about it, and I will promise not to mention it to any one.' 'Well, but look here,' said he; 'you know a fellow will never be damned for doing the best he knows how.' 'Well, then,' said I, 'the best way I know of is, to go home and think and pray about it.' 'Well,' said Young, 'I shall leave it with Brother Joseph, whether it would be best for you to have time or not.' 'Well,' said Joseph, 'I see no harm in her having time to think, if she will not fall into temptation.' 'O sir!' said I, 'there is no fear of my falling into temptation.' 'Well, but,' said Brigham, 'you must promise me you will never mention it to any one.' 'I do promise it,' said I. 'Well,' said Joseph, 'you must promise me the same.' I promised him the same. 'Upon your honour,' said he, 'you will not tell.' 'No, sir; I will lose my life first,' said I. 'Well, that will do,' said he; 'that is the principle we go upon. I think I can trust you, Martha,' said he. 'Yes,' said I, 'I think you ought.' Joseph said, 'She looks as if she could keep a secret.' I then rose to go, when Joseph commenced to beg of me again. He said it was the best opportunity they might have for months, for the room was often engaged. I, however, had determined what to do. 'Well,' said Young, 'I will see you to-morrow. I am going to preach at the school-house opposite your house. I have never preached there yet; you will be there, I suppose.' 'Yes,' said I. The next day being Sunday, I sat down, instead of going to meeting, and wrote the conversation, and gave it to my sister, who was not a little surprised; but she said it would be best to go to meeting in the afternoon. We went, and Young administered the sacrament. After it was over, I was passing out, and Young stopped me, saying, 'Wait, Martha; I am coming.' I said, 'I cannot; my sister is waiting for me.' He then threw his coat over his shoulders, and followed me out, and whispered, 'Have you made up your mind, Martha?' 'Not exactly, sir,' said I; and we parted. I shall proceed to a justice of the peace, and make oath to the truth of these statements, and you are at liberty to make what use of them you may think best.

> "Yours respectfully,
>
> "MARTHA A. BROTHERTON.

"Sworn to and subscribed before me, this 13th day of July, A.D. 1842.

> "DU BOUFFAY FREMON,
> "Justice of the Peace for St. Louis County."

CHAPTER XVIII.

Marriage—The Age for Marrying—Seventy and Seventeen—
Women privileged to choose their own Husbands—Some Women
make a Choice—Joseph's Widows—"Serving for seven Years"—
"Celestial Marriages"—Baptism and Marriage for the Dead—Saving
one's Ancestors ad infinitum—Marrying "for Time and for
Eternity"—The Register at Salt Lake City, from which the World
shall be judged—Difficulties of "proxy" Marriages—"Proxies" for
the Empress Josephine and Napoleon I.—"The next best Thing"—
Joseph's unproductive Polygamy—Divorce—Woman's solitary
Privilege—Divorce for ten Dollars!—Re-marrying—"Affinity"—
Shocking Instance of self-fulfilling a "Revelation"—Perverted
Heroism—Brother Hyde's Argument—The Woman with seven
Husbands—Statistical Facts.

THE dominant principle of Mormonism is marriage, and the theory that men and women are not perfect without each other. The man is not perfect without the woman, nor is the woman without the man, in the Lord.

Every man and every woman must be married some time or other. They cannot otherwise attain to glory, and would be "angels," or servants to the Celestial Saints. The woman ought to be married but once; the man may be married as often as he pleases, if he can provide for his wives and their families. There is no particular age specified as proper for marriage, but the younger the girl is, the better. It is seldom that there are any girls married under fifteen years of age; but sixteen is a very sweet age, and very desirable for men, themselves ranging in years from forty-five to seventy and over. An unmarried girl in Utah is old at twenty, and it is rarely the case that any attractive girl passes out of her teens before she is wedded.*

The boys seldom marry so early, but if capable of supporting themselves, the accumulation of property and experience are neither very necessary to becoming a husband. The teachings of the priesthood have

---

* Since the above was written, the Utah Legislature has entertained a bill as follows: "A bill has been offered and referred to a committee regulating marriage. It provides that males of fifteen years and females of twelve years of age may contract marriage, with the consent of parents or guardians."—*New-York Herald*, Jan. 27th, 1872.

generally discountenanced prudential preparations that are common elsewhere. The chief object has been rather to encourage an increase of "the kingdom," than to seek the personal happiness of the married pair.

In any other community, it would be remarked if a man of fifty, sixty, or seventy years of age should be paying his addresses to a girl of seventeen. In Utah, there is no attention paid to it; and not infrequently, married men with several wives may be seen courting and marrying girls much younger than their own daughters. It is a great wrong to the girls. They are too young to see the consequences of their folly at the outset, and the men who seek them for wives are too selfish to draw their attention to the error.

It is very amusing to see a vain, silly old man trying to be young again—dyeing his hair, and aping the fancies of juvenile courtship. This sight is any thing but rare among the Mormons. I knew a man who objected to his daughter being married, as she was only a few months over sixteen. The married man who was courting the young lady, tersely replied to the father, "Yes, she is very young; she is six months younger than my sister whom you are courting." The sarcasm of the answer was enough, and in the course of time he got the daughter.

In the first years of polygamous experience, the elders tried in their teachings to give the institution of the patriarchs as favourable an appearance as possible, and told the sisters who had been neglected, that it was *their* "privilege" to choose their own husbands. This had some practical results; but the acknowledgment of it as a principle has never been much dwelt upon in the pulpit, as it has its inconveniences.

After the death of Joseph Smith, something had to be done for his numerous "widows;" and when the church was travelling across the plains, this "privilege" was extended to them to "choose" their future husbands. Very reluctantly Brigham accepted the preference of one of these "widows," while another of them manifested in a similar way her preference for his counsellor—Heber.

A lady called one day upon a prominent bishop, north of Salt Lake City, whom I knew very well, and sought his counsel "in the interest" of her daughter. The mother related that a young man wanted to marry the daughter, but she did not love him; she had a preference for a gentleman already married. What was she to do? That was the subject upon which she wanted the bishop's counsel. With a ready answer for every one, the bishop saw no difficulty. "Go," said he, "to the married man, and tell him that your daughter loves him, and it is his duty to marry her." The task was soon accomplished; the kind mother smiled and blushed a little, and then said, "Bishop, *thou* art the man!" The bishop could do no other than follow his own "counsel." He was in comfortable circumstances, and the young lady shortly after became wife number six or seven of his household.

Many such cases of the sisters choosing husbands have occurred, and sometimes with very satisfactory results. When it is really a case of affection on the lady's part, and the selected husband is a liberally disposed man, the affair goes off as well as any marriage of his own choosing; but when the arrangement is not an "affinity" affair, the lady receives very little attention, and often lives to repent of her choice.

A very excellent Englishwoman is said to have entered Brigham's family as a domestic, and from her devotion to her faith, and affection for the Prophet, it is related that she served, like Jacob in the house of Laban, seven years, to obtain her choice. She is a woman of good sense, and illustrates, in her quiet and almost solitary life, the tenacity of affection, even if only coldly returned. With a son that she has added to the Prophet's family, she lives apparently contented. Another lady was less fortunate. The Prophet passed through the form of sealing and registering her name upon the "Book of Life," but there the marriage ended. She lives in all the loneliness of married spinsterhood. Brigham honoured the law of "privilege," and permitted her to be called by his name.[1]

What I have written of marriage hitherto has only been that which appertained to *this* world. I have now to give the Mormon views of a continuance of this marriage in the celestial world.

The Mormon priesthood claim that there is no legal and holy marriage outside of their church, and that all the Gentiles are, therefore, in the sight of God, living in sin. If this is true of the present age, it must necessarily be true of all the ages that have intervened, from the days of the fishermen of Galilee, to the advent of Joseph Smith and Brigham Young; for the latter claim that no true priesthood has been upon the earth till restored by Peter, James, and John, to Joseph Smith.

As all earthly associations are the foundations for eternal institutions, the marital relations naturally claim the highest and first attention of the Saints. The glory of a Saint in the world to come is, therefore, predicated upon the foundation laid here for that glory. Woman is the glory of man; children are the glory of woman; the more wives, the greater glory to the man; the more children, the greater glory to the woman.

Out of this faith comes the novel doctrine that it is not only the duty of men to multiply wives to themselves here, but that it also devolves upon them to see that all their relatives who have died are placed in a position in the world to come, where they also can have wives and children associated with their names, and thus increase their glory. Believing also in the rejuvenation of the aged beyond the veil, it is not uncommon to learn of some lady of sixty winters being "sealed" to a brother of half her age, and bearing *his name* before the community.

With a blooming bride of seventeen on one side, the Mormon elder may occasionally be seen (though not often) at his family table, with a grandmotherly lady at his other side, and both are his wives. The younger one seeks his glory *now;* the other will when hereafter she is rejuvenated, seek his glory in the next world. These are matters on which explicitness is not particularly necessary. It is, however, very creditable to the faith of a young Mormon elder for him to provide for the declining years of the aged spinster or widow. When the old lady has money in her own right, she can literally say that "she eats her own bread and wears her own apparel;" and it is seldom that the condition of which I have written is seen without some such consideration.

With this explanation, the reader will readily understand the doctrine, not only of Mormon men and women being married themselves for time and eternity, but they will also comprehend what is meant by "proxy wives" and "proxy husbands." For illustration: a man and his wife in Salt Lake City are married by the priesthood; they are married legally—as "the Lord" wants it. There is nothing that can separate this man and wife in time and in eternity but adultery or "apostasy," unless the priesthood find some other reason, which they sometimes have done.

A record of Mormon marriages is preserved in the archives of the church, and only out of these records the world will be judged. It is therefore necessary that the names of my father and mother, and every other person's father and mother should be recorded on the books in Salt Lake City as man and wife, otherwise they would be as "angels," strolling about in the upper regions without any particular marital relationship. Should, however, my husband and myself agree that we shall be married as "proxies" for my father and mother, or for his father and mother, then we go to the "Endowment House" and personate the dead, each according to sex, and that is recorded. By this devotion and care on our part, Mr. and Mrs. Stenhouse, the elder, would then, but not before, be duly entitled to be husband and wife in the other world. As Mr. Stenhouse *père* had but one wife, his glory would necessarily be very limited, and it would become the duty of Mr. Stenhouse *fils* to see that he had some extra wives sealed to him for his father. As a dutiful son, the living, believing Stenhouse should see that his grandfather, great-grandfather, and all *their* fathers, right back to the first ages of Christianity, or even, possibly, as far back as old father Adam, were secured the same privileges.

To be consistently careful of his progenitors, and their happiness and glory in the world to come, the same attentions and courtesies should be extended to all my husband's brothers, and to his uncles, as well as to all my brothers, uncles, etc., up to the beginning of time. The mothers are necessarily cared for in the marriage with fathers; but all our sisters and aunts have to be provided for in the same way. They must all be married, and the men clothed with the glory of numerous wives, and the women with the glory of many children.

As in life all the marriages have not been pleasant, it would be somewhat difficult to determine, among our dead, who wanted to know each other then, and be reunited in eternal marriage as they had been on earth. Besides these, difficulties innumerable and insurmountable spring up. I might be looking out for some maiden aunt or spinster sister who had never had their hearts touched by the tender passion, or perhaps might have set their affections on some particular person, and then to seal them to another would be rather awkward. In all this it would be very cruel if some were forgotten, or if others should be united, when perhaps they had waited with anxiety for death to set them free.

I am afraid that I am getting lost in the magnitude and extent of the Mormon obligations for the dead, and I shall, therefore, stop here upon that point.

I was much amused at learning, in Salt Lake City, that a French lady of my acquaintance had been baptized as "proxy" for the Empress Josephine, while her son had stood for Napoleon I. How much further the mother and son carried their admiration for the imperial pair, I know not; but it would be consistent for them to have been proxies for Josephine and Napoleon in marriage, and for the son to have recorded in the archives of the "Endowment House" that he had stood proxy for Napoleon to be ordained a Mormon elder. Following that, he could also have had "sealed" to Napoleon any maiden of Utah, or any number of maidens who had an admiration for the prisoner of St. Helena.*

Illustrative of the folly, if not profanity, to which some carry this teaching, I was told of a lady who once asked Brigham Young if she could not be "sealed" to Jesus Christ, as one of His wives. Brigham replied that he could not go thus far, but he would do the next best thing, and that was to have her "sealed" to Joseph Smith.[2] Had the lady to whom I refer been an ignorant semi-savage of Asia or Africa, or a squaw of the Rocky Mountains, this could readily have been understood; but when I assure the reader that the lady in question was educated in New-England, and held a respectable social position there before she embraced Mormonism, the terrible extent of her credulity can be imagined.†

---

* General Washington has also in a similar way been kindly cared for by the Mormons. Judge Adams, of Springfield, was baptized as proxy for him, and he is now a member of the "Church and Kingdom" established by Joseph Smith.

† The Mormon Apostles insist that Jesus Christ was a polygamist; that the sisters Martha and Mary were two of his wives, and that the marriage at Cana of Galilee, when the water was turned into wine, was one of Christ's bridal feasts. According to the Mormon faith, the lady alluded to above was, therefore, not so inconsistent in her request as might otherwise be supposed. Yet few persons can hear of such a desire being expressed, without considering it to be simply a bold profanity. Had I not heard the statement from the most reliable source, I should not have even named it.

Consistently with all this complication of marriages, another distinctive feature in Utah Polygamy is the raising up of children to the dead. When one of the prominent Mormons died some years ago, his five or seven wives, with their families and property, passed over to the care of his young nephew—one of the Apostles. The nephew had already two or three wives of his own, but that was a small consideration, and he assumed the extra responsibility. All the offspring of this plural marriage are the children of the deceased, and are to be "claimed" by him in the resurrection.

Though the object in instituting Polygamy is said to have been the "raising up of a holy seed," it is not a little surprising that Joseph Smith, through whom the revelation is given, notwithstanding his numerous wives, had no children born to him in Polygamy. Since his death, however, his brethren have done well for him, and his posterity is numerous. One of the finest families of Brigham Young will one day pass away to the account of Joseph, his predecessor. The lady was sealed to Joseph for time and eternity, and she is therefore wholly his. But Joseph died; and, as the widow was young and handsome, from respect to the dead, Brigham assumed the responsibility of being a proxy husband to her during her lifetime. Devotion to the deceased, of course, demands that no love beyond that of brotherly and sisterly affection should spring up between them.

All this has, theoretically, a very devotional turn; but I am afraid humanity has something to say in it, as the lady in question has a very large family to Joseph,[3] while another lady of Brigham's household has but one daughter to the dead Prophet, and other wives of Joseph have had a similarly diversified experience.[4]

With these numerous classifications of marriage, some from affection and others from necessity, or faith, or obligation, it would be natural to look for a law of divorce almost as large and liberal as that of the marriage itself. This is the case. It is easy to get married in Utah, and it is quite as easy to get unmarried. But the leading actors are reversed. Men marry the women: the women divorce the men; and this is about the only rational and just thing there is in connexion with the Mormon marriages.

The causes of divorce are as numerous as the ordinary disagreement between individuals; and the facility of obtaining a divorce leads often to very strange complications.

The first wife among the Mormons is not intentionally more privileged than the twentieth wife; but no first wife ever forgets that she is the *legal* wife of her husband, and that the priesthood cannot interfere with her status. Should the first wife have cause of complaint and seek for a divorce, she applies to the courts of law and obtains protection and alimony.*

* I am assured by a leading attorney in Salt Lake City that during the last twelve months, more than one hundred first wives have called upon him to enter suit for divorce and alimony.

All the other wives were married to the husband by the priesthood, and can only be released from him by the priesthood.

All law contention is avoided in the Mormon divorce cases, and they are also unattended with expense. A young wife presents herself at Brigham's office and complains of her husband. Brigham listens. If he has any personal interest in the absent husband, he will probably defer his decision, and afford him an opportunity of being heard in his own defence. Should it be otherwise, and Brigham would rather humble the husband if he can, he readily accepts the woman's statement. The clerk is instructed to "make out the papers." The discontented wife signs them, and her marriage is dissolved. The husband is notified that he is "wanted at the office." He goes—it may be without any knowledge of the nature of the business—and is informed that his wife Ignatia had been there, and had related all his "brutality" to her, and his "shocking neglect," his greater preference for some other wife, or that he had stayed two days more in every week with his favourite—Susannah, than he had with her or with Mary Jane, and *she* "was not going to stand it." The husband may supplicate, promise better behaviour, or suggest a more just disposition of his hours and affection, and then the signing of the papers is deferred. Other husbands take dissatisfied wives at their word, thankful for the opportunity of sundering ties that were irksome to both. He watches the occasion of Brigham's absence from the office, goes round in a great hurry, sees the clerk, asks for the papers and signs them. He then hands ten dollars to the clerk, and beats a retreat from the office without giving any opportunity for repentance, and rejoices in the glory of being once more a free man—"a one-wifed bachelor!"[5]

This divorce business has about as many ludicrous phases as the marriage is stamped with cruel severity. In the marriage ceremony, the husband and wife are "sealed up unto eternal life." Nothing but adultery can unloose those bands. Yet it frequently occurs that a dissatisfied wife "gets a bill" of divorce and marries again another man to whom she is "sealed up" also to "eternal life;" and cases are known of women being "sealed up" to "eternal life" to three and four different husbands. And after all this professedly sacred service has been performed, Brigham in some of his comical humours will tell the people in the Tabernacle that "the divorce is not worth the paper it is written upon; but the people insist upon getting them, and the ten dollars is pin-money for my wives." What a picture to contemplate! What reflections arise upon purity! He first teaches Polygamy as the marital relations of the purest and the highest

But he has discountenanced their proposed proceedings, as far as he was concerned, as he regarded it as a very unpleasant business and not unattended with danger. Besides which, he believed that up to the present time the situation of affairs in Utah was not so favourable for such proceedings as might shortly be expected.

in the heavens: he introduces it with the grandest promises: it becomes intolerable, and for peace' sake he gives divorces and then gets into confusion. The truth is that Brigham now begins to realize that he has more on his hands than he knows what to do with.

Women are to be met with in Utah with even a much larger married experience than many of the men. I know a good-natured soul who has had *four* husbands. I first knew her at my house as a laundress. Ever since that, whenever I chance to meet her, I expect to hear something interesting. She now lives in the country, and only comes into the city about once a year. The last time I saw her she came up smiling good-naturedly, and said—"What do you think, Mrs. Stenhouse? I have just seen *two* of my old husbands! One I knew was here, but I did not expect to see the other." She seemed to look upon this rencontre as a cheerful and amusing incident, and from her manner while speaking of them, I should think that she was on very excellent terms with both. Their divorce had caused no bitterness.

When any woman has not been seen for some length of time, a little caution is necessary in addressing her by name. She may have been Mrs. Smith when you last spoke to her: have become Mrs. Jones, or Robinson, and be now Mrs. Smith again! I have generally waited to hear something which might indicate if any change had taken place before I would venture to address her by the name which she had borne when I last saw her. It is not uncommon in Utah for a wife to leave her husband, marry again, be divorced, and go back to her first husband.

This changing round from one husband to another is, however, not altogether the result of personal caprice alone, and the indelicacy of such "trading" of husbands and wives cannot be charged entirely to the fickleness of the persons interested. Faith, as taught by the priesthood, has been a disturbing element in married life.

Though the word "affinity" is not used by the Mormons, its meaning has, in fact, been often illustrated among them. Wives in Utah, as well as elsewhere, have passed from one husband to another; but the worst of the matter is, that in Utah a divine revelation is claimed for these proceedings. In connection with the "affinity" doctrine elsewhere, the parties satisfy themselves and act on their own responsibility. If they blunder, and are punished for their mistake, they have only themselves to blame; but when "revelation" is claimed as authority for what is done, one of the parties is generally the innocent victim of the other.

To avoid wounding the feelings of an innocent and excellent lady, I withhold names; but I may say that I know of a lady in Salt Lake City who was many years ago married to a man of about her own age. She is a very handsome woman. A certain man officiating at the marriage ceremony in the "Endowment House," is said to have remarked to some members of his family that he had that day married to another man a sister who *ought* to have been *his own* wife.

As every word falling from *his* lips is looked upon as a divine "revelation," his wives very naturally regarded what he now said in that light. His statement was not long in finding its way to the newly married wife. She, with the usual faith and confidence of the Saints in all that is uttered by *him*, believed what she heard, and looked upon her marriage with the young man as a mistake which would have to be set right some day, and so became very unhappy. After having borne two children to her husband, and only a few months before the birth of her third child, she became the wife of the *"great" man!*

Terrible as the trial *must* have been to her young husband, he was forced to accept the situation, and remained in fellowship with the church for several years afterwards. He is now amongst the Liberals of Utah. The lady is still young and very good looking, but she is made to realize most keenly that she is only *one of a number* of wives; while her "priestly" husband is spending his leisure hours with a more recent favourite.[6]

But this is by no means a solitary instance of the kind. One of the "Twelve Apostles" met with his death from the hands of a husband who considered himself outraged in his wife leaving him, adopting the new faith, and marrying the apostle; and although the Mormons very much regretted his death, the most intelligent and thinking portion of them felt that in the situation of the husband they might have done the same thing. No "Gentile" could interfere with a Mormon wife in Utah to the same extent without being visited by "judgment."[7]

Many instances could be given of ladies leaving their husbands under the impression that they, though good men, were not as able to "exalt" them as other men in the priesthood. Two ladies in Salt Lake, whom I know and have already alluded to, while they were in Nauvoo became the sealed wives of Joseph Smith and yet still maintained their relationship to their own husbands.[8] This is very revolting, and exhibits to what extremes faith will sometimes conduct people. These ladies to-day think that that which the world would universally condemn was an act of the noblest heroism. Their names, if printed here, would perfectly astonish many who personally know and respect them. I do not doubt for a moment that they conscientiously thought that they were worthy of the highest honor for believing the "revelation" of "the Lord," through "His servant," and accepting the position of handmaids to "the Anointed."

Enough has been written already to set the most devoted Saint thinking over the crooked paths of Polygamy. I have not attempted to enter into any argument hitherto, but I think I may venture to conclude this chapter with a word to Brother Hyde about his statement justifying the practice.

"Brother" Orson puts forth perhaps the best argument that has ever been given in its favour. But let us see what this argument is. He says:

"Some man will perhaps marry a wife of his youth. She dies. He loved her as he loves himself, and her memory ever lingers about his heart. He marries another, and she dies, and he loved her equally as well. He marries a third, and so on, and he loved them all. By-and-by he dies, and he dies with devoted affection and love to them all. Now, in the resurrection, which of these wives shall he claim? There is no difference in his love to any of them; and they have all, perhaps, borne children to him. He loves the children of one mother as well as the children of another. What say you? Which shall he have in the resurrection? Why, let him have the whole of them; to whom are they more nearly allied?

"There is a case opposite to this, where a woman married a husband, and he died, and so on, until she had been married to seven husbands; and then *she* also died. The question was asked the Savior—'Whose wife will she be in the resurrection, for they all had her?' A curious answer was returned—'In the resurrection they neither marry nor are given in marriage; but are as the angels of God in heaven.'"

Brother Hyde appears willing that *the woman* with her seven husbands should be "as the angels"—whatever that condition may be; but he would rather himself decide the fate of his own sex, and he very generously says of *the man* with seven wives, "Let him have them all; to whom are they 'nearer' allied?" Be just, Brother Hyde, and allow to the poor woman who has had seven husbands *the whole* of them: who deserves them better? She might similarly have loved *all* her husbands; and if the argument is good for the man, it is good for the woman. Why should *she* not be permitted to have them all in the other world, instead of being compelled to become "an angel"?

The question arises in my mind—If all these seven brethren are faithful members of the church, and if their only chance of glory and "exaltation in heaven" consists in the number of wives and children which each has, why should the unfortunate six be sentenced to be kept out in the cold—wifeless, and with only a faint taste of the bliss of Paradise? Why, also, should *only one* be favoured? And, then, *which* ought to be *that one!*

It is, I think, very evident that Brother Hyde expressed only the desires of his poor, weak, erring nature when he said—"Let him have them all, to be sure!"

Brother Hyde has provoked statistics. The women of Utah who have listened to so many sermons in the Tabernacle, about the women so far outnumbering the men in the world, and hence the necessity of Polygamy, so that every woman should have a husband, will be interested in the perusal of the following table, which certainly does not prove the assertion.

TABLE

OF MALE AND FEMALE POPULATION OF THE TERRITORY OF UTAH IN 1870.

	Counties.	Males.	Females.	Total.
1	Beaver	1010	997	2007
2	Box Elder	2842	2013	4855
3	Cache	4068	4161	8229
4	Davis	2232	2227	4459
5	Iron	1123	1154	2277
6	Juab	1027	1007	2034
7	Kane	776	737	1513
8	Millard	1429	1324	2753
9	Morgan	995	977	1972
10	Piute	69	13	82
11	Rich	1020	935	1955
12	Rio Virgin	250	200	450
13	Salt Lake	9019	9318	18,337
14	San Pete	3274	3512	6786
15	Sevier	19	—	19
16	Summit	1349	1163	2512
17	Tooele	1159	1018	2177
18	Utah	6174	6029	12,203
19	Wahsatch	642	602	1244
20	Washington	1532	1532	3064
21	Weber	4112	3746	7858
	Total	44,121	42,665	86,786

In the above table, for which I am indebted to the Census Bureau at Washington, the reader will perceive that in polygamous Utah there are two thousand and fifty-six *more males than* females![9]

Brigham Young at Home.

CHAPTER XIX.

Domestic Life in Polygamy—Management of Families—
Separate Homes—Half a dozen Wives under one Roof—Internal
Arrangements—The "Odd Day" for the first Wife—"Generosity"—
How six Wives are visited—The Misery of poor Polygamists—The
greater Misery in a wealthy House—"The Kingdom"—The Tale of
the Doors and Windows—Fruitless good Intentions—Illustrative
Instance of the Effects of Polygamy and Monogamy—An economi-
cal Wife, and her Object—Wives in various Places—Utilizing the
Services of Wives—A Husband's Difficulties—Brigham Young—His
"Homes"—Mrs. Young: Nineteen of Her!—Wives and "proxy"
Wives—The Bee-Hive House—The Lion House—Six other
Houses—Domestic Relations—Brigham's Favourite—The Prophet
in the Ball-Room—His Proscenium Box at the Theatre—Delusion of
Utah Women—Can this be from God?

In every conversation upon Polygamy in Utah, the first question usually asked is, "How are the women managed? do they all live
together—or how?"

There is no fixed principle regulating men in the management of
their families. Every one is at liberty to do as he thinks best; and, with the
greatest diversity of judgment and circumstances, there are scarcely two
families alike. Where the husband is wealthy, separate homes are generally provided for the wives. Still, some wealthy men have all their families
together under the same roof. When this is the case, if the wives number
half a dozen or more, the "living" arrangements are ordered with a view
to economy. If there is harmony in the household, some deference may
be paid to the first wife, and perhaps she may be excused from part of the
domestic duties; but as a general thing, all the wives take week and week
about in the management of the house. The work of the kitchen, the
laundry, etc., is done by hired "help."

In such a house there is a common dining-room, large enough to
seat the wives and the eldest and youngest children. Of course the table
is often not large enough for all the children, and then there is a second
table for the others. In such an establishment privacy is unknown. Each
lady, however, has her own apartment.

In a very large house, with many wives, there is greater safety and peace for the husband than in a small house, with only two wives. When there are only two apartments, the husband is supposed to be in the one or in the other; and if there is any disposition to be bitter, the occupied room at once furnishes the object for the attack from the vacant room. In a large house, there are some advantages. The whereabouts of the husband is not so easily discovered, and the unhappy or jealous wife is at a loss to know on whom she should vent her ire. On this account, even men of small means prefer to have three wives instead of two, as the jealousy is then divided, and the wives do not well know which of the two others is her greatest enemy.

The husband who provides separate homes for his wives has to divide his time between them. Some men go from house to house, spending a day with one wife and a day with another, and so on until he has visited them all. Then he begins again where he first set out, and travels over the same road as before. Where the wives are not more than three in number, each wife generally has the society of her lord for two days in each week; and when the husband desires to show any preference to his first wife, the odd day in the seven is accorded to her, and this is rarely objected to; but not infrequently the extra day falls to the lot of the youngest and last wife—this very pious and impartial man justifying his preference by a kindly word to his wives about their all having had "their day," and that it was nothing but right that the young bride should have "her day" also. To such a delicate appeal to their generosity, and to such an exhibition of his manifest disinterestedness, and desire to be just, these loving wives could of course make but little objection!

A house with two wings is very popular among the men with two wives. The centre door opens into the parlour, which serves for the reception of visitors to both families. Two doors are sure to be seen—one to the right, another to the left, conducting to the family apartments of each wife. The husband spends one week on one side of the house, and the following week he goes to the other side of the house; and in the mean time he keeps trotting from one side to the other every day, to preserve peace in his family.

I have in my mind a prominent man in Salt Lake City, who is the husband of half a dozen wives; he divides his time after this fashion: The first week, he stays with the first wife; the next week he is with the second; then he goes back again to the first wife for another week. He then passes the fourth week with the third wife, and back he goes again to the first wife, and so on forward and backward, until he has blessed them all with his presence. By this arrangement, the first wife has the largest share of her husband's society. The truth, however, requires that I should state that the last wife in this particular family was a young and very good-looking girl, and she resided with the first wife. Thus while the husband was showing his devotion to his first wife, he was rewarded by the society of his younger one. The other wives only got a week of his society in about every eleven weeks; they have thus each about five weeks of his society in every year.

When abundant wealth can supply all the wants of numerous wives and children, and furnish every accommodation that a growing family demands, much of the jealousy and ill-feeling so common to Polygamy can in some degree be avoided. But when poor men have families growing up in some old, dilapidated house, and huddled together, it is a very painful experience. Polygamy with riches is bad enough; but Polygamy with poverty is terrible.

It is said that many men in Utah have entered into polygamic life with two wives under one roof, and with but a very doubtful partition in the bed-room. But even for this those poor people were hardly to be blamed. "Build up the kingdom! build up the kingdom!" has been drummed into their ears till all good sense and propriety were driven out of their heads. It is very common, however, to see families of two or three wives living together in one small house—the women with separate bed-rooms, but with only one kitchen to accommodate them all, and with one room that serves as dining-room and parlour—all for "the Kingdom's" sake.*

A row of doors and windows may be seen in every settlement in Utah, and even still in Salt Lake City they may be noticed. To each door and window there was a wife, a fire-place, a bedstead, three chairs, and a table. When the family of either wife increased and required more room, a shed would be added behind. This was "celestial" marriage in Utah. Yet I have known more misery to exist in a handsome residence, and more ill-feeling between two wives rolling in abundance there, than probably was ever felt in some of those mud-roofed cottages of doors and windows where half a dozen wives resided.

Poverty is ill to bear in Polygamy. It is a terrible physical affliction, and develops the lowest feelings in both women and children, who are ever afraid that other wives and their children are getting more than their

---

* I have frequently mentioned in this work the word "Kingdom." To my "Gentile" readers, this expression will probably not be very clear, and it is only right that I should give a word of explanation. The Mormon doctrine is, that in the other world, a man's children and descendants will form his "Kingdom." Hence it is that they are anxious to have numerous families, as the more children a man has, the greater will be his power and glory hereafter, as their patriarch and monarch. A knowledge of this doctrine will give the reader a better insight into much that has been written, and will explain why it is that Polygamy has taken such hold upon the minds of the Mormon people, and how natural it is that the idea of a future "kingdom," if once believed, should enter so deeply into their thoughts and language, and so largely influence the practice of their lives.

share of bread, potatoes, and molasses—the staples of such a home—but in the houses of the rich, with every thing in abundance at hand, it is there that the green-eyed monster—jealousy, has the fullest rein. The mind, thus unoccupied with the cares of providing for a home, is the more at liberty to count the hours of a husband's absence, to brood over the remembrance of the last kind look which he gave to the other, or to note the more delicate shade of the last silk dress, or the richer shawl, which she did *not* get. I have seen such women; I have heard them confidentially tell their woes; and I have watched them pine away to that physical weakness which makes life a burden.

Possibly the other lady was innocent of ever doing any thing intentionally wrong, and quite as likely, too, the lord of the mansion was as careful as man could be to guard his tongue, to control his eyes, and to measure all his acts, and knew not why his wife should pine and always have her headaches and retire to her own apartment. With, or without cause, the sensitive woman is afflicted, and not infrequently she it is who suffers most who has the most attention. One kind, insinuating glance of the husband to the other wife obliterates from the afflicted one's memory the ten times greater acts of kindness that he has shown to her. All is forgotten in an instant; the waters of Lethe pass over the tablets of her memory, and the recollections of the pleasantest hours of her life are washed away for ever.

The effects of Polygamy are singularly illustrated in the appearance and condition of two sisters (twins) who reside in Salt Lake City. The contrast between the two ladies is very striking, although in many respects they resemble each other so strongly that it is almost impossible even for their most intimate friends to distinguish the one from the other when apart. Sometimes even their husbands have ludicrously mistaken them. One of these ladies is the wife of a liberal, kind-hearted man, but he is a Polygamist, and has three other wives besides herself. The other sister is the wife of a monogamist; and, of course, is the sole mistress of his heart's affections.

When, however, the sisters are together, a marked dissimilarity can be observed between them. The wife of the Polygamist—good-hearted man, as he is—has a touching look of care and sorrow constantly dwelling upon her features, for she has but a share in her husband's love. The wife of the monogamist has no such sad expression on *her* face; for small as her husband's heart may be, she knows that she *alone* rules therein—its sole queen and mistress.

I knew two wives—very pleasant ladies and naturally kind-hearted—who tried the Polygamic life in its varied phases. They were unhappy together and they separated, and tried the experiment of living in different parts of the city. That was, however, still worse than before. When the ladies were both living together, either lady could at once see whether her husband's hat and overcoat were in the hall; but when he had a second home, he was gone entirely, and no trace of him was left behind. When both were in one house, prudence might suggest to the husband the number of the absent hours; but out of the house, he might find a thousand business excuses for a prolonged absence; none of which the suffering one would believe implicitly. Besides, when all together, in the same house, one table served for both wives, and the husband could not, of course, "get a better dinner in one house than in the other."

Women naturally seek the happiness of their husband, even though they may be bitter against him and Polygamy. They try to preserve his favour and make their homes as attractive as possible, so that he may always be pleased when he comes to see them. Out of their frequently poor allowances for the maintenance of their families, and what their own labour may add thereto, some women try to be exceedingly economical while they are living by themselves, so that when it comes to "their turn" to receive the husband, he may be well entertained. I have one lady in view who earned her husband's flattering opinion for economy in this way, and by some unlooked for change in his family, this good opinion has been of some service to her.

That is the course adopted by a woman of years and experience. Young and thoughtless wives sometimes try the opposite experiment, and when their husbands come to see them they are always poor, suffering—always needy; they never have enough of any thing. The effort at creating sympathy is not half as successful as the pleasant home and smiling welcome of more experienced ladies. Many a woman has missed her opportunity from want of a proper knowledge of human nature and good cookery.

Some of the leading men have wives in different parts of the Territory; which is, of course, very convenient when travelling. It is quite common to find a man with one family in the city and another a few miles in the country. The city residence is necessary in the pursuit of business, while the country wife overlooks the farm and dairy.

Many of the patriarchs in the country are very judicious in their selection of wives—that is, if they have comfortable homes. I remember many years ago reading a letter in a newspaper from a "brother" in the south of Utah. He had one who was a good housewife, another who was a good weaver, another was a good seamstress; and all his ambition then was to find another wife who could teach the children.

Some men are not quite so fortunate in their patriarchal relations. They do not seem to know how to dispose of themselves and keep peace in their families. In the language of the teachers, these are "weak men, who fall in love with one wife, and are not smart enough to conceal it from the others." Perhaps something occurs in course of time to break in upon his sweet communion with the favourite, and he leaves her and goes to another wife. Then the unfortunate patriarch has the favourite's indignation added to the complaints of the other wives, and his latter condition is worst of all. No amount of "teaching" in the world would make such a family happy. Women are argus-eyed, and nothing can escape their notice.

No man with weaknesses should ever think of Polygamy.

Of the privacy of Brigham Young *as a man,* I shall not write—no, not a word. His wives and children are as sacred to me as I would desire my own family to be with the public. But *as the head of a system,* I have no scruples to speak of him, and of the example of "celestial marriage" which he sets before the world. He cannot consistently object, as he has repeatedly told the people to follow him as he follows Christ; and as he permits no one to question him, the natural conclusion is that his family is the pattern of the patriarchal order.

Very extravagant statements have been published of the number of Brigham Young's wives and children. How many he has had from the time he courted Miss Martha Brotherton until now, it would be difficult to estimate. Some of his wives are dead; others have left him, and many probably have been sealed to him who strayed away like those of Brother Heber, and he knew not whither they went.

Of Brigham's present family I am personally acquainted with nineteen of his wives. Before he was a Mormon, he had *a* wife and family, but of that lady I know nothing. Two of her daughters are in Utah.[1]

His Mormon family begins with his first, *legal,* wife, who is still living—Mrs. Mary Ann Angel Young. She is probably about his own age, but is physically less preserved, and looks much older. She is a most excellent and amiable lady, and bears traces of having had her full share of earthly troubles.[2] She is the mother of his three prominent sons, Joseph A.; Brigham, Jr.; John W., and two daughters—Alice and Luna. Each of the sons has three wives.[3] The first daughter is the third of four wives in a polygamic household. The other daughter is the first wife of a young man, and has for a companion wife her father's daughter by another mother. The eldest daughter, Alice, has also her half-sister as an associate wife in her husband's household.

The *legal* wife of Brigham is:

I.   Mrs. Mary Ann Angel...

His Polygamic Wives are:

II.	Mrs. Clara Decker, ⎫	(sisters).....................
III.	Mrs. Lucy Decker, ⎭	

IV.   Mrs. Emeline Free ....
V.   Mrs. Harriet Cook...
VI.   Mrs. Twiss ....
VII.   Mrs. Eliza Burgess ....
VIII.   Mrs. Susan Snively...
IX.   Mrs. Lucy Bigelow..   Young
X.   Mrs. Harriet Barney Seagers ....
XI.   Mrs. Martha Bowker ....
XII.   Mrs. Margaret Pierce ....
XIII.   Mrs. Amelia Folsom ....
XIV.   Mrs. Mary Van Cott Cobb...
XV.   Mrs. Eliza Ann Jay Webb...

His "Proxy" Wives are:

XVI.   Mrs. Emily Partridge...
XVII.   Mrs. Zina D. Huntington Jacobs ....
XVIII.   Miss Eliza R. Snow..
[These were formerly "sealed" to Joseph
Smith, and are now "Proxy" wives to Brigham.]

Also—

XIX.   Mrs. Augusta Cobb..
[who was "sealed" to Joseph Smith *since* his death.][4]

Besides these, there may very likely be other ladies "sealed" to Brigham, but I myself know personally no more than the above named.

Brigham's first home in Utah was in a little cottage called "The White House," which every visitor to Salt Lake will notice on the hill-side, north of "The Eagle Gate." In that house Mrs. Young, the first, is domiciled. She is much loved by her children, and with their attention and affection, this good old lady probably long ago became indifferent to the additions that have been made to her husband's dominions. She is much beloved by the people for her own worth.

In the "Bee-Hive House," the official residence of *Governor* Young, adjoining his office on the east, there is but one lady occupant—Mrs. Lucy Decker Young. There is a privacy about this dwelling that no one invades. It is here that the Prophet has his own private bed-room, and at this house he breakfasts—when he has been at home over night.

In the "Lion House"—a very long, narrow building on the west of the business office—the larger number of his wives reside. The basement floor is used for kitchen, dining-room, pantry, and a general receptacle for the odds and ends of a large family. The first floor has a passage up the centre, where probably half a dozen of the wives with small families have their rooms on the right-hand side. On the left, at the entrance, is the parlour, and the other rooms on that side are occupied by mothers with larger families, and ladies who have a little more than ordinary attention. The upper floor is divided into twenty square bed-rooms.

There is no extravagance in the furniture of the homes of these wives, but they are comfortable and kept neat and clean.

It is in this "Lion House" where he usually dines at three P.M. Mrs. Twiss Young is housekeeper, and excellently fitted for the duties of that position. At three punctually the bell rings, and the mothers, with their children, move down to the dining-room, and all are seated at a very long table, that has had to be lengthened by turning round at the end of the room. Each mother has her children around her. Brigham sits at the head of the table, with his favourite—when in the house—*vis-a-vis*, or on his left, and any visitor sits on his right hand. The repast is frugal, but ample. Brigham is a sober and exceedingly economical man. This is the first time he sees his family.

In the evening, at seven o'clock, the bell again rings, and the mothers and the children fill the sides and ends of the parlour. When they are all seated, the Patriarch enters, takes his seat by the parlour table, and chats quietly with those who may go in with him to prayers. When all the members of the family are assembled, the door is closed; they kneel, and he prays for all—for Zion, and for the "Kingdom." That is the last they see of him, unless they seek him privately.

Outside of the wall that surrounds these houses he has wives occupying six other houses. One other wife is far down South, another is at the farm, and one "proxy" wife lives with her son-in-law.

The wives of Brigham have all good homes, have the necessaries of life, and are comfortably, respectably, and neatly dressed. With the exception of the one who is called his "favourite," and her growing rival, there is no indication of extravagance among them.

Up to an addition of late years, the community heard nothing of his family but what was pleasant and creditable to them. His wives are kind and faithful mothers, seeking to live the religion they have been taught, and ambitious to increase the glory of their "lord." They are women who would be regarded with respect in the most moral community of any country; and are as far from resembling the Sultanas of an Eastern harem as one thing can be different from another. Most of them are women of devout faith. I know them all personally—some of them intimately; and, while I have heard from some, with heavy hearts, of their difficulties in bearing "*the* cross" which all Mormon women have to carry, they have tried, I know, to be submissive, and I think it is due to them that I should make the present recognition of their goodness of disposition and purity of soul.

With his family he is said to be kind; but it is supposed to be more the awe which his position as Prophet inspires, than the love which they bear him as a man, which renders him successful in managing them. At the same time, that sweet familiarity is destroyed which should exist between husband and wife, father and children. He aims to be looked upon more as a ruler than as the head of a family.

With such a number of wives, he cannot possibly wait upon them in visiting, frequenting the ball-room, or places of public entertainment. With the exception of his reigning favourite, whoever she may happen for the time to be, no one expects his attentions. At the theatre, which is his own, a full number of seats are reserved, and his wives attend when they please or they remain at home. They sit in the body of the parquette, among the rest of the people; but one of the two proscenium boxes is reserved for him, and beside him is a chair for the favourite Amelia.

When he goes to the ball-room, the same special attention is manifest. He dances first with the favourite, and, if half a dozen more of his wives have accompanied them, he will dance with each of them once in the course of the evening; but with the favourite he dances as frequently as any youth in the ball-room with his first maiden love. The Apostles and leading men of the community, who dance attendance upon him and desire his favour, are sure to seek the pleasure of her hand and place her in the same cotillion with Brigham, who is thus able all the evening to enjoy her company.

This favouritism is ill-looked upon by the Saints, and, in their estimation, savours more of Turkey than of the "Celestial Kingdom." Were there greater devotion, or greater virtue in her, the people might find some argument for his defence; but the circumstance, whenever alluded to in society, is generally answered with a smile or a shrug of the shoulders.

Some Apostles look with pain upon this boyishness of the Prophet, and deplore it. Most of them are attached to their first wives, and have shown to them consideration and attention which has not always pleased Brigham. I have heard more than one of them express the wish that Brother Brigham's devotion to the fair sex had more direction toward his first wife. It is but just to the reigning favourite to state that she has not been wanting in kindness and respect to Mrs. Young.

Brigham has had his favourites before; and, if he were to live many years longer, with the privilege hitherto enjoyed by him of doing just what he pleased, he doubtless would lose his fancy for his present toy and seek another. One of his recent wives is a very handsome lady, and his attentions in that direction are already very marked.[5]

As I write, the thought comes over me,—What infatuated beings the women of Utah have been, with all these evidences of human weakness and passion exhibited by the "Priesthood" continually before their eyes, that they should ever believe that there is even a shadow of divinity in Polygamy! How could they imagine for an instant that it was possible for such a doctrine to emanate from God, or from that Adorable Being who looked upon woman with the sweetest tenderness that humanity could express! What a terrible infatuation! It is fearful to contemplate!

CHAPTER XX.

Gentiles in Utah—Mormon Women not allowed to mingle
with them—Restrictions and Prejudices—Women and Men kept
apart in the Tabernacle and the Theatre—Keeping a Gentile
Boarding-House—Times changed—Mormon Girls marrying Gentile
Husbands—Why they prefer the Gentiles—Reasons of Jealousy—
The Looks of Mormon Women—False Notions—The Railway working Changes—An Appeal to Congress—The wisest Course to be
adopted—To the Women of Utah.

FOR many years there were very few Gentiles in Utah. Most of these
were merchants and their clerks, and teamsters. There were also two or
three Federal officials. Although they were but few, their influence was
always dreaded by the Mormon leaders; and the Tabernacle and Meeting-
Houses resounded with something disparaging to the Gentiles. Some of
them doubtless commanded very little respect. But it mattered not how
much others might be respected elsewhere, how pure and blameless their
lives, it was enough that they were Gentiles, and a worse thing still to be
a gentlemanly or educated Gentile. The pleasant manners of a cultivated
life were set down as the wiles of the Evil One to seduce the simple and
trusting maidens of the flock, and rendered the gentleman an object
of suspicion and distrust. The rough and uncultivated could be easily
guarded against and easily exposed.

No young woman could possibly accept any attentions from a
Gentile without being disgraced—it was an unpardonable sin, and she
was certain to be denounced and abused in the Ward meetings. It was a
risk of reputation for any woman to be seen talking to a Gentile. It mattered not where they might have met before—at the store, or at a friend's
house, or even before they had gone to Utah—to recognize a Gentile in
the street was to avow an intimacy which was associated with a suspicion
of the vilest conduct. For any family to entertain gentlemen who brought
letters of introduction from friends abroad was not impossible, it is true;
but the less they had of this kind of thing the better. If these gentlemen
were simply passing through Salt Lake City, an invitation to the theatre
might be accepted by any member of the family; but they would be very

thankful when it was over, knowing well that all eyes were upon them. But if this friend happened to prolong his visit, and should chance to give a second invitation for the theatre or a carriage-drive, some falsehood had to be conjured up as an excuse for declining.

Some toleration was extended in the case of my husband, as he was an editor, and necessarily had many visitors whom he took pleasure in entertaining; but it was considered by many pious friends that we had more of that kind of association than was beneficial. At the present time, I have little doubt that our leaving the church is attributed to this cause.

I would not have permitted my daughters, had they had such a desire, to have accepted any attentions from a Gentile. Not that I believed it was wrong—I knew better—but I was afraid of the bitter tongue of scandal, which I knew was ready to wag. A very sweet little girl who lived near us, and who had associated with my daughter while growing up, became acquainted with Gentile ladies and visited them at home. There, naturally, she became acquainted with Gentile gentlemen; and as she was very good-looking she received attentions which were to her agreeable, particularly in her lonely situation. Of course, the acquaintance with my daughter had to be stopped, although I believed this little girl pure and spotless. The scandal against her as she grew up became of the very vilest character, and her offence was simply associating with the Gentiles. Had her faith in the Mormon Church been unshaken, she would certainly not have formed such acquaintances; but the poor girl was disgusted with the wretched phases of Polygamy constantly before her eyes—her mother could have told an awful tale of sorrow.

Another very beautiful young Mormon lady, the daughter of a gentleman who, when living, was one of the highest dignitaries of the church, was once chosen for her handsome appearance to represent the goddess of liberty in a Fourth of July procession. When Brigham heard it, the committee were rebuked and the young lady insulted by their afterwards refusing to accept her, although she had been specially invited—her unfitness being that she kept Gentile society.

These young ladies are now married to very respectable Gentiles.

When the United States army went to Utah in 1858, one half of the old Tabernacle was appropriated to the sisters, and the other half to the brethren. The centre of the new Tabernacle is now devoted exclusively to the sisters—no husband or brother sits near them. When Brigham built the theatre it was also specially partioned off. The Mormon families occupied the parquette, and the Gentiles had the first circle. Of course, the poorer classes had no souls to contaminate, were less cared for, and Gentiles and Mormons sat together in the second and third circles.

At one time, the Saints were not permitted to keep Gentile boarders and retain good standing in the church. Some persons would persist in doing so; but it was a source of great scandal, and they subjected themselves to attacks in the sermons. It was told them that Gentile society would bring a pernicious influence into their families. But what a change has come over the affairs of Utah! One of Brigham Young's own wives, the one who was once the reigning favourite, now keeps Gentile boarders. Not long ago, I made some remarks about the inconsistency of this to a very good sister, who by-the-by was doing the same thing herself, and was also one of the persons most opposed to our receiving Gentile company. She replied that the times had changed, and that Brigham Young could not be responsible for what his wives did; they would do as they pleased. This excuse was worse than none; for every one in Salt Lake City knows that none of Brigham Young's wives would do any such thing without his permission. The wife alluded to is as obedient as any he has got, and a very excellent lady with a large family.[1] It enables her probably with her numerous children to procure many things which they might otherwise have to dispense with, and as long as "there is money in it," and his treasury is saved, Brigham will "wink at it," as he says the Lord does at certain things among the Saints. I could mention Mormons who have had a very bad name for years for keeping Gentile boarders. They will doubtless now feel better since it has become respectable and no longer renders them liable to "damnation."

Notwithstanding the vigilance of the priesthood, several young ladies of highly respectable families have preferred Gentile husbands, and have left the Territory. These have invariably been traduced, and every rumour of misfortune occurring to them afterwards was a sweet morsel to be retailed with very ill-disguised gratification. For any lady to be spoken of with respect or as holding a good position after leaving the church is particularly obnoxious to the devoted Mormons, and any evil which may befall such a person is regarded as a judgment from heaven. Kind-hearted and fraternal as the people are, the rulers seem to rejoice in nothing so much as the misery or ill-fortune of any one who has left the church.

It is not strange that spirited, proper-feeling girls should find the society of Gentiles acceptable. There need be no mystery about it. The Mormon boys and young men have heard so much of polygamic preaching, and have had so much of its practice before their eyes, that many of them never can visit the Mormon girls without speaking of it. I have frequently heard sensitive young maidens relate that boys, when visiting, were in the habit of speaking of their "privileges;" telling what they would do when they got married; how they thought that they would take two wives at once, to begin with; how they would live with them afterwards, etc.

Girls of the slightest feeling and intelligence are naturally shocked at this kind of talk, even though it has no practical effect on them. Polygamy is disagreeable enough in any form, but when made a subject of boasting by silly boys and ignorant men, it is doubly offensive. In Gentile society, the girls are at least spared conversation on such subjects; and, when they are by themselves, they do not fail to remark it to each other. In polygamic Mormonism, woman is a convenience; in a proper Gentile home, woman is a companion, and this comparison is really more apprehended than any immoral conduct. A polygamous wife, who is one of many, who sees her husband only occasionally, and that generally as a favour, cannot well see a Gentile lady at home without comparing situations. It makes them unhappy, and that in a great measure is why the Mormons have been taught to avoid Gentile society.

Writers upon Utah have said that the Mormon women were extremely homely and coarse-looking. This is very unjust, for, doubtless, nowhere is there to be found—taking them as a whole—a more fresh, happy, and good-looking set of girls than among the Mormons. It is only after marriage that many of them lose their elasticity of step, their joyous, happy looks, and that animation of countenance which makes even a homely face look beautiful at times. On some of their faces may be detected a deep melancholy; but, if they can be diverted from their sad thoughts for ever so short a time, they become animated, and even, it may be, beautiful. Add to this secret sorrow which casts a gloom upon their countenances, the little opportunity which they have of cultivating their taste for dress, and it will not be wondered at if the Mormon women are not always very beautiful to a man who is captivated by outward appearances. Many of these women are taught to be satisfied with simple clothing, and it is constantly drummed into their ears that love of dress is a sin in the sight of God. Thus this love of the beautiful, which is a part of woman's nature, has to be crushed out entirely, and that, too frequently, by her own husband, whose example is entirely opposed to his teaching; for a Mormon, if he can afford it, is very scrupulous in his own dress. Those very men who are most severely economical with their wives, and who think that they should be satisfied with homespun and sunbonnets, are they who are the soonest captivated by an elegantly-dressed and fashionable woman, and often become perfectly infatuated about her.

This has been a cause of much discontent among the women of Utah; for they very justly feel that if they had as fine feathers, they might make just as handsome birds.

I remember, at one of the parties, a lady was very nicely dressed, and one of the principal authorities of the Church said to her, "Sister, don't you think that you spend too much time and thought on your dress?" She answered, "Do you think so? After all, a person looks a great deal better when they give a little attention to their dress. You, Brother Kimball, look a great deal better since you have worn a coat of broadcloth, cut in the fashionable style." He simply answered that it was not his wish to wear other clothes than what he used to, but that his wives insisted upon his doing so. Men in Utah are not guilty of following the advice of their wives, except it be in this one particular; for Brigham himself has said that "it is a disgrace in the sight of heaven for a man to follow his wife."

In Utah, as well as elsewhere, there are certainly women to be found who never had any good looks to lose, or a sensitive nature to contend with; but it is not true to assert this as a characteristic of the whole community. The women of Utah are like women of their class everywhere.

The construction of the Pacific Railroad, the discovery of the great wealth in the mountains of Utah, and the free expression of the sentiments of thinking men who have outlived and abandoned Mormonism, have given the death-blow to Polygamy. Were there none but Mormons in the Territory, it might have lived on so long as they were willing to remain in poverty; but with prosperity, and the changed circumstances which are ever certain to follow wealth, Polygamy is a doomed institution.

Whatever, in the providence of God, may be the action of Congress toward Utah, if the word of a feeble woman can be listened to, let me respectfully ask the Honourable Senators and Representatives of the United States that, in the abolition of Polygamy, if such should be the decree of the nation, let no compromise be made where subtilty can bind the woman now living in Polygamy to remain in that condition. Legalize, if Congress will, the marriages that have been made, and legitimatize the children born in that wedlock, if such can be done, for the women and children are innocent; but let one proviso ever remain, that any wife living in Polygamy, at the time of the passage of that Act of Congress, shall be then and ever afterwards free to abandon that relationship when her conscience shall so dictate, without legal hindrance, and that she and her children shall be provided for as if she had been his first and legal wife whom the courts of law had separated "for cause."

I have now completed my task, and am about to lay down my pen. I shall, I know, be condemned by those hymn-singing, devotional women, who, childless and husbandless here, dream of the glories of the world to come, while they never knew the duties, the obligations, the sweet and hallowed sympathies of the world in which they live. In their eyes, I have doubtless committed the "unpardonable sin." I have written for the suffering and sorrowing women in Polygamy. *They* will understand me, and to *them* I appeal. Before the Great Tribunal I will cheerfully meet their verdict.

APPENDIX.

The Revelation on Polygamy is a curious document to the unbeliever. To him it bears every mark of imposture. To the Saints it is as sacred a document as the decalogue given to Moses upon Mount Sinai. To a person who has once believed it from the teachings of the Mormon priesthood, and who has lived under its threatenings, but who has finally outgrown the whole religion, the Revelation reads like a strained effort, on the part of Joseph Smith, to justify, under the sanction of a commandment, the leadings of his own passions. Whatever its origin, whoever its author, no document was ever given to any community that caused so much misery and accomplished so little good. There is no evidence of God in it. From beginning to end, it is man, and weak man only.

In glancing over it, the intelligent reader will be rather astonished to find that it entirely escaped the notice of "the Lord," that the Patriarch Isaac was not a Polygamist. There are also many other statements which no one but a true believer would be apt to receive with implicit faith. But the reader will be able to form his own judgment from the document itself, which I shall now place before him.

CELESTIAL MARRIAGE:

A REVELATION ON THE PATRIARCHAL ORDER OF MATRIMONY, OR PLURALITY OF WIVES.

Given to Joseph Smith, the Seer, in Nauvoo, July 12th, 1843.

1. Verily, thus saith the Lord unto you, my servant Joseph, that inasmuch as you have inquired of my hand, to know and understand wherein I, the Lord, justified my servants, Abraham, Isaac, and Jacob; as also Moses, David, and Solomon, my servants, as touching the principle and doctrine of their having many wives and concubines: Behold! and lo, I am the Lord thy God, and will answer thee as touching this matter: Therefore, prepare thy heart to receive and obey the instructions which I am about to give unto you; for all those who have this law revealed unto them must obey the same; for behold! I reveal unto you a new and an everlasting

covenant, and if ye abide not that covenant, then are ye damned; for no one can reject this covenant, and be permitted to enter into my glory; for all who will have a blessing at my hands shall abide the law which was appointed for that blessing, and the conditions thereof, as was instituted from before the foundations of the world: and as pertaining to the new and everlasting covenant, it was instituted for the fulness of my glory; and he that receiveth a fulness thereof, must and shall abide the law, or he shall be damned, saith the Lord God.

2. And verily I say unto you, that the conditions of this law are these: All covenants, contracts, bonds, obligations, oaths, vows, performances, connections, associations, or expectations, that are not made and entered into, and sealed, by the Holy Spirit of promise, of him who is anointed, both as well for time and for all eternity, and that too most holy, by revelation and commandment, through the medium of mine anointed, whom I have appointed on the earth to hold this power, (and I have appointed unto my servant Joseph to hold this power in the last days, and there is never but one on the earth at a time, on whom this power and the keys of the priesthood are conferred,) are of no efficacy, virtue, or force, in and after the resurrection from the dead: for all contracts that are not made unto this end, have an end when men are dead.

3. Behold! mine house is a house of order, saith the Lord God, and not a house of confusion. Will I accept of an offering, saith the Lord, that is not made in my name! Or, will I receive at your hands, that which I have not appointed! And will I appoint unto you, saith the Lord, except it be by law, even as I and my Father ordained unto you, before the world was! I am the Lord thy God, and I give unto you this commandment, that no man shall come unto the Father but by me, or by my word which is my law, saith the Lord; and every thing that is in the world, whether it be ordained of men, by thrones, or principalities, or powers, or things of name, whatsoever they may be, that are not by me, or by my word, saith the Lord, shall be thrown down, and shall not remain after men are dead, neither in nor after the resurrection, saith the Lord your God: for whatsoever things remaineth are by me; and whatsoever things are not by me shall be shaken and destroyed.

4. Therefore, if a man marry him a wife in the world, and he marry her not by me, nor by my word; and he covenant with her so long as he is in the world, and she with him, their covenant and marriage is not of force when they are dead, and when they are out of the world; therefore, they are not bound by any law when they are out of the world; therefore, when they are out of the world, they neither marry, nor are given in marriage, but are appointed angels in heaven, which angels are ministering servants, to minister for those who are worthy of a far more, and an exceeding, and an eternal weight of glory; for these angels did not abide my law, therefore they cannot be enlarged, but remain separately

and singly, without exaltation, in their saved condition, to all eternity, and from henceforth are not Gods, but are angels of God for ever and ever.

5. And again, verily I say unto you, if a man marry a wife, and make a covenant with her for time, and for all eternity, if that covenant is not by me, or by my word, which is my law, and is not sealed by the Holy Spirit of promise, through him whom I have anointed and appointed unto this power, then it is not valid, neither of force, when they are out of the world, because they are not joined by me, saith the Lord, neither by my word; when they are out of the world, it cannot be received there, because the angels and the Gods are appointed there, by whom they cannot pass; they cannot, therefore, inherit my glory, for my house is a house of order, saith the Lord God.

6. And again, verily I say unto you, if a man marry a wife by my word, which is my law, and by the new and everlasting covenant, and it is sealed unto them by the Holy Spirit of promise, by him who is anointed, unto whom I have appointed this power, and the keys of this priesthood, and it shall be said unto them, Ye shall come forth in the first resurrection; and if it be after the first resurrection, in the next resurrection; and shall inherit thrones, kingdoms, principalities, and powers, dominions, all heights and depths, then shall it be written in the Lamb's Book of Life, that he shall commit no murder whereby to shed innocent blood; and if ye abide in my covenant, and commit no murder whereby to shed innocent blood, it shall be done unto them in all things whatsoever my servant hath put upon them, in time, and through all eternity, and shall be of full force when they are out of the world; and they shall pass by the angels, and the Gods, which are set there, to their exaltation and glory in all things, as hath been sealed upon their heads, which glory shall be a fulness and a continuation of the seeds for ever and ever.

7. Then shall they be Gods, because they have no end; therefore shall they be from everlasting to everlasting, because they continue; then shall they be above all, because all things are subject unto them. Then shall they be Gods, because they have all power, and the angels are subject unto them.

8. Verily, verily I say unto you, except ye abide my law, ye cannot attain to this glory; for strait is the gate, and narrow the way that leadeth unto the exaltation and continuation of the lives, and few there be that find it, because ye receive me not in the world, neither do ye know me. But if ye receive me in the world, then shall ye know me, and shall receive your exaltation, that where I am, ye shall be also. This is eternal lives, to know the only wise and true God, and Jesus Christ whom he hath sent. I am He. Receive ye, therefore, my law. Broad is the gate, and wide the way that leadeth to the death; and many there are that go in thereat; because they receive me not, neither do they abide in my law.

9. Verily, verily I say unto you, if a man marry a wife according to my word, and they are sealed by the Holy Spirit of promise, according to mine appointment, and he or she shall commit any sin or transgression of the new and everlasting covenant whatever, and all manner of blasphemies, and if they commit no murder, wherein they shed innocent blood—yet they shall come forth in the first resurrection, and enter into their exaltation, but they shall be destroyed in the flesh, and shall be delivered unto the buffetings of Satan, unto the day of redemption, saith the Lord God.

10. The blasphemy against the Holy Ghost, which shall not be forgiven in the world, nor out of the world, is in that ye commit murder, wherein ye shed innocent blood, and assent unto my death, after ye have received my new and everlasting covenant, saith the Lord God; and he that abideth not this law can in nowise enter into my glory, but shall be damned, saith the Lord.

11. I am the Lord thy God, and will give unto thee the law of my Holy Priesthood, as was ordained by me, and my Father, before the world was. Abraham received all things, whatsoever he received, by revelation and commandment, by my word, saith the Lord, and hath entered into his exaltation, and sitteth upon his throne.

12. Abraham received promises concerning his seed, and of the fruit of his loins—from whose loins ye are, namely, my servant Joseph—which were to continue, so long as they were in the world; and as touching Abraham and his seed, out of the world, they should continue; both in the world and out of the world should they continue as innumerable as the stars; or, if ye were to count the sand upon the seashore, ye could not number them. This promise is yours also, because ye are of Abraham, and the promise was made unto Abraham; and by this law are the continuation of the works of my Father, wherein He glorifieth himself. Go ye, therefore, and do the works of Abraham; enter ye into my law, and ye shall be saved. But if ye enter not into my law, ye can not receive the promises of my Father, which He made unto Abraham.

13. God commanded Abraham, and Sarah gave Hagar to Abraham, to wife. And why did she do it? Because this was the law, and from Hagar sprang many people. This, therefore, was fulfilling, among other things, the promises. Was Abraham, therefore, under condemnation? Verily, I say unto you, Nay; for I, the Lord, commanded it. Abraham was commanded to offer his son Isaac; nevertheless, it was written, Thou shalt not kill. Abraham, however, did not refuse, and it was accounted unto him for righteousness.

14. Abraham received concubines, and they bare him children, and it was accounted unto him for righteousness, because they were given unto him, and he abode in my law: as Isaac also, and Jacob did

none other things than that which they were commanded; and because they did none other things than that which they were commanded, they have entered into their exaltation, according to the promises, and sit upon thrones; and are not angels, but are Gods. David also received many wives and concubines, as also Solomon, and Moses my servant; as also many others of my servants, from the beginning of creation until this time; and in nothing did they sin, save in those things which they received not of me.

15. David's wives and concubines were given unto him, of me, by the hand of Nathan, my servant, and others of the prophets who had the keys of this power; and in none of these things did he sin against me, save in the case of Uriah and his wife; and therefore, he hath fallen from his exaltation, and received his portion; and he shall not inherit them out of the world; for I gave them unto another, saith the Lord.

16. I am the Lord thy God, and I gave unto thee, my servant Joseph, an appointment, and restore all things; ask what ye will, and it shall be given unto you, according to my word; and as ye have asked concerning adultery, verily, verily I say unto you, if a man receiveth a wife in the new and everlasting covenant, and if she be with another man, and I have not appointed unto her by the holy anointing, she hath committed adultery, and shall be destroyed. If she be not in the new and everlasting covenant, and she be with another man, she has committed adultery; and if her husband be with another woman, and he was under a vow, he hath broken his vow, and hath committed adultery; and if she hath not committed adultery, but is innocent, and hath not broken her vow, and she knoweth it, and I reveal it unto you, my servant Joseph, then shall you have power, by the power of my Holy Priesthood, to take her, and give her unto him that hath not committed adultery, but hath been faithful, for he shall be made ruler over many; for I have conferred upon you the keys and power of the priesthood, wherein I restore all things, and make known unto you all things, in due time.

17. And verily, verily I say unto you, that whatsoever you seal on earth shall be sealed in heaven; and whatsoever you bind on earth, in my name, and by my word, saith the Lord, it shall be eternally bound in the heavens; and whosoever sins you remit on earth shall be remitted eternally in the heavens; and whosoever sins you retain on earth shall be retained in heaven.

18. And again, verily I say, whomsoever you bless I will bless; and whomsoever you curse I will curse, saith the Lord; for I, the Lord, am thy God.

19. And again, verily I say unto you, my servant Joseph, that whatsoever you give on earth, and to whomsoever you give any one on earth, by my word, and according to my law, it shall be visited with blessings, and not cursings, and with my power, saith the Lord, and shall be without

condemnation on earth, and in heaven; for I am the Lord thy God, and will be with thee even unto the end of the world, and through all eternity: for verily I seal upon you your exaltation, and prepare a throne for you in the kingdom of my Father, with Abraham, your father. Behold, I have seen your sacrifices, and will forgive all your sins; I have seen your sacrifices, in obedience to that which I have told you: go, therefore, and I make a way for your escape, as I accepted the offering of Abraham, of his son Isaac.

20. Verily I say unto you, a commandment I give unto mine handmaid, Emma Smith, your wife, whom I have given unto you, that she stay herself, and partake not of that which I commanded you to offer unto her: for I did it, saith the Lord, to prove you all, as I did Abraham; and that I might require an offering at your hand, by covenant and sacrifice: and let mine handmaid, Emma Smith, receive all those that have been given unto my servant Joseph, and who are virtuous and pure before me; and those who are not pure, and have said they were pure, shall be destroyed, saith the Lord God! for I am the Lord thy God, and ye shall obey my voice; and I give unto my servant Joseph, that he shall be made ruler over many things, for he hath been faithful over a few things, and from henceforth I will strengthen him.

21. And I command mine handmaid, Emma Smith, to abide and cleave unto my servant Joseph, and to none else. But if she will not abide this commandment, she shall be destroyed, saith the Lord; for I am the Lord thy God, and will destroy her if she abide not in my law; but if she will not abide this commandment, then shall my servant Joseph do all things for her, even as he hath said; and I will bless him, and multiply him, and give unto him an hundred fold in this world, of fathers and mothers, brothers and sisters, houses and lands, wives and children, and crowns of eternal lives in the eternal worlds. And again, verily I say, let mine handmaid forgive my servant Joseph his trespasses, and then shall she be forgiven her trespasses, wherein she has trespassed against me; and I, the Lord thy God, will bless her, and multiply her, and make her heart to rejoice.

22. And again, I say, let not my servant Joseph put his property out of his hands, lest an enemy come and destroy him, for Satan seeketh to destroy; for I am the Lord thy God, and he is my servant; and behold! and lo, I am with him, as I was with Abraham, thy father, even unto his exaltation and glory.

23. Now as touching the law of the priesthood, there are many things pertaining thereunto. Verily, if a man be called of my Father, as was Aaron, by mine own voice, and by the voice of him that sent me, and I have endowed him with the keys of the power of this priesthood, if he do any thing in my name, and according to my law, and by my

word, he will not commit sin, and I will justify him. Let no one, therefore, set on my servant Joseph; for I will justify him; for he shall do the sacrifice which I require at his hands, for his transgressions, saith the Lord your God.

24. And again, as pertaining to the law of the priesthood: If any man espouse a virgin, and desire to espouse another, and the first give her consent; and if he espouse the second, and they are virgins, and have vowed to no other man, then is he justified; he cannot commit adultery, for they are given unto him; for he cannot commit adultery with that that belongeth unto him, and to none else; and if he have ten virgins given unto him by this law, he cannot commit adultery, for they belong to him; and they are given unto him—therefore is he justified. But if one or either of the ten virgins, after she is espoused, shall be with another man, she has committed adultery, and shall be destroyed; for they are given unto him to multiply and replenish the earth, according to my commandment, and to fulfil the promise which was given by my Father before the foundation of the world; and for their exaltation in the eternal worlds, that they may bear the souls of men; for herein is the work of my Father continued, that He may be glorified.

25. And again, verily, verily I say unto you, if any man have a wife who holds the keys of this power, and he teaches unto her the law of my priesthood, as pertaining to these things; then shall she believe, and administer unto him, or she shall be destroyed, saith the Lord your God; for I will destroy her; for I will magnify my name upon all those who receive and abide in my law. Therefore, it shall be lawful in me, if she receive not this law, for him to receive all things whatsoever I, the Lord his God, will give unto him, because she did not believe and administer unto him, according to my word; and she then becomes the transgressor, and he is exempt from the law of Sarah, who administered unto Abraham according to the law, when I commanded Abraham to take Hagar to wife. And now, as pertaining to this law: Verily, verily I say unto you, I will reveal more unto you, hereafter; therefore, let this suffice for the present. Behold, I am Alpha and Omega. Amen.

The three sons of Joseph Smith,[1] who, it should be remembered, still cling to the original doctrines of Mormonism, have for years valiantly combated the charge of Polygamy made against the Prophet; but in the face of so much testimony against him, it appears difficult for them to fully satisfy themselves that there was not something wrong in his ideas of marriage. It must be extremely unpleasant for them to make such an avowal, but it would be the easiest way of getting out of the difficulty. In collating matter for this appendix, I met the following, from the pen of Alexander H. Smith, the second son of the Prophet:

"The stories about that article [the revelation] are so numerous, and so conflicting, that I do not believe that he ever received a revelation from *God* on the matter. The very fact that so much strong testimony had been produced, and did exist, as we have shown from the Book of Mormon, and Doctrine and Covenants, satisfies me that it is folly for any sane man to think that Joseph Smith needed to ask God concerning a matter that His will was so plainly manifest on as the one in hand. There are those who say that the revelation 'was received over a five-gallon keg of whiskey.' There are those who say 'the original was burned;'* but strange to say, they all say 'that it was burned,' and all seem to agree that one person burned it. It is evident that a supposed copy of the revelation has been palmed off upon the people, by a designing set of men, who have certainly lost the priesthood they once held, and have made money and women their only pleasure, that they might gratify to the fullest extent their lustful desires and wicked purposes."

The reader will see from the concluding sentence, which is rather more forcible than polite, the opinion which the sons of the Prophet entertain for their father's successors.

Italicizing the word "God" in the above was the work of Mr. Smith, and evidently intended by him as a reluctant admission that his father *had possibly something to do with it.* The further allusion to the "keg of whiskey" is also a partial admission of alleged occasional habits of the Prophet. But the revelation to Joseph is too shrewdly worded, and looks too much like the results of a battle between him and the "Elect Lady"—his wife, Emma, to have owed its inspiration to the "keg." Besides this, the subtle way in which the priesthood therein entwines its authority around the woman, threatening her at one moment with damnation, and the next attracting her with promises of glory, evinces too much system and calculation for such an origin. The true story is the best—Joseph had himself entered into practical Polygamy, and a revelation was necessary to appease his wife, Emma, and to satisfy his brother, Hyrum, who had some "conscientious scruples."

Mr. Smith, however, continues:

"Should we admit the truth of this so-called revelation, there is not a man on earth, neither has there been since the death of the martyr, who holds the keys to administer the ordinances of celestial marriage according to the revelation itself, for it is stated emphatically that 'there is never but one on the earth at a time on whom this power and the keys of this priesthood are conferred.' So by their own witness they are condemned. For Brigham has time and again said he was not a 'prophet nor the son of the prophet,' and none but a prophet can hold the keys of this priesthood. I give one more feature of the beautiful document:

* Mrs. Emma Smith is understood to have thrown it into the fire.

"'Verily, verily, I say unto you, if a man marry a wife according to my word, and they are sealed by the Holy Spirit of promise according to mine appointment, and he or she shall commit any sin or transgression of the new and everlasting covenant whatever, and all manner of blasphemies, and if they commit no murder whereby they shed *innocent* blood, yet shall they come forth in the first resurrection and enter into their exaltation.'

"Here is licence given to any one who enters this system of things to lie, steal, bear false witness, use the name of God in vain, blaspheme at will, and do all manner of wickedness except the shedding of 'innocent blood,' and by them taught, if a man be a Gentile and unconverted his blood is not innocent, he is a sinner, consequently there is no crime in killing him; provided, that you have a wife or two sealed to you by the holy celestial knot. This clause alone should reveal its origin."

In conclusion he adds:

"Now may God save this people from *this great plague spot that cankers and corrodes the soul, alienates it from God,* and fits it only for Satan's kingdom."—*Polygamy: was it an original tenet of the Church?* pp. 7, 8, 9.

CHOICE EXTRACTS FROM MODERN APOSTLES.

FROM THE FIRST SERMON PREACHED ON POLYGAMY IN THE TABERNACLE, SALT LAKE CITY, BY THE APOSTLE ORSON PRATT, AUGUST 29TH, 1852.

"The Lord ordained marriage between male and female as a law through which spirits should come here and enter into the second state of existence." * * * "Then is it not reasonable and consistent that the Lord should say unto His faithful and chosen servants, that had proved themselves before Him all the day long; that had been ready and willing to do whatsoever His will required them to perform—take unto yourselves more wives, like unto the patriarchs, Abraham, Isaac, and Jacob, of old—like those who lived in ancient times, who walked in my footsteps, and kept my commands?" * * * * * "What will become of those individuals who have this law taught unto them in plainness, if they reject it? [A voice in the stand, 'They will be damned.'] I will tell you: THEY WILL BE DAMNED, *saith the Lord God Almighty.*" —*Journal of Discourses*, vol. i. pp. 58, 63, 64.

"We are created for the express purpose of increase."—*J. of D.,* vol. i. p. 93.

"Suppose that I had the privilege of having only one wife, I should have had only three sons, for those are all that my first wife bore; whereas I now have buried five sons, and have thirteen living. It is obvious that I could not have been blessed with such a family if I had been restricted to one wife; but by the introduction of this law I can be the instrument in preparing tabernacles for those spirits which have to come in this dispensation."* —*Brigham Young, J. of D.*, vol. iii. p. 264.

"The fleshly body of Jesus required a Mother as well as a Father. Therefore the Father and Mother of Jesus, according to the flesh, must have been associated together in the capacity of Husband and Wife; hence the Virgin Mary must have been, for the time being, the *lawful* wife of God the Father: we use the term *lawful* Wife, because it would be blasphemous in the highest degree to say that He overshadowed her or begat the Saviour unlawfully. * * It was also lawful in Him, after having thus dealt with Mary, to give her to Joseph her espoused husband. Whether God the Father gave Mary to Joseph for time only, or for time and eternity, we are not informed. Inasmuch as God was the first Husband to her, it may be that He only gave her to be the wife of Joseph while in this mortal state, and that he intended after the resurrection to again take her as one of His own wives to raise up immortal spirits in eternity."

"One thing is certain, that there were several holy women that greatly loved Jesus—such as Mary, and Martha her sister, and Mary Magdalene. If all the acts of Jesus were written, we, no doubt, should learn that these beloved women were his wives."—*Orson Pratt, Seer*, pp. 158–9.

"The grand reason of the burst of public sentiment in anathemas upon Christ and his disciples, causing His crucifixion, was evidently based upon Polygamy, according to the testimony of the philosophers who rose in that age. A belief in the doctrine of a plurality of wives caused the persecution of Jesus and His followers. We might almost think they were 'Mormons.'"—*Elder Jedediah M. Grant, Counsellor to Brigham, Young, J. of D.*, vol. i. p. 346.

"Jesus was the bridegroom at the marriage of Cana of Galilee." "Now there was actually a marriage; and if Jesus was not the bridegroom on that occasion, please tell who was." "We say it was Jesus Christ who was

---

* It seems never to have occurred to Brigham Young that if all the wives whom he had married each had had a husband to herself, the spirit immigration of which he speaks so much, and in which he professes so deep an interest, would have found ten times more facility for earthly existence. His monopoly, therefore, of from fifty to a hundred wives, instead of carrying out the purpose of "the Lord," has only hindered it. He seems to have thought nothing of the women fulfilling the "full measure" of their creation. It has been with him all the time only "I." "When I labour in the kingdom of God, *I labor for my own dear self, I have only self constantly before me; the object of my pursuit is to benefit my individual person*, and this is the case with every person who ever was or ever will be exalted." That is exactly Brigham's portrait, drawn by his own hand, August 8th, 1870.

married, to be brought into the relation whereby he could 'see his seed' before he was crucified." "I shall say here, that before the Saviour died, he looked upon his own natural children, as we look upon ours; he saw his seed, and immediately after that he was cut off from the earth."—*Orson Hyde, President of the Apostles, J. of D.*, vol. ii. pp. 79, 80, 81, 82.

"The woman who marries out of this priesthood marries for hell."—*O. H.*

HOW THEY SAID IT WAS.

"Instead of a plurality of wives being a cause of sorrow to females, it is one of the greatest blessings of the last dispensation; it gives them the *great privilege* of being united to a righteous man, and *of rearing a family according to the order of heaven;* instead of being compelled to remain single, or marry a wicked man who will ruin her and her offspring, she can enter a family where *peace and salvation reign;* where *righteousness abounds;* where the head of the family stands forth as a patriarch, a prince, and *a saviour,* to his whole household; where *blessings unspeakable* and *eternal* are sealed upon them and their generations after them; *her glory is eternal,* and *her joy is full.* Rejoice, then, ye daughters of Zion, that you live *in this glorious era!*"[2]

HOW IT REALLY WAS.

Jedediah M. Grant, in the Salt Lake Bowery, September, 1856, uttered the following:

"We have women here who like any thing but the Celestial Law of God, and if they could break asunder the cable of the Church of Christ,* *there is scarcely a mother in Israel but would do it this day.* And they talk it to their husbands, to their daughters, and to their neighbours, and they say *they have not seen a week's happiness since they became acquainted with that law, or since their husbands took a second wife.*"

In a sermon published in the *Deseret News*, October 1st, 1856, Brigham Young tells the story.

"Men will say—'My wife, though a most excellent woman, *has not seen a happy day since I took my second wife.*' 'No, not a happy day for a year,' says one; and another has not seen a happy day for five years."

"I am going to set every woman at liberty, and say to them, Now go your way—my women with the rest; go your way. And my wives have got to do one of two things: either round up their shoulders to endure the afflictions of this world, and live their religion, or they must leave; for I will not have them about me. I will go into heaven *alone* rather than have them scratching and fighting around me. I will set all at liberty. 'What, first wife

---

* Polygamy the cable of the Church of Christ!

too?' Yes, I will liberate you all. I know that there is no cessation to the everlasting whinings of many of the women in this territory; I am satisfied that this is the case; and if the women will turn from the commandments of God, and continue to despise the order of Heaven, [Polygamy,] *I will pray that the curse of the Almighty may be close to their heels, and that it may be following them all the day long.* And those that enter into it (the celestial law) and are faithful, I will promise them that they shall be queens in heaven and rulers to all eternity."

"Now if any of you will deny the plurality of wives and continue to do so, *I promise that you will be damned.*"—*J. of D.*, vol. iii. p. 266.

This hardly comports with the Apostle Pratt's picture of a family, "where *peace* and salvation reign," and it is not a little amusing to read of the promises from his pen of "this glorious era," when the women were to "rejoice" because of the high honours and privileges conferred upon them; "the glorious prospects" which were opening before them, and the "freedom" in the dales of Utah. Polygamy in Utah is the martyrdom of civilized, Christian womanhood, and the enslavement of every noble instinct in man.

EPILOGUE

The 1872 *Exposé of Polygamy*
Compared with the 1874 *"Tell It All"*

Stenhouse's "pamphlet," *Exposé of Polygamy: A Lady's Life among the Mormons*, had twenty chapters and 221 pages. When it reappeared two years later with the new title of *"Tell It All": The Story of a Life's Experience in Mormonism*, it had forty-three chapters, a larger page size, and 623 pages. How did the slim volume expand so? A comparison of the two editions shows Stenhouse not only expanded and detailed her original accounts of experiences but also added entirely new material, often in new chapters. Sometimes the latter technique involved creating composite stories and including material outside of Stenhouse's own experience, unlike the original firsthand narrative. What follows is a brief description of how the original chapters compare with the more numerous ones in the 1874 version. It can serve as a guide for readers who wish to more closely compare Stenhouse's treatments of specific subjects in the two books.

The opening chapters of the two books demonstrate the first method, expansion. Stenhouse covers the same topics and timespan in both books—how she came to write the book and an account of her early life until her return to England from teaching in France—but with much more detail in the second version. As an example of even greater elongation, while chapter 2 in the *Exposé* describes Stenhouse's introduction and conversion to Mormonism up through her marriage to a Mormon elder, those events take up three chapters (2, 3, and 4) in *"Tell It All,"* which also include events from early Mormon church history outside Stenhouse's experience, such as the 1856 handcart disaster.

In chapter 5 of *"Tell It All"* we see an example of Stenhouse adding a complete chapter focusing on a topic that was either not included or only mentioned in the original. This chapter 5 is devoted to explaining details about Mormon meetings, experiences, and miracles, items which are only briefly touched on here and there in early chapters of the *Exposé*.

Chapters 3 through 7 of the *Exposé* describe the Italian and Swiss missions and the return to England, once again events that are fleshed out in chapters 6 through 11 of *"Tell It All."* Chapter 8 of the original book covers the voyage across the ocean, the Stenhouses' life in New York, and the trip across the plains to Salt Lake City, including some first impressions of the city. In *"Tell It All,"* instead of a single chapter this part of the story takes up eight chapters–essentially all of chapters 12 through 19.

Once Stenhouse is in Salt Lake City, the chronology of her memoir is less clearly delineated, and more additional filler chapters appear in the *"Tell It All"* version. Chapter 20 of *"Tell It All"* describes Brigham Young's wives and family life, an expansion of information that appears late in the *Exposé* in chapter 19. This is followed in *"Tell It All"* by three chapters (21, 22, and 23) explaining unusual Mormon doctrines and recounting some church history, including the Reformation and the Mountain Meadows Massacre—all topics not found in the *Exposé*.

The next four to six chapters in each version deal with general impressions and comments about polygamy (chapters 9 through 12 in *Exposé* but 24, 26 through 28, and 33 in *"Tell It All"*). Chapter 25 in *"Tell It All"* is entirely devoted to Stenhouse's trip to the Endowment House, which was described with minimal detail as a portion of chapter 12 in the *Exposé*. Chapter 13 of the *Exposé* expands to three chapters (29 through 31) in *"Tell It All"* that cover the same material, and chapter 14 of the *Exposé* also expands to three (32, 34, and 36) in *"Tell It All."*

Chapter 15 of the first book—dealing with the onset of dwindling confidence in Brigham Young, the move of the *Telegraph* to Ogden, the Stenhouses' leaving Mormonism and being attacked on the street—is described in greater detail in chapters 39 and 41 of *"Tell It All."* Chapter 16 in the original has general comments on polygamy, while chapter 17—Martha Brotherton's account of Brigham Young's attempted seduction of her—was omitted from *"Tell It All."* Chapters 18 of *Exposé* and 34 of *"Tell It All"* deal with proxy marriages and work for the dead, and chapters 19 of *Exposé* and 33 of *"Tell It All"* discuss domestic arrangements in Mormon homes.

Toward the end of *"Tell It All"* are several more new chapters. Chapter 35 describes Mormon festivities and Brigham Young's stores; chapter 37 is largely devoted to describing Orson Pratt's uncaring behavior toward a plural wife; and chapter 38 focuses on T. B. H. Stenhouse's unsuccessful courtship of a third potential wife.

There are also throughout *"Tell It All"* several sections inserted describing in great detail Stenhouse's conversations/letters with two women, "Mary Burton" and Stenhouse's "talkative friend," Ann. Stenhouse explains that these are the only people in her account for whom she has not used real names, and they are likely composite portraits. Toward the end of the book each receives a whole chapter: the account of Mary's sad end appears in chapter 40 and that of Ann's trials in chapter 42.

The final chapters in each book (20 and 43) are similar to one another, discussing Mormon dealings with Gentiles, Fanny's life since leaving Mormonism, and recent changes within Mormonism, including the waning popularity of polygamy.

Aside from how the content changed and expanded from the first version to the second, a difference in tone also distinguishes one from the other. This difference is noticeable from the very beginning. In the *Exposé* Stenhouse's initial description of her experience in Mormonism is straightforward and a bit wistful. Chapter 1 begins:

> I was once a Mormon woman, and for over twenty years I have lived among Mormons. Their faith was once mine as truly as any words can express; their thoughts were the same as mine; their hopes were my hopes; their religious opinions were in sympathy with my own. But that was in the time past. It *seems* long past, and yet it was, as I may say, only a little while ago—a few months, which I might almost count upon my fingers. Yet now all this is changed, and I have learned to see matters in another light.

Contrast this with the first page of *"Tell It All"* where she describes "my own experience—the story of a faith, strange, wild, and terrible it may be, but which was once so intimately enwoven with all my associations that it became a part of my very existence itself."

As another example of the difference in approach and intent between the two versions, the *Exposé* takes only a few short pages (chapter 8) to note briefly the fact of the Stenhouses' ocean voyage, give a quick description of the Mormon brethren her husband worked with in New York, and provide a short account of their trip across the plains to Utah. However, when Stenhouse covers this same time period in *"Tell It All"* (eight full chapters), she also includes items such as (1) a conversation with "Mary Burton" recounting stories about "Danites," or "Avenging Angels;" (2) detailed accounts of how she believes Mormon leaders swindled the emigrating Saints by making money on their provisions—as well as deceiving Stenhouse, leaving her and her family without their luggage and provisions they had brought for the ship's voyage; (3) how church leaders in New York mistreated the emigrants who could not find work; (4) a description of Mary Burton's change from a gentle, clear-eyed girl into a woman with fanatical religious zeal and unwavering trust in church leaders; (5) a detailed account of the handcart disaster of 1856 and the culpability of Brigham Young and other church leaders in creating the tragedy; (6) conversations about esoterica of church theology regarding polygamy, such as whether all wives or only the first wife will be queen in heaven; and (7) a lengthy account of Brigham Young's rise to church leadership, along with pointed criticism of Young as cruel, cowardly, miserly, and dishonest regarding church finances. This additional matter clearly seems designed to sensationalize by casting the Mormon leaders in as negative a light as possible, piling up example upon example of unsavory behavior, a tactic noticeably absent in the *Exposé*.

Ronald W. Walker, in "The Stenhouses and the Making of a Mormon Image" (64), has pointed out that Stenhouse plucked much of her added material in *"Tell It All"* from other works. In particular, her inclusion of the 1856 handcart emigration disaster, the description of the Mormon Reformation of 1856–57, and the story of the Mountain Meadows Massacre look to be "thinly disguised rewritings of materials quoted in her husband's book" (*Rocky Mountain Saints*, published in 1873, the previous year). These along with the lengthy stories about her apparently fictionalized friend Mary Burton made up a large part of the expanded *"Tell It All."* Together, they described some of the more explosive or scandalous elements in Mormon history or lore. But while elaborating on these subjects attempted to add both historical heft and titillation to Stenhouse's book, this was at the expense of the straightforward approach and general credibility that characterized the *Exposé*.

Overall, the narration in the *Exposé* is forthright and honest, expresses genuine emotion, and conveys a kindly, understanding stance toward others, while in *"Tell It All"* one can see in the added text a heightened dramatic approach and much more critical judgment, particularly of Mormon church leaders. In the intervening two years, having been challenged to "tell it all" and perhaps encouraged by her publisher to include more lurid elements, Stenhouse's memoir morphed from a heartfelt story of disillusion and betrayal to a detailed indictment of all facets of her previous religion and its leader.

APPENDIX

List of Editions

Most of the books listed here were viewed at either the Church of Jesus Christ of Latter-day Saints Church History Library (CHL) or the Brigham Young University Library (BYU). The four-digit numbers following the entries correspond to the numeration in Chad J. Flake and Larry W. Draper, *A Mormon Bibliography 1830 to 1930: Books, Pamphlets, Periodicals, and Broadsides Relating to the First Century of Mormonism* (Provo: Brigham Young University Press, 2004). Metric measurements also follow the practice in that work.

1872

Fanny Stenhouse's earliest version of her life in Mormonism was published by American News Company. (My first edition has a personal notation on the inside dated April 9, 1872.) A second edition by American News is identical to the first except for the notation "Second edition."

The book was also published later in the year by Russell Brothers Publishers, but with "*Exposé of Polygamy*" omitted from the title. There were apparently two editions of this as well, as I have viewed a first edition in private ownership although Flake only lists a second edition. I deduced that the Russell Brothers edition came later than that of American News Company by a comparison of the advertisements in the back for *Rocky Mountain Saints*, by Stenhouse's husband, T. B. H., which was published in 1873. The ad in the American News Company edition says that the book "will be ready shortly," while the one in the first Russell Brothers edition, otherwise virtually identical, says, "*In press*, [my italics] and will be ready shortly," which seems to imply a later date, closer to actual publication.

Curiously, Flake also lists an edition put out the same year by American News Company but under the truncated title ("*A Lady's*

Life . . ."). I have not been able to see this edition at the few distant librar-
ies where it is held.

These are all very small books, with spine heights measuring 19 to
21 cm. (7.5 to 8.25 in.) and consisting of 221 pages. The content is identical except for publishing details and extra matter such as advertising.

Editions

    *Exposé of Polygamy in Utah: A Lady's Life Among the Mormons. A Record
of Personal Experience as one of the Wives of a Mormon Elder during a Period
of more than Twenty Years.* By Mrs. T. B. H. Stenhouse, of Salt Lake City.
Illustrated by H. L. Stephens. New York: American News Company, 119
Nassau Street/ New York: S. W. Green, Printer, 10 and 18 Jacob Street.
[8385]

    (Same) Second edition. New York: American News Company. [8386]

    *A Lady's Life Among the Mormons. A Record of Personal Experience as one of
the Wives of a Mormon Elder, during a Period of more than Twenty Years.* By Mrs.
T. B. H. Stenhouse, of Salt Lake City. Illustrated by H. L. Stephens. New
York: Russell Brothers Publishers, 28 30 32 Centre Street. [Not in Flake]

    (Same) 2nd edition. New York: Russell Brothers, publishers. [8387]

    (Same) New York: American News Company. [8388]

1873

The single edition printed (in English) in 1873 is the one listed below,
published in London. It is titled identically to the Russell Brothers 1872
edition and has the same content except that where the 1872 editions
had nine illustrations, this one has none. The volume is slightly smaller
in size (17 cm., or 6.5 in.) and has only 176 pages. The smaller number
of pages is due to (1) omitting the illustrations, (2) using Roman numer-
als for the prefatory material, and (3) a smaller typeface and less leading
between lines. Page headings are different, with "A Lady's Life" on verso
pages and "Among the Mormons" on recto pages rather than the "What I
know about Polygamy" on both in the 1872 editions.

Editions

    (Same) London: George Routledge and Sons, The Broadway,
Ludgate. Printed by Woodfall and Kinder, Milford Lane, Strand, W.C.
[8389]

    A Spanish edition was also published in 1873:

    *Vida de una senora entre los Mormons; producto de la experiencia personal
de un de las espousa de un sacerdote Mormon, durante un periode de mas de
viente anos.* Mexico, Imprinta de Ignacia Escalante. [8401]

1874

Two years after its first appearance, Stenhouse's book underwent a profound transformation and expansion. It almost tripled in pages, from 221 to 623, grew from twenty chapters to forty-three (plus a farewell note, "L'Envoi"), and sported a new title claiming to "*Tell It All.*" It also included a publisher's notice describing the new edition and an "introductory preface" by Harriet Beecher Stowe. Stenhouse's earlier preface was expanded to explain this new version of her story. The book is not only thicker than the earlier slim volumes but otherwise larger (height, 23 cm., or 9 in.). There are twenty-seven illustrations, including a portrait of Fanny Stenhouse at the beginning.

Editions

"*Tell It All.*" *The story of a life's experience in Mormonism. An autobiography: By Mrs. T.B.H. Stenhouse of Salt Lake City, for more than twenty years the wife of a Mormon missionary and elder.* With introductory preface by Mrs. Harriet Beecher Stowe. Hartford, Conn.: A. D. Worthington & Co. [Listed as 8390 by CHL, but Flake only lists the edition below, the one with multiple publishers.]

(Same) Hartford, Conn.: A. D. Worthington & Co.; Chicago: Louis Lloyd & Co.; San Francisco: A. L. Bancroft & Co. [8390]

(Same) Cincinnati, Ohio: Queen City Publishing Company. [8391]

(Same) Cincinnati, Ohio: Queen City Publishing Company; St. Louis: Excelsior Publishing Co. [Listed as 8391 by CHL, but Flake doesn't include Excelsior in his listing.]

1875, 1876, 1877

For the next three years, the 1874 edition was reprinted by the same publishers as well as some additional ones. These editions all were exact reprints, sometimes even with the same advertisements at the end, and all bore the original 1874 copyright.

1875 Editions

(Same) Hartford, Conn.: A. D. Worthington & Co., publishers; Chicago: Louis Lloyd & Co. [8392]

(Same) Hartford, Conn.: A. D. Worthington & Co., publishers; Cincinnati, Ohio: Queen City Publishing Co.; St. Louis: Excelsior Publishing Co.; Chicago: Louis Lloyd & Co.; San Francisco: A. L. Bancroft & Co. [8393]

(Same) Hartford, Conn.: A. D. Worthington & Co., publishers; Cincinnati, Ohio and St. Louis, Mo.: A. G. Nettleton & Co. [8393a]

1876 Edition

(Same) Hartford, Conn.: A. D. Worthington & Co., publishers; Chicago, Ill., Cincinnati, Ohio, and St. Louis, Mo.: A. G. Nettleton & Co. [This edition is listed as 8394 in BYU catalog, but Flake does not list other locations or publishers besides Hartford and Worthington in 8394; he does list multiple cities in 8395, but calls it a publisher's dummy. It looks like the copies at both BYU and CHL show Nettleton as publisher (Flake's 8395), although Flake says the 8394, with just Worthington as publisher, is at CHL. Flake in 8395 does not list Nettleton, making it appear that it is Worthington at all four locations.]

1877 Edition

(Same) Hartford, Conn.: A. D. Worthington & Co.; Chicago, Ill., and Cincinnati, Ohio: A. G. Nettleton & Co.; London, Ontario: J. M. Chute & Co. [8395a]

1878, 1879

The 1878 edition of "*Tell It All*" contained 655 pages instead of 623 because of the addition of three chapters at the end describing the Mountain Meadows Massacre and the confession and execution of John D. Lee. This addition was a response to the publication of the *Life and Confessions of John D. Lee* and the news of Lee's execution by firing squad, both of which occurred in 1877, following Lee's conviction for his involvement in the massacre twenty years previously (1857), thus reviving interest in that horrendous event. Otherwise the content remained the same, including the twenty-seven illustrations. An 1879 edition repeated this format.

1878 Edition

"*Tell It All*": *The story of a life's experience in Mormonism. An autobiography: By Mrs. T. B. H. Stenhouse, of Salt Lake City, for more than twenty-five years the wife of a Mormon missionary and elder.* With introductory preface by Mrs. Harriet Beecher Stowe. Including a full account of the Mountain Meadows massacre, and of the life, confession and execution of Bishop John D. Lee. Fully illustrated. Hartford, Conn.: A. D. Worthington & Co., publishers. Chicago, Ill., and Cincinnati, Ohio: A. G. Nettleton & Co.; St. Louis, Mo.: J. H. Chambers & Co.; London, Ontario: J. M. Chute & Co. [8396]

1879 Edition

(Same) San Francisco: Hawley, Rising & Stiles. [Not in Flake]

1880, 1882, 1883(?)

Another change in title, content, and format appeared in 1880. "*Tell It All*" is replaced by "*An Englishwoman in Utah.*" There are now only 404 pages, a smaller size (22 cm., or 8.5 in.) and sixteen illustrations. A new (older-appearing) portrait of Fanny Stenhouse replaces the original. The preface by Harriet Beecher Stowe remains. Stenhouse's own preface is modified from the 1874 version by omitting some sections. The table of contents lists only the title of each chapter instead of giving detailed descriptions of the content, two of the forty-three chapters are omitted, and the order of chapters is changed. At the end, after the two chapters on the execution and confession of John D. Lee, a chapter that in the 1878 edition was entitled "The guilt of Brigham Young for the Mountain Meadows massacre" is now called "Killing a rival prophet" and tells the story of the suppression of the dissident Morrisite sect.

The 1882 edition, described as a "new and cheaper edition," is even smaller (20 cm., or 8 in.) and has only fourteen illustrations. Orson Pratt's portrait has replaced Fanny Stenhouse's at the front, perhaps because it was Pratt who officially announced the Mormon doctrine and practice of polygamy in 1852.

1880 Edition

An Englishwoman in Utah: The story of a life's experience in Mormonism. An autobiography: By Mrs. T.B.H. Stenhouse, of Salt Lake City, for more than twenty-five years the wife of a Mormon missionary and elder. With introductory preface by Mrs. Harriet Beecher Stowe. Including a full account of the Mountain Meadows massacre, and of the life, confession, and execution of Bishop John D. Lee. London: Sampson Low, Marston, Searle, & Rivington; London: Gilbert and Rivington, printers. [8398]

1882 Edition

(Same) New and cheaper edition. London: Sampson Low, Marston, Searle, & Rivington. [8399]

Possible 1883 Edition

(Same)

["There is a tipped in errata sheet that follows the last page of text, p. 404, but it does not represent changes for this book. According to an advertisement of a book dealer, there was a second issue of the second edition published in 1883 with a correction leaf. This errata leaf may belong to the 1883 edition. Flake's bibliography does not have an entry for an 1883 edition." From the expanded book description of the 1882 edition above, M270.07 S825t 1882b., CHL catalog.]

1888

This is similar to the 1880 and 1882 editions, but with a new title, "*The tyranny of Mormonism, or an Englishwoman in Utah.*" Like the 1882 edition, there are only fourteen illustrations, and the portraits of Fanny and Brigham Young that were in the 1880 edition are missing.

Edition
> *The tyranny of Mormonism, or an Englishwoman in Utah. An autobiography, by Fanny Stenhouse of Salt Lake City. For more than twenty-five years the wife of a missionary and elder.* With an introductory preface by Mrs. Beecher Stowe. London: Sampson Low, Marston, Searle & Rivington, Limited. [8400]

1890

Sixteen years after its first printing, the "*Tell It All*" title reappeared on a reprinting of the 1878 edition but with a copyright date of 1874. It included the "younger" portrait of Fanny, all twenty-seven illustrations, the detailed table of contents, and a final chapter on "the guilt of Brigham Young for the Mountain Meadows massacre."

Edition
> "*Tell It All*": *The story of a life's experience in Mormonism. An autobiography: By Mrs. T. B. H. Stenhouse, of Salt Lake City, for more than twenty-five years the wife of a Mormon missionary and elder.* With introductory preface by Mrs. Harriet Beecher Stowe. Including a full account of the Mountain Meadows massacre, and of the life, confession, and execution of Bishop John D. Lee. Fully illustrated. Hartford, Conn.: A. D. Worthington and Company. [8397]

1971

Reprints of the 1888 edition appeared in 1971. They are 404 pages, are short by two chapters of the original "*Tell It All*" version, and have a variety of illustrations. Reprints after the nineteenth century, although they include the title "*Tell It All,*" no longer seem to enclose it in quotation marks. The Centaur and Praeger editions in 1971 appear to be identical, the one published in Great Britain and the other in the United States.

Editions
> *Tell It All: The tyranny of Mormonism, or, an Englishwoman in Utah. By Mrs. T.B.H. Stenhouse.* Editor James Morris. Travellers' classics. Fontwell,

Sussex: Centaur Press; Woking, Surrey: Unwin Brothers Ltd., printers. [facsimile of 8400]

(Same) New York and Washington: Praeger Publishers. Printed in Great Britain. [facsimile of 8400]

2003

In 2003 Kessinger Publishing reprinted in an 8 x 11 ½ -inch paperback format what appears to be the original "*Tell It All*" version of 623 pages. This reprint begins with Stenhouse's dedication "To my children," omitting her portrait, the title page, and the page showing printing and copyright information. Otherwise it follows exactly the 1874 version. It has the list of twenty-seven illustrations (Stenhouse's portrait is listed here as the frontispiece, though the actual portrait is not included), the publishers' notice, prefaces by Harriet Beecher Stowe and by Stenhouse, and the detailed table of contents showing forty-three chapters plus L'Envoi. Unfortunately, the publishers give no reference as to which edition or year this reprint was copied from and no place of current publication. They also list Harriet Beecher Stowe as essentially a co-author on the cover and the spine.

Edition

Stenhouse, Fanny, and Harriet Beecher Stowe. *Tell it All* [no colon] *A Woman's Life in Polygamy*. Whitefish, Montana: Kessinger Publishing.

Notes

Introduction

1. The following brief summary of the history of polygamy in the Mormon church up to the time when Stenhouse wrote is drawn principally from the following accounts: B. Carmon Hardy, *Doing the Works of Abraham: Mormon Polygamy, Its Origin, Practice, and Demise*, Kingdom in the West: The Mormons and the American Frontier, vol. 9 (Norman, Oklahoma: Arthur H. Clark, 2007); Richard Van Wagoner, *Mormon Polygamy: A History*, 2nd edition (Salt Lake City: Signature Books, 1989); and Lawrence Foster, *Religion and Sexuality: The Shakers, the Mormons, and the Oneida Community* (Urbana and Chicago: University of Illinois Press, 1984).

2. Arrington and Bitton's comment is in *The Mormon Experience: A History of the Latter-day Saints* (New York: Alfred A. Knopf, 1979), 230. The conclusion that "the reality for most women was probably a mixture of faith and frustration" is that of Kahlile Mehr, "Women's Response to Plural Marriage," *Dialogue* 18 (fall 1985): 87. Mehr's article (84–98) focuses on women's motivations in entering into polygamy. The most common justification he finds is obedience to church revelations and authority along with hope of salvation, but notes that some women married polygamously in hopes of a higher celestial glory as well as for romantic or economic reasons. The examples he cites also show a great deal of heartache, resistance, and stoic acceptance on the part of the women. He notes (95) that the divorce rate among polygamists was 9 percent compared to 1 percent among monogamists, an indication of greater struggles and unresolved issues in polygamous marriages. Other authors have drawn similar conclusions. B. Carmon Hardy, in his massive study of Mormon polygamy, *Doing the Works of Abraham*, provides in chap. 4, "'Her Comfort Must Be Wholly in Her Children'—Polygamy at Home" (145–84), extensive examples of private attitudes toward polygamy that are largely at odds with the public statements of happiness often attested to mostly by men but also by women. These accounts of private feelings are quite remarkable, given the general defensiveness among Mormons about the doctrine and the Victorian reluctance to discuss intimate affairs publicly. Hardy concludes that "The emotional burdens of those living the Principle, especially women, seem undeniably wounding. At the same time, religious conviction clearly played an immense role in Latter-day Saint responses to plural marriage. The succinct conclusion of Samuel Bowles may have said it best: 'Their religion is of course the great reason for polygamy; it is the excuse of the men; it is the reconciliation of the women'" (184). For other detailed examples of the differences between women's public and private expressions about polygamy see Van Wagoner, *Mormon Polygamy*, especially chap. 9, "Women in Polygamy," 89–104. Van Wagoner says that "Mormons

nearly always entered polygamy because they believed it was essential to their salvation, that God required it of them" (90) and quotes George S. Tanner, a "prominent Utah educator and polygamous son," who stated, "I doubt there was a woman in the church who was in any way connected with Polygamy who was not heartsick. . . . They would not admit it in public because of their loyalty to the church and their brothers and sisters. . . . the women try to be brave, but no woman is able to share a husband *whom she loves* with one or more other women" (93). The accounts provided by Van Wagoner emphasize the emotional distress of the women, their resolve to bear the burden of polygamy because of the religious command, and the loss of a truly loving relationship between a husband and wife. An excellent book-length firsthand account by a polygamous wife is Annie Clark Tanner, *A Mormon Mother* (Salt Lake City: University of Utah Press, 1973), which was originally published in 1941. Tanner, who remained a faithful member of the Mormon church, is forthright in portraying the heartache, disappointment, and anguish she experienced as a plural wife and describing the personal and social repercussions of the practice. See also Jessie L. Embry, *Mormon Polygamous Families: Life in the Principle,* Publications in Mormon Studies, vol. 1 (Urbana and Chicago: University of Illinois Press, 2001), especially chap. 13, "Participant Evaluation of Polygamy" (187–94), which has several accounts essentially saying that while women generally accepted polygamy as a commandment, they felt that it was a great trial even though in most cases they found ways to accept the heartache and learned to live in relative peace. It is quite clear, then, that Stenhouse's description of polygamy as she observed and experienced it—most obviously in terms of the motivation in agreeing to enter polygamy and the emotional effects experienced—is validated by the abundance of other personal stories now available.

3.   See Maureen Ursenbach Beecher, "The 'Leading Sisters': A Female Hierarchy in Nineteenth Century Mormon Society," *Journal of Mormon History* 9 (1982): 25.

4.   T. B. H. worked for newspapers most of his life, maintaining a relationship with the *New York Herald,* for one, long after he left Utah. He also wrote and published a massive history of Mormonism, *Rocky Mountain Saints: A Full and Complete History of the Mormons* (New York: D. Appleton and Company, 1873), perhaps the most authoritative Mormon history of its time and still valuable today.

5.   Sir Richard Francis Burton, *The City of the Saints and Across the Mountains to California,* edited by Fawn M. Brodie (New York: Alfred A. Knopf, 1963), 247.

6.   William Hepworth Dixon, *White Conquest,* vol. 1 (London: Chato and Windus, Piccadilly, 1876), 208.

7.   She also said Stenhouse was "born a Frenchwoman," which is not entirely inaccurate, since many Channel Islanders were bilingual and since political control of the Channel Islands has changed hands many times. Thus Stenhouse might have been "French" depending on governance at the time, although her heritage was English. Olympe De Joaral Audouard, "A Travers L'Amérique: Le Far West [Crossing America: The Far West]," translated by Hugh McNaughton, in Michael W. Homer, ed., *On the Way to Somewhere Else: European Sojourners in the Mormon West, 1834–1930,* Kingdom in the West: The Mormons and the American Frontier, vol. 8 (Spokane: Arthur H. Clark, 2006), 123–24, 136.

8. See the *Deseret News*, December 7, 1864, for a complimentary review of her performance. The information about Stenhouse's midwifery comes from the John Lyon family. Lyon knew the Stenhouses well, spent time in New York during the time they lived there, and traveled to Utah in the same company with them. T. Edgar Lyon provided the midwifery information to LeJeune Young Decker, Carolyn Young Hunsaker's aunt. Carolyn Young Hunsaker, email to Linda DeSimone, April 26, 2007.

9. Carolyn Young Hunsaker, Stenhouse family records, copy in possession of Linda DeSimone.

10. See chapter 15, note 1.

11. From *The Revolution*, July 5, 1871, printed in the *Salt Lake Daily Tribune*, July 19, 1871, p. 4; *Salt Lake Herald*, July 8, 1871.

12. *Salt Lake Tribune*, July 12, 1871; August 10, 1871.

13. Letter of March 18, 1872, *Salt Lake Daily Tribune*, March 20, 1872.

14. *Salt Lake Daily Tribune*, March 20, 1872.

15. *Salt Lake Herald*, March 30, April 4–11, 1872; *Salt Lake Daily Tribune*, April 11, 1872.

16. Claudia L. Bushman, ed., *Mormon Sisters: Women in Early Utah* (Cambridge, Massachusetts: Emmeline Press Limited, 1976), 26, 178–86.

17. *Salt Lake Daily Tribune*, April 11, 1872, p. 2.

18. *Deseret Evening News*, April 11, 1872, p. 3.

19. *Salt Lake Daily Tribune*, July 10, 1872, p. 2.

20. Winifred Young Rosenthal, "The Profit," microfilm of typescript, 1973, 127, Church of Jesus Christ of Latter-day Saints, Church History Library-Archives, Salt Lake City, Utah (hereafter cited as LDS Church History Library-Archives). Stenhouse says only that "a lady-friend, with whom I was visiting, suggested again '*the book*;' and she would not permit me to leave her house, until she had exacted from me a promise that it should be written." "*Tell It All*," viii.

21. *Mormon disclosures!! Polygamy!!* . . . (Chicago?: s.n., 1872?), 15–16. LDS Church History Library-Archives.

22. *Harper's New Monthly Magazine*, no. 294, November 1874, 886.

23. Ronald W. Walker, *Wayward Saints: The Godbeites and Brigham Young* (Urbana and Chicago: University of Illinois Press, 1998), 301.

24. *Salt Lake Daily Tribune*, May 8, 1873.

25. *Woman's Journal*, March 29, April 5, 1873, as cited in Lola Van Wagenen, "Sister Wives and Suffragists: Polygamy and the Politics of Women Suffrage 1870–1896" (Ph.D. diss., New York University, 1994),107.

26. *Harper's Bazaar*, June 14, 1873, 380.

27. *Salt Lake Daily Tribune*, April 16, 1874, p. 4; November 4, 1874, p. 4.

28. *Salt Lake Herald*, June 28 and July 3, 1874; *Salt Lake Tribune*, June 25, June 30, July 3, and November 20, 1874.

29. *Salt Lake Daily Tribune*, February 23 and November 2, 1875; July 23, 1876; Van Wagenen, 113.

30. Interestingly, Ann Eliza Webb Young's first Mormon visitor after breaking with her former life was none other than Stenhouse's daughter, Clara Stenhouse Young, who came to see her at the hotel where she was staying. A second visit was more strained, and Ann Eliza didn't invite her back, since by then "I felt sure that she had come to spy." Irving Wallace, *The Twenty-Seventh Wife* (London: Arthur Barker, 1961), 235–36, 247–48; Van Wagenen, 187–88. Clara's granddaughter Winifred Young Rosenthal (daughter of

Walter Stenhouse Young, Clara's oldest son) says that her great aunt, Susa Young Gates, once passed on this information about Ann Eliza during a visit to the family just before World War I broke out: "'You know, Walter,' Aunt Susa went on more confidentially, 'Major Pond told me years ago that Ann-Eliza never wrote one word of her book or lectures. She used your Grandmother Stenhouse's first pamphlet as a starter, and memorized it, she admitted to me. Then Major Pond secured a ghost-writer or two, and away they went.'" Rosenthal, 152.

31. Wallace, 235. Since Ann Eliza left Brigham Young in 1873, it is not likely that she is here describing *"Tell It All,"* which was not published until 1874. It is also possible that this account refers to a book written by someone other than Stenhouse. Still, it is a revealing view of the effect of critical writings on Brigham Young.

32. Rosenthal, 180.

33. *Salt Lake Daily Tribune,* June 12, 1875, p. 4.

34. *Salt Lake Daily Tribune,* November 2, 1875, p. 2.

35. Ibid.; *Salt Lake Daily Tribune,* July 23, 1876, p. 4.

36. Charles R. Savage, Diary, June 5, 1877, L. Tom Perry Special Collections, Harold B. Lee Library, Brigham Young University, Provo, Utah.

37. Savage, Diary, March 5, 1878.

38. Savage, Diary, following a date of November 23, 1895.

39. *Journal History of the Church of Jesus Christ of Latter-day Saints, 1830–1972,* LDS Church History Library-Archives, Salt Lake City, Utah, March 10, 1882, p. 6.

40. Carolyn Young Hunsaker, "'Dear Father . . .': The Life of Clara Federata Stenhouse Young Agramonte, 1850–1893," typescript, 1991, 18. Copy in possession of Linda DeSimone, also available at the J. Willard Marriott Library, University of Utah; Utah History Research Center (Utah State Historical Society); LDS Family History Library, and other locations.

41. Douglas Simms Stenhouse, "Thomas Brown Holmes Stenhouse and Fanny Warn," in *Antecedents of Douglas Simms Stenhouse: A Four-Part Introduction, Listing by Generations, Notes and References Written for My Children,* typescript, III, 16. Copy in possession of Linda DeSimone.

42. Hunsaker, Stenhouse family records; Walker, *Wayward Saints,* 15–16.

43. Rosenthal, unpaged introduction to Part II, between pages 128 and 129; Winifred Young, "The Third Wish," typescript, 23–24, in possession of Carolyn Young Hunsaker.

44. Winifred Young, 28, 46.

45. Obituary, *Deseret News,* April 19, 1904.

46. *Salt Lake Tribune,* April 19, 1904, p. 4.

47. Douglas Simms Stenhouse, III, 16. Actually, although her given name does not appear on the marker, it does say "Stenhouse" on the top, at least in one photograph, although another photograph shows no name. The story goes that the name was cut into the top of the stone but has eroded over time, so family members have "painted" it again, either on the marker or on the photograph (or perhaps both). In some photos a faint outline of the letters can be discerned with imagination and a sharp eye. The marker also shows a birth year of 1830, which was calculated based on the best guess of whoever (probably her children) provided the information for her death certificate, which lists her age as 74 "as nearly as I can ascertain." Hunsaker, Stenhouse family records; email from Carolyn Young Hunsaker to Linda DeSimone, April 18, 2007, and conversation in person with Hunsaker, May 31, 2007.

Chapter 1

1. Fanny Stenhouse's parents were John Warn, a " florist and gentleman's gardener," and Elizabeth (Betsy) Hill. John Warn's death certificate says "formerly a gardener," and his wife's identifies her as "widow of John Warn gentleman's gardener." Stenhouse was somewhere in the middle of the eleven children in the family. (Birth dates of the children are sometimes approximate or missing in the family records.) Hunsaker, Stenhouse family records, and email of April 25, 2007, from Carolyn Young Hunsaker to Linda DeSimone.

Chapter 2

1. Stenhouse's date of birth has been reported variously as anywhere from 1826 through 1829 (and even 1830 on her cemetery marker). Her own reckoning in this book points to an 1828 birth, assuming that her birthday was in April, as reported elsewhere, because she would have been twenty-one years old in the summer of 1849 if, as she reports, she left for France at age fifteen and stayed there six years. Her *Deseret News* obituary notes her birth date as 1829, which Stenhouse herself claims as the year of her birth in the expanded version of her story (*"Tell It All,"* 32), and which may explain why many later sources cite this year. She also states there (33) that she left for France at age fourteen. Both the Southampton LDS records (right after her baptism on August 11, 1849) and her marriage certificate (February 6, 1850) claim she is twenty-two, which would mean an 1827 birth year. The following year, thirteen months after her marriage, the 1851 census showing Clara as three months old (which would have been in March 1851) lists Stenhouse as being twenty-three, which would again support a birth year of 1827—unless, given her April birthday, she was jumping ahead a month and was considered "almost" twenty-three, in which case we are back to 1828. Emigration records showing her as twenty-seven in November 1855 also support the 1828 date. The family historians have used various years but often come back to 1826 based on parish records which show Stenhouse's birth date as April 12, 1826, and her christening date as April 23, 1826. (The family hired a professional researcher to extract information on the Warn family from the St. Helier parish records.) If the christening date is correct, it seems that Stenhouse knocked one year off her age at the time of her baptism and marriage (to make her birth year 1827), another year off by the time she emigrated a few years later (1828), and a third year off by the time she wrote her second book, citing an 1829 birth year, in 1874. Or, she simply had a poor memory. Southampton records of members, LDS Family History Library, microfilm #087,032; Hunsaker, "'Dear Father . . . ,'" 5, 22; Hunsaker, Stenhouse family records, and telephone conversation with Hunsaker March 28, 2007.

2. Stenhouse's rapid attachment to the Mormon church must have also been a strong one, since she doesn't mention here the Frenchman, Constant De Bosque, to whom she was engaged and who hoped to marry her. *"Tell It All,"* 36–38.

3. Thomas Brown Holmes (T. B. H.) Stenhouse had also baptized Fanny six months earlier. Born in Dalkeith, Midlothian, Scotland, in 1824, the twelfth child of a large family, he had converted to Mormonism in 1845 at the age of twenty-one and had become a diligent and charismatic missionary by the time he met the Warn family. His birth records show his name as Thomas Brown Stenhouse. He added the "Holmes" later in tribute to Milton Holmes, the elder who baptized him. Hunsaker, Stenhouse family records.

Chapter 3

1. Stenhouse's description of her attitude at the time is affirmed by the account of Thomas Margetts, president of the London Conference, in the *Millennial Star* (12:219): "I must say a word in regard to Sister Stenhouse. The resignation with which she bore the trial of parting with her husband, was praiseworthy indeed—a resignation which proved she loved her partner, and at the same time showed she loved her God more, and was willing to give the choicest treasure on earth for the cause of God."

2. This was Thomas Margetts, who (see previous note) had praised Stenhouse's response to her husband's call to the Italian mission. See also *"Tell It All,"* 104–5. Margetts had married in 1845 and had four children between 1846 and 1850. He died a few years later, on September 4, 1856, along the North Platte River. I could find no record of a second marriage by him to a young woman after the time of which Stenhouse writes. www.FamilySearch.org.

3. Lorenzo Snow left Italy for England in late January or early February 1851. Along the way he spent a month with T. B. H. Stenhouse in Geneva. (Stenhouse had been transferred to Switzerland the previous November, when he was also ordained a high priest.) Snow was in England at least by April, and T. B. H. was there at least by mid-May. Thomas C. Romney, *The Life of Lorenzo Snow* (Salt Lake City: Deseret Book, 1953), 124, 128–29.

Chapter 4

1. Stenhouse reported that at this London Conference in June 1851 "Mr. Stenhouse and I were ordained and set apart by four of the Twelve Apostles—namely Lorenzo Snow, John Taylor, Franklin D. Richards, and Erastus Snow." This may be the first instance of a Mormon woman being "ordained" or set apart for missionary work. Fanny Stenhouse, personal letter to "My dear sister," November 4, 1898, microfilm, LDS Church Library-Archives.

2. Clara Federata, named after one of Stenhouse's sisters, Federata or Fredretta, was born December 13, 1850. Stenhouse does not mention the death of her father, John Warn, on June 9, 1851, in Southampton. He had been living in a home for the aged and infirm and would have been about sixty-three years old. Hunsaker, "'Dear Father . . . ,'" 3, 22.

3. The second child was Lorenzo, most likely named after Lorenzo Snow. He was born April 5, 1852, and would have been a few months old when they moved in June. *"Tell It All,"* 121.

4.   Stenhouse's benefactor, Mr. B., was Serge Louis Ballif, cultured and well educated in Switzerland and Russia. He was a great support to the Stenhouses
in their missionary efforts in Switzerland and emigrated to Utah with a
Swiss company in 1854.

Chapter 5

1.   This took place in January 1853. Fanny was given a copy of the revelation
printed in the *Millennial Star.* "*Tell It All,*" 131. Polygamy had first been
admitted publicly in a speech at the Salt Lake City Tabernacle, the site of
gatherings of the general church membership, by Orson Pratt on August
19, 1852.
2.   Clara became the fourth wife of Joseph A. Young, Brigham Young's oldest son, on March 4, 1867, at the age of sixteen. He was thirty-two. Besides
those Stenhouse mentions, two more sons were born to Clara and Joseph
before his untimely death in 1875. Their sons were Walter Stenhouse
(1868); Junius (1870); Kane Lester (1872), later known as Lester K.; and
Eugene Jared (1874). Hunsaker, Stenhouse family records.
3.   This was Madame Ballif, the former Elise Lacoultre. She was married to
Serge Louis Ballif in 1848, and they had three daughters in Switzerland
before emigrating to Utah. Andrew Jenson, *Latter-day Saint Biographical
Encyclopedia* (Salt Lake City: Andrew Jenson History Company, 1920), 3:
305–6.

Chapter 6

1.   James Marsden was president of the London Conference at this time.

Chapter 7

1.   The fourth child was Serge Marsden, named after Serge Ballif and James
Marsden. The second daughter (and third child) was Emelia Eliza, also
known later as Minnie, born September 7, 1853, and probably named after
Lorenzo Snow's sister, Eliza Roxcy Snow, who had written a poem of praise
and encouragement addressed to Stenhouse the month before this daughter's birth:

"TO MRS. STENHOUSE, SWITZERLAND.

Sister, you are counted worthy
Toils and sufferings to partake,
Which your dear devoted husband
Now endures for Jesus' sake.

Be not fearful or desponding,
Though from home you're far away,

For the Lord our God will give you
Grace according to your day.

Wreaths of honor, crowns of glory,
Robes of pure, celestial white,
Will be given to all the faithful—
All who in the truth delight.

Be not weary in well-doing:
Be thou blest—be of good cheer,
For your name is known in honor
By the Saints—the faithful, here.

Snow, Eliza R., "To Mrs. Stenhouse, Switzerland," in *Poems, Religious, Historical, and Political*, vol. 1 (Liverpool, London: F. D. Richards, 1856), 223–24.

Chapter 8

1. The Stenhouses sailed on the ship *Emerald Isle*, with T. B. H., who was listed as a "photographic artist," serving as a member of the presidency among the 350 Mormons on board the ship. The account from the *Millennial Star* of the voyage describes a reasonably uncomplicated passage, with no sickness except sea-sickness, two deaths of children, and three marriages. Hunsaker, "'Dear Father . . . ,'"5.

2. Stenhouse describes these four men more fully in "*Tell It All*," 186–89. The Apostle was John Taylor, who married Margaret Young in Westport, Connecticut, September 27, 1856. One of the High Priests was William Ivins Appleby, who married Margaret's sister, Mary Young, November 6, 1858, after returning to Salt Lake. He died in 1870. I have not been able to definitely identify the other two, but Charles C. Dulin and Alexander Ott are possible candidates, as both worked on *The Mormon*. Dulin did not become a High Priest until April 1857, so may well have been the Seventy at this time, and seems to have disappeared from Mormon society after his time with *The Mormon*. Ott traveled around the Eastern Mission a great deal and worked especially among the German saints. John Taylor's son, George, also worked for *The Mormon* but, as he never married, would not have been one of the four polygamous brethren described here by Stenhouse. *The Mormon*, Papers, 1857–1858, LDS Church Library-Archives; *Journal History of the Church of Jesus Christ of Latter-day Saints*, October 5 and November 2, 1856; April 5 and 15, May 28, July 7, 9, 11, 16, and 18, August 24, September 5, 1857; Dec. 15, 1914; Samuel W. Taylor, *The Kingdom or Nothing: The Life of John Taylor, Militant Mormon* (New York: Macmillan Publishing Co., 1976), 183; www.FamilySearch.org.

3. By this time Stenhouse had six children. Ida Lulu arrived on March 8, 1857, and George Thomas, born March 10, 1859, was only a few days old when the family was told to be ready to leave New York in two weeks to join emigrants from England, with Stenhouse's husband being put in charge of that company. Preparations and the trip to Florence required time, and

Stenhouse was also peeved at having to wait there in camp an additional three weeks, due to "mismanagement" by church agents. They left Florence June 26, 1859, with the Edward Stevenson company of 350 people and 54 wagons, arriving in Salt Lake City September 16, 1859. "*Tell It All*," 238–41; Hunsaker, "'Dear Father . . . ,'" 6.

Chapter 9

1. Stenhouse comments further on the revelation in the appendix to her book, where she provides a full text for the reader. Also see chapter 14 for her description of how she came to read the revelation a second time.

Chapter 10

1. Brigham Young, however, was not averse to granting divorces, and in chapter 18 Stenhouse describes how easily divorces could be obtained by wives unhappy in their marriages.

Chapter 11

1. Stenhouse identifies this man as Orson Pratt in "*Tell It All*," 521–24. The wife described here (actually his ninth) is Eliza Crooks, whom he married in Liverpool in 1857. She died in Tooele on January 9, 1869. Orson Pratt married Margaret Graham on December 28, 1868, when he was fifty-seven and she was not quite seventeen. www.FamilySearch.org.
2. Not quite. T. B. H.'s first polygamous marriage took place November 28, 1863, a little more than four years after the Stenhouses arrived in Utah.

Chapter 12

1. The date of her endowment and sealing to her husband was October 29, 1859, only about a month after their arrival in Salt Lake City. Index card to Endowment House Temple Records, no. 2237, Book C, page 94. A full chapter in "*Tell It All*" (Chapter 25, 352–69) gives a more detailed account of Stenhouse's experience in the Endowment House.

Chapter 13

1. This was Serge Ballif, who had eventually settled in Cache County. This visit as well as Stenhouse's visit to Madame Ballif likely occurred in 1860. "*Tell It All*," 385–86, 393, 405–6.
2. Madame Ballif would eventually have nine children before she died May 13, 1872. www.FamilySearch.org.

3. The second wife was Henriette Jeanette Vuffrey, whom Serge Ballif married February 8, 1857. She bore him ten children and died in 1924 in Idaho. www.FamilySearch.org.

4. Stenhouse notes in *"Tell It All"* (346–51) that she began her millinery work in 1859, only a month after arriving in Salt Lake, and describes there how Brigham Young purchased several of her hats for his wives. Less than a year after her arrival, she was advertising as a "milliner, dress and cloak maker," located at "First House west of Tabernacle." *Deseret News*, August 8, 1860. Later she had a millinery shop on 1st South "between E & W Temple." *Salt Lake City Directory*, 1873, 69.

5. Caroline (Carrie) Grant was then the sixteen-year-old orphan daughter of Jedediah M. Grant, Brigham Young's counselor, who had died in 1856. Her mother, Caroline Van Dyke Grant, had died in September 1847 on the trail to Utah, when Carrie was only two years old. See *"Tell It All"* 409–32 for a full account of the relationships among Fanny, Carrie, and T. B. H. Although Stenhouse always refers to her as "Carrie," others say she was always known as "Caddie" (or Caddy), at least as a small child. Mary Grant Judd, *Jedediah M. Grant: Pioneer—Statesman* (Salt Lake City: Deseret News Press, 1959), 68, 116; Gene A. Sessions, *Mormon Thunder: A Documentary History of Jedediah Morgan Grant* (Chicago, Urbana, London: University of Illinois Press, 1982), 294.

6. She was Belinda Marden Pratt, daughter of Parley P. Pratt (deceased—see chapter 18, note 7) and Belinda Marden. Born in 1848, she was fifteen years old when she and T. B. H. married.

7. See note 5 above. After her ten-month illness, Carrie asked to be sealed to T. B. H. following her death. A more detailed account of Fanny's relationship with Carrie in her dying days is in *"Tell It All"* 440–51. Carrie died June 20, 1863.

Chapter 14

1. Stenhouse's seventh child, Thomas Brown Holmes Jr., had been born February 13, 1862, around the time that all the events involving Belinda Pratt began. The marriage date of T. B. H. Stenhouse and Belinda was November 28, 1863. Fanny Stenhouse was at this time pregnant with Walter, her eighth child, who would be born the following June.

2. T. B. H. was also sealed to Caroline Grant on this occasion, with Fanny acting as proxy. *"Tell It All,"* 454.

3. Actually she had been married just short of fourteen years, from February 1850 to November 1863.

4. The "favoured damsel" this time was sixteen-year-old Zina Presendia Young, daughter of Brigham Young and Zina Diantha Huntington Jacobs Young.

5. Stenhouse never explains the outcome of the courtship here but does to some extent in *"Tell It All"* (536–47). Zina apparently had a dream which convinced her to break off her engagement to T. B. H. Soon thereafter in October of 1868, she married forty-year-old Thomas Williams, a clerk in her father's office, becoming his third wife. He died unexpectedly six years later, and she was left a widow with two young sons. A decade later, Zina became the third wife of Charles O. Card, founder of Cardston, Alberta (Canada), and had several more children by him. She died in Salt Lake City

in 1931. Martha Sonntag Bradley and Mary Brown Firmage Woodward, *4 Zinas.* (Salt Lake City: Signature Books, 2000), 247–71.

6. In *"Tell It All"* (541) Stenhouse describes this re-reading as taking place around the time of her husband's courtship of Zina. But since Zina was married to Thomas Williams in 1868 and Stenhouse first read the revelation in 1853, it was closer to a fifteen-year gap at most, rather than seventeen years, unless Stenhouse actually did the re-reading at a later time than she describes here.

7. Some early Mormon leaders suggested decades later (1870s and 1880s) that the revelation was actually received at an earlier time, as early as 1831, and only written down in 1843. See Linda King Newell and Valeen Tippetts Avery, *Mormon Enigma: Emma Hale Smith,* 2nd ed. (Urbana and Chicago: University of Illinois Press, 1994), 64. Richard Van Wagoner has pointed out that Joseph Smith "never claimed to have received the sealing power of plural marriage until 3 April 1836." *Sidney Rigdon: A Portrait of Religious Excess* (Salt Lake City: Signature Books, 1994), 292. Van Wagoner also believed that "while Smith may have justified biblical polygamy at an early period in his life, the revelation on celestial marriage was a document contemporary to 12 July 1843." *Mormon Polygamy: A History,* 57.

Chapter 15

1. Fanny and T. B. H. Stenhouse were already associated with a group of English-born Mormon intellectuals in a reform movement, often called the New Movement, also referred to as Godbeites, after the leader, William S. Godbe. The movement had both secular and spiritual elements. Godbeites advocated the separation of church and state in Utah and the development of the state's mineral resources. They opposed Brigham Young's authoritarian rule, especially in economic concerns. They were also spiritualists and mystics and hoped to reform Mormon theology along more modern and intellectual lines. See Ronald W. Walker, *Wayward Saints: The Godbeites and Brigham Young* (Urbana and Chicago: University of Illinois Press, 1998).

2. It was probably not all that unusual for Joseph A. Young to drop in to visit the Stenhouses, as he was their son-in-law. But it is notable that Stenhouse describes him here as Brigham Young's son and not her son-in-law.

3. It seems inexplicable why Stenhouse would do this and deliberately "out" her husband. Perhaps it was her way of moving the process along in the direction she desired, but it is not clear whether her husband was in agreement with her action.

4. Actually Brigham Young backed off and did not disfellowship T. B. H. Stenhouse with the rest of the men, instead dismissing the charges against him. Stenhouse continued to defend church interests both in Salt Lake and the East through 1869. Walker, "The Stenhouses and the Making of a Mormon Image," *Journal of Mormon History* I (1974), 60–61.

5. T. B. H. Stenhouse was excommunicated as requested on August 17, 1870, while Fanny's request was not acted upon until several years later on October 5, 1874. Excommunication File, LDS Church Archives, as noted in Walker, "The Stenhouses," 62.

6. Stenhouse describes in *"Tell It All"* how she and her husband were squirted with "disgusting filth" (580), actually "diluted excrements," according to a newspaper account. *Salt Lake Herald,* August 23, 1870, p. 3.

7.   In response to the claim that the attack may have been because of a "personal difficulty," the *Salt Lake Tribune* (August 27, 1870) said that "religious fanaticism *was* at the bottom of the whole transaction. Men don't utter such phrases as the sanctimonious, 'Do your duty brethren' in relation to matters of private pique or personal animosity."

Chapter 16

1.   Stenhouse identifies the woman as Eliza R. Snow. "*Tell It All*," 430–31.

Chapter 17

1.   Martha Brotherton was a young English convert who had arrived in Nauvoo late in 1841. The experience described here took place in January 1842. Martha may have spoken of her experience or written letters back to England, as rumors were circulating about it in Nauvoo shortly afterward. Hyrum Smith, Joseph's brother, spoke in an April church meeting to try to contradict this story, and Martha was labeled a "mean harlot" by the Nauvoo newspaper, *The Wasp*, in August. Still, after her death she was sealed by proxy to Brigham Young at the Endowment House in Salt Lake on August 1, 1870. Van Wagoner, *Mormon Polygamy: A History*, 20, 26, 39.

2.   The book was John C. Bennett's *The History of the Saints*. Bennett had asked Martha to tell her story publicly, which she did in the affadavit provided here. The "Dear Sir" refers to Bennett, as the asterisks at the beginning originally read "General John C. Bennett." Bennett describes Martha Brotherton as "a very good-looking amiable, and accomplished English lady, of highly respectable parentage, cultivated intellect, and spotless moral character." John C. Bennett, *The History of the Saints; or An Exposé of Joe Smith and Mormonism*, 3rd ed. (Boston: Leland & Whiting, 1842), 236–40.

3.   The letter first appeared on July 15, 1842, in the *St. Louis Bulletin* and was later published widely in both America and Europe.

Chapter 18

1.   The woman who worked herself up from a domestic in Brigham Young's household to a wife was Eliza Burgess, Young's only English wife. She married Young in 1852, and her son Alfales was born in 1853. The other woman mentioned here, the wife in name only living in "married spinsterhood," is harder to identify, since Leonard Arrington notes that about thirty women were sealed to Brigham Young but had no marriage relation at all. However, Stenhouse probably was referring here to Martha Bowker Young, since she describes Martha in "*Tell It All*" as follows: "Martha Bowker Young is a quiet little body, with piercing dark eyes, and very retiring. Brother Brigham acts toward her as if he had quite forgotten that he had ever married her, and she lives in all the loneliness of married spinsterhood." "*Tell It All*," 279, 280; Leonard J. Arrington, *Brigham Young: American Moses* (New York: Alfred A. Knopf, 1985), 329, 420–21.

2.   Stenhouse identifies her as Augusta Adams Cobb (*"Tell It All,"* 290), whom Brigham Young married for time only.

3.   This wife is likely Emily Partridge, the only one of Brigham Young's wives previously sealed to Joseph Smith who had a "very large family" by Young. (Emily had seven children.)

4.   This is Zina Diantha Huntington Jacobs, and her "one daughter" by Young is Zina Presendia, who was courted unsuccessfully by Stenhouse's husband, T.B.H. Stenhouse.

5.   It is interesting that Stenhouse does not mention here that this is exactly how her husband's divorce from Belinda Pratt came about in November 1869, shortly after the financially disastrous experiment of publishing the *Telegraph* in Ogden, the return of the newspaper to Salt Lake, and the beginning of the Stenhouses' involvement with the Godbeite reform movement. As Fanny tells it, Belinda was jealous that Fanny, rather than she, had been invited to accompany T. B. H. to San Francisco where Fanny's eldest son, Lorenzo, was critically ill. Belinda filled out the divorce papers, and T. B. H. was summoned to Brigham Young's office. T. B. H. waited for a time when he knew Brigham would not be in the office and, while out riding with his son-in-law Joseph A. Young, had him stop at the office, persuaded Joseph to sign as one of the witnesses, paid the ten-dollar fee, and brought his copy of the bill of divorce back to Fanny, telling her to take good care of it, "for it makes me a free man again." *"Tell It All,"* 554–57. The years of T. B. H.'s marriage to Belinda (1863–1869) were fruitful ones for him in terms of fatherhood, as his two wives produced six children, in alternating years. Fanny's final three children arrived at two-year intervals. She delivered her eighth child, Walter, with whom she was pregnant at the time of T. B. H. and Belinda's marriage, on June 22, 1864; her ninth child, Fanny Maud, on June 27, 1866; and her tenth and final child, Blanche Hortense, on July 30, 1868. Belinda's daughters, born in the odd rather than even years, were Louisa, born on January 12, 1865; Florence Pratt, born on July 16, 1867 (she died on August 5); and Flora Bella, born on May 23, 1869. After her divorce from T. B. H., Belinda married Henry Julius Smith in 1871, had one son by him, and after divorcing him married Amos Milton Musser in 1872, by whom she had six additional children. Hunsaker, Stenhouse family records and email to Linda DeSimone, April 26, 2007; www.FamilySearch.org.

6.   Stenhouse identifies her as "Harriet Barney Seagers Young." Harriet was born in 1830 so was still relatively young—just past forty—and had been married to Brigham Young in 1856. An "Elder Sagurs" was the leader of the "liberal" Godbeite group in Tooele in 1870. *"Tell It All,"* 279; Arrington, 420; Walker, *Wayward Saints*, 205.

7.   Parley P. Pratt was killed on May 13, 1857, in Arkansas by Hector McLean. McLean's wife, Eleanor Jane McComb McLean, had converted to Mormonism in San Francisco and eventually left McLean because of his abuse. She became Pratt's twelfth wife in November 1855. A good account is Steven Pratt, "Eleanor McLean and the Murder of Parley P. Pratt," *BYU Studies* 15 (winter 1975), 225–56.

8.   One of these women is certainly the aforementioned Zina Diantha Huntington Jacobs Young, the mother of Zina Presendia, whom Stenhouse's husband, T.B.H., courted unsuccessfully. The second might be any one of a number of women, since Todd Compton has pointed out that ten other women were polyandrous wives of Joseph who continued to live with their

own husbands. Todd Compton, *In Sacred Loneliness: The Plural Wives of Joseph Smith* (Salt Lake City: Signature Books, 1998), 15–23.

9.   Stenhouse's arithmetic seems to be off by six hundred. Subtracting the total females in the territory (42,665) from the total males (44,121) gives a difference of 1,456, not the 2,056 that Stenhouse claims.

Chapter 19

1.   These are Elizabeth and Vilate, daughters of Miriam Angeline Works. They were in their forties at this time. Each married and bore eight children and lived in Salt Lake City into old age. Arrington, 120; www.FamilySearch.org.
2.   Mary Ann Angell Young was two years younger than Brigham, having been born in 1803.
3.   Although Joseph A. Young had made Stenhouse's daughter Clara his fourth wife in 1867, an earlier plural wife, Thalia (or Athalia) Elizabeth Grant, whom he had married during the Reformation (1856–57), was, according to the 1860 census, back living at her father's home in Bountiful and had reclaimed her maiden name. So, Joseph only would have had three wives at this time. Letter from Barbara Young Brown to Carolyn Young Hunsaker, July 22, 2004, copy in possession of Linda DeSimone..
4.   All of the wives listed here are described in more detail in *"Tell It All,"* 275–90.
5.   Since the "reigning favourite" at this time was Amelia Folsom, whom Brigham Young married in 1863, the only more recent wives who might fit this description are Mary Van Cott Cobb (married 1865) and Ann Eliza Webb (married 1868). Arrington, 420–21.

Chapter 20

1.   This is likely Emmeline Free, a previous favorite and the mother of ten.

Appendix

1.   These are Joseph Smith III, born 1832; Alexander Hale Smith, born 1838; and David Smith, born 1844.
2.   This quotation is found in Orson Pratt, *The Seer,* vol.1, no.10 (October 1853; Photo reprint, Salt Lake City: Eborn Books, 1990), 155. In the last paragraph of her comments Stenhouse attributes this passage to "Apostle Pratt" when she quotes briefly from it.

Index